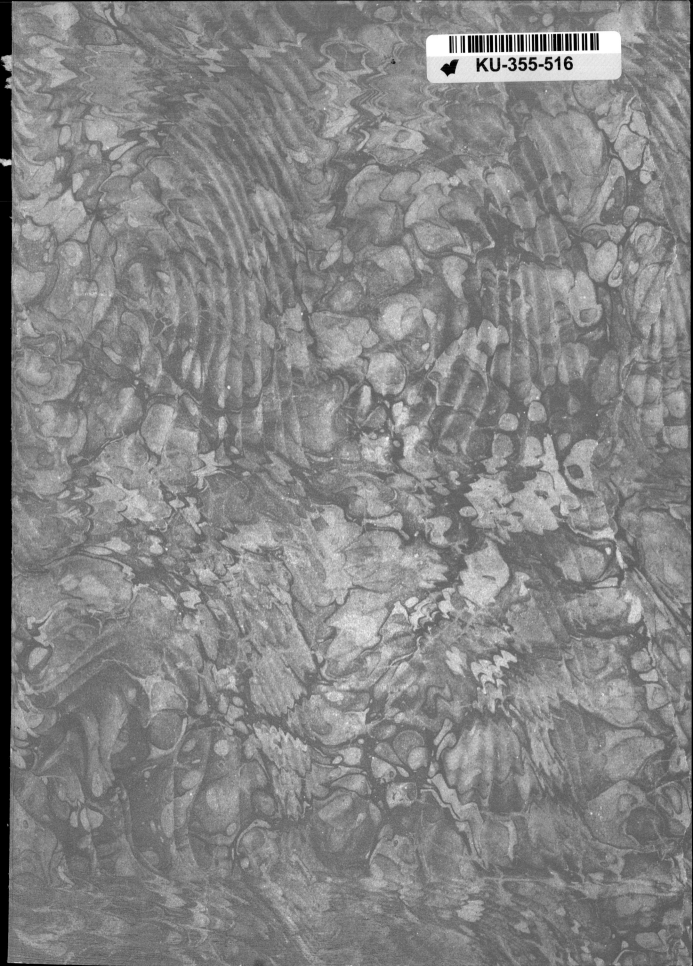

NEWNES'
PICTORIAL KNOWLEDGE

THE POOL OF LONDON

If you stand upon London Bridge and turn your face towards the Tower Bridge, you are looking down upon the Pool of London, one of the most historic stretches of waterway in the world. Here you may see ocean-going ships being loaded and unloaded by huge cranes, which pick up the merchandise as with a giant's hands. In the view you will be able to include the Tower of London, Custom House and a great many churches and other interesting buildings.

[*Frontispiece.*

NEWNES'
PICTORIAL KNOWLEDGE

VOLUME 3.

AN EDUCATIONAL TREASURY
and
CHILDREN'S DICTIONARY

General Editor
H·A·POLLOCK

Associate Editor
ENID BLYTON

Technical Editor
A.C.MARSHALL

Art Editor
A·H·J·HUMPHREYS

The HOME LIBRARY BOOK COMPANY
(GEORGE NEWNES LTD)
23 & 24. TAVISTOCK STREET, W.C. 2.

First Edition	.	.	June, 1930
Reprinted	.	.	January, 1931
Reprinted	.	.	August, 1931
Reprinted	.	.	January, 1932
Reprinted	.	.	August, 1932
Second Edition	.	.	May, 1933
Reprinted	.	.	February, 1934
Reprinted	.	.	December, 1934

PRINTED IN GREAT BRITAIN
BY THE WHITEFRIARS PRESS LTD.
LONDON AND TONBRIDGE

CONTENTS OF VOLUME THREE

PAGE

THE STORY OF THE WORLD AND ITS PEOPLES—
THE EMPIRE ON WHICH THE SUN NEVER SETS (Contd.)

THE STORY OF THE WORLD AND ITS PEOPLES—
SOME JEWELS OF THE EMPIRE'S CROWN

THE STORY OF THE WORLD AND ITS PEOPLES—
OUR NEIGHBOURS AND FRIENDS IN OTHER LANDS

CONTENTS OF VOLUME THREE

PAGE

THE STORY OF THE WORLD AND ITS PEOPLES— OUR NEIGHBOURS AND FRIENDS IN OTHER LANDS

Colour Plates

Photo=tone Supplements

Folding Model

The Story
of the
World and
its Peoples

Great Britain
and Ireland—
the Fortunate
Isles

Humphrey Joel.

A FARM IN THE "GARDEN OF ENGLAND"

Here is the homestead of a farm in Kent, the county to which we refer as the "Garden of England." It is such pictures as this that bring people from our overseas dominions to what they all call "Home." Note the oast-house, which is typical of those parts of the country where the soil is suitable for the growing of the hop plant. Oast-houses are really kilns in which hops or malt are dried. Sussex, Hampshire, Hereford and Worcester grow hops, but Kent is the principal county for this crop.

THE HOME OF THE ENGLISH

ONE of the most wonderful stories in history is that which tells how a little group of islands, which were inconsiderable and far away in the outer world of the Greeks and the Romans, became the Motherland of the greatest Empire that the world has ever seen.

That little group of islands is the British Isles—our Homeland, and the Motherland of the Overseas Dominions, themselves the homes of citizens of the Empire who look towards the little Motherland with affection as the real home of the British race to which they are proud to belong.

There must be something remarkable about these islands which have become the centre of an Empire that covers about one-fifth of the lands of the globe and is the home of at least a quarter of the world's people.

People and Geography.

What is it? Is it the people themselves? It is true that the British race has most of the qualities of empire builders, but it is also true that they possess these qualities largely because of the geography of their Homeland.

That is one of the reasons why geography is interesting. Geography, of course, tells us of strange lands and peoples, and of the wonderful things that are being done in other parts of the world. But, in addition to this, it does help to explain what the peoples of a land have done in the past, and what they are doing at the present time ; and it may help us to foresee what they can do in the future—if they choose. *If they choose*—that is important—for some peoples have not taken advantage of the geography of their land, perhaps because they did not choose, perhaps because they have not been able and energetic enough. Geography often shows us what splendid chances nations have missed, as well as those which they have taken and used to make their country a better place in which to live.

The British race must have used most of the advantages which Nature gave them when she made the British Isles as she did, and placed the islands where they are.

The Fortunate Islands.

It is a fact that we have in our Homeland one of the best climates in the world. Yet we often grumble at our weather—more often in fun than in real anger—and look upon it as a series of practical jokes played upon us by Mother Nature, all through the four seasons.

Have you friends abroad ? Listen to what they say on coming " Home " for a holiday—for all the citizens of the British Empire look upon the little Motherland as home, even if they were not actually born there, and long to visit it.

Will F. Taylor.

LAND'S END

In this picture we see Land's End, which is the most westerly point of the mainland of Great Britain. It is a familiar landmark to travellers. Those who are homeward bound welcome it as marking the entrance to the English Channel, whilst outward bound voyagers feel that here they are really saying good-bye to the Motherland. The lighthouse just off Land's End is known as the Longships. The longest continuous journey you can take in the British Isles is from Land's End to John o' Groats, a distance of about 800 miles.

Photochrom.

THE NEEDLES

Many ocean liners travelling to or from the great deep-water port of Southampton pass through the Solent, and both passengers and crew keep a close look-out for the Needles, which are depicted above. The Needles are really rocks of chalk at the westernmost end of the Isle of Wight, near Alum Bay. A very tall pillar of chalk, from which the point really takes its name, fell down nearly 200 years ago.

One will say, " Thank God for a sight of fields of living green once more " ; another will love to feel the beat of the rain upon his face and the bluster of the wild west wind ; for these men have come from thirsty lands of blazing sunshine where water is the most precious thing on earth.

Yet another from a country where winters are bitter and cruel will say how fortunate he is to come home for Christmas, knowing he will have no need to fear frostbite if he goes out, and that if he journeys by road or by rail his car or his train will not be buried deep in snow drifts.

Mineral Wealth.

It is true that occasionally the weather is unpleasant ; but it does not last long, and better weather soon wipes away disagreeable memories of the bad days that precede it.

You have only to journey—even a little—in other lands to know what a wonderful little Homeland is yours, and what a good climate it has for work and for play.

Besides the advantage of a genial climate, the British Isles possess rich stores of coal and iron as well as other useful minerals.

Luckily most of the coal is near enough to the sea to make it easy for cargoes to be sent away to other lands for sale ; and what is more important still, the iron is near enough to the coal for the best use to be got out of both.

Iron makes the steel for machinery of all kinds, and coal provides the power to drive it. Our factories, our railways and our steamships to-day are still largely coal-driven, although electricity and oil are beginning to play a very important part in manufacture and in transport. It is our wealth of coal and iron that has made Britain a great manufacturing country, and dotted the seaways of the world thickly with British steamers made of British steel, driven by British coal, carrying British goods to all parts of the world that can be reached by sea-going vessels, and bringing home again the foodstuffs for Britain's millions of workers and raw materials for her busy factories.

When we think over all the advantages possessed by the land in which we live we see that very few countries are as fortunate as ours in their natural wealth, their fertility, their climate, and their position in the world of to-day.

In the visits we shall make to different parts of our Homeland in the following pages, we shall understand many things if we remember that all things we have and use are the gifts of the Earth, and that the rocks of which our land is built up decide not only its particular types of scenic beauty, but very often the kind of work people do and the ways in which they live and move and have their being.

The Beauty of our Island Home.

Our Homeland is a beautiful land. Even those of our race who have travelled far and have seen the wonders of the lands beyond the seas are glad to return and enjoy the scenery of their own country once more.

J. Dixon-Scott.

SHAKESPEARE'S CLIFF

Most travellers by sea know the Shakespeare's Cliff at Dover, which is illustrated above. It is an enormous chalk cliff, rearing its great wall sheer from the sea to a height of more than 350 feet. If you are crossing from Calais or Boulogne you are not long at sea before you observe this and other of the " White Walls of Old England." They stand like monster sentinels welcoming every visitor and speeding the parting guest.

LONDON AND THE THAMES BASIN

THE GUARD AT BUCKINGHAM PALACE

Here is the east front of Buckingham Palace, the London residence of their Majesties the King and Queen. It was built originally by the Duke of Buckingham, who held the office of Keeper of the Mulberry Garden, at a time when an effort was made to raise up a great silk industry in this country. Interest is added to this photograph by the marching-off of the Guards, headed by their regimental pet and band. The Changing of the Guard is a daily event, always watched by large numbers of Londoners and visitors.

" I go hence
To London, to the gathering place of
Souls."—*E. B. Browning.*

LONDON is the heart of the British Empire and the Imperial Port on the River Thames—" the avenue of Empire and the highway of the world."

Although for sheer size and population London is closely rivalled by New York, London has what New York can never possess—a wonderful history that can be traced in her buildings and monuments in almost unbroken sequence from Roman times to the present day. We could fill this book with the tale of London, and still leave the story unfinished.

The beginnings of London were in the little village that grew up by the first London Bridge, which was built by the Romans, and was crossed by the Roman road that we know as Watling Street. Even then London was a port for ships carrying goods to and from the Roman city of Verulamium (St. Albans). But many long years had to pass before it had grown enough in size and importance to become the capital of England.

The Tower, built by Bishop Gundulf under William the Conqueror, reminds us that it was in the Norman era that London became the centre of government ; and from the Conqueror's time until now the Tower has been a storehouse of history. Westminster Abbey, re-built in the eleventh century—" our national Valhalla," as Dean Inge calls it—is a monument that enshrines within its walls historical memories that reach back in a continuous chain to the very day on which its foundation stones were laid.

J. Dixon-Scott.

This is considered to be the busiest spot in the world, for here converge no fewer than seven of the most important thoroughfares in the centre of the City of London. The building with columns is the Royal Exchange, from the steps of which a new sovereign is always proclaimed. On the left is the Bank of England, sometimes known as the "Old Lady of Threadneedle Street."

J. Dixon-Scott.

A view of Trafalgar Square, one of London's best-known open spaces, which was laid out in memory of the great sea battle. The Nelson Column is surmounted by a figure of the Admiral, three times his real height. The National Gallery comes to the north of the Square. Scarcely one visitor to London could fail to pass Trafalgar Square, for it is a hub of the West End.

J. Dixon-Scott.

The Houses of Parliament as seen from the Surrey side of the Thames. The clock in the tower on the right strikes its hours upon a bell weighing many tons, which goes by the name " Big Ben." You have probably heard its voice on the wireless. The present Houses of Parliament were built in the time of your great-grandparents, the first stone being laid in 1840.

J. Dixon-Scott.

With the trees and open, pastoral space of the Green Park, it is hard to believe that this photograph was taken in the very heart of London. The highway to the left is Piccadilly, and that to the right Constitution Hill. The Wellington Arch, through which only His Majesty the King may drive, is surmounted by a chariot and four horses.

The name London really belongs to the City, which extends from where old Temple Bar once stood, to Bishopsgate and Aldgate, and from Thamesside north to the lines formed by Finsbury Square, Barbican and Holborn. To-day there is the County of London, which at the last census (1931) had a population of 4,385,825 people.

What is London ?

But London to most people now means the mighty growth of human settlement that includes the distant suburbs and still day by day is pushing its way outwards in every direction where there is land for it to grow. This Greater London had in 1931 a population of 8,202,818 souls—the greatest town the world has ever seen.

London is the focus of British roads and railways ; all the world's seaways lead to it, and its docks provide accommodation for ships of all the seafaring nations of the globe. It is the great brain of British business, and a banking centre whose interests are not only British, but world-wide. It is a great manufacturing centre, too, with a wider variety of products than any other manufacturing city in the world. It is the centre of a government that is still a model for the liberty-loving nations of to-day, and the home of a Parliament that is known all the

J. Dixon-Scott.

TOWER BRIDGE

Were it not for the fact that the wide roadway of the Tower Bridge is made to lift, ships could not enter that famous strip of water, the Pool of London. Tower Bridge, which takes its name from the nearby Tower of London, cost more than a million pounds sterling, and is the last bridge towards the mouth of the Thames. During the day ships are signalled by semaphores like those used on railways and at night by lamps. Each bascule or " leaf " of the bridge weighs 1,000 tons. The top span connecting the Gothic towers is 142 feet above high water mark, and is used by foot passengers.

HOME OF THE "BEEFEATERS"

The Tower of London is so old that it contains one portion of wall made by the Romans, whilst the White Tower was built in the reign of William the Conqueror. The stronghold was originally surrounded by a moat and has served as a fortress, a place of royal residence, and a prison. To this day the Crown Jewels are kept within its walls. The warders of the Tower wear a uniform that dates back to Edward VI., and are known as "Beefeaters."

The site of public execution was on Tower Hill. Within the Tower itself, however, may be seen the spot where a headsman's block stood for the beheading in privacy of persons of high degree.

SOME MARKETS OF MIGHTY LONDON (1)

The vast and ever-increasing population of Greater London calls for enormous markets to which wholesale dealers may bring their wares, and where the retailers may gather to buy. Here is an early morning scene in the Central Meat Market at Smithfield. The thing that strikes us most is the absolute cleanliness of all the arrangements for handling the meat.

In this photograph we see Billingsgate. To study London's great fish market at its best one needs to be there in the very early morning, for the main business of the day is completed whilst we are at breakfast. In the ninth century it is believed that Billingsgate was a fish market, and the name has existed since 1282. Much of the fish bought and sold still comes by water.

Sport and General.

One of the sights of London is Caledonian Market on Fridays. On these occasions what is known as the pedlars' market is held, when curios, antiques, china and similar goods are displayed for sale at stalls, and also by the roadside. The Caledonian Market is at Islington.

Topical Press.

Once upon a time the Abbots of Westminster possessed a convent near St. Martin-in-the-Fields; and, naturally, the convent had a garden. So arose in course of evolution the name Covent Garden, which is now London's great market for fruit, vegetables and flowers. Here a market has been held for 300 years. As the seasons come round one may see home-grown market garden produce, Christmas holly and mistletoe, and fruit from almost every part of the world.

WORKERS OF THE MARKETS

The men who work in London's markets are types in themselves, and once a man has become attached to the vocation he is unlikely to change. The men above are fish porters. Because of Billingsgate's heavy loads, which they carry on their heads, many of the boxes of fish streaming with water from the melting ice, they wear leathern hats coated with a waterproofing substance.

Any year, mostly during the month of June, you may see a bevy of women of all ages clustered together in an odd corner of Covent Garden Market, London. Their work is to shell culinary peas so that the buyers do not have the trouble of handling the pods. In September one might watch the same women, with blackened fingers, getting walnuts from their green outer shells.

A KING OF THE BASKET-CARRIERS

Here is "Jim," one of the champion basket-carriers of Covent Garden Market, getting into good form for the porters' sports, at which basket-carrying is one of the features. This man has a score of half-bushel baskets balanced securely on his head, and the fruit and vegetable porters prefer to carry their loads in this manner. Unfortunately, baskets (which were certainly used in the time of Moses) are rapidly giving place to machine-made wooden boxes for the wares of Covent Garden.

WHERE KINGS AND QUEENS ARE CROWNED

Albert Hester.

The High Altar in Westminster Abbey, which is one of the most beautiful in any English place of worship. On this site there was a church in the eighth century, and the Abbey has been used throughout the reigns for royal coronations, weddings and funerals. Many of our sovereigns are buried here, and also illustrious people in all walks of life. Few are aware that the House of Commons met in the Chapter House of the Abbey for nearly three centuries.

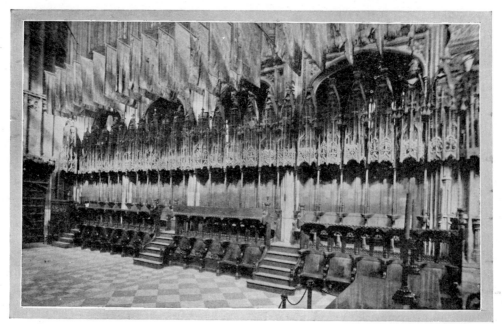

H. N. King.

In the Henry the Seventh Chapel at Westminster Abbey, as shown above, are the stalls of the Knights of the Bath, with their banners above. The Order of the Bath is one of the greatest honours conferred for military or civil service to King and Country.

INSIDE THE HOUSES OF PARLIAMENT

Walter Scott.

In this photograph you obtain a very clear idea of what the House of Lords is like inside. In the centre, the two raised chairs are the thrones, with the distinguished strangers' gallery just above. The galleries at the sides are for peeresses. Just beyond the table you see the woolsack, occupied by the Lord Chancellor. For centuries a sack of wool has been the official seat.

Walter Scott.

Here is the actual Chamber of the House of Commons. You will notice particularly the Speaker's chair. It is the Speaker who presides over the proceedings, and he has a residence provided within the Houses of Parliament. In this room are made the laws by which we are governed, and here our taxes are levied. The Government benches are on the right of the Speaker.

MY LORD MAYOR'S GILDED COACH

If you go to Kensington Gardens, to a point near the Long Water, you will see Sir George Frampton's fine statue of the children's hero, Peter Pan. Peter, the boy who never grew up, is surrounded by fairies, and there is no more delightful effigy in London.

November the Ninth is a most important occasion in London, for it is then that the Lord Mayor's Show is held, when the chief magistrate of the City proceeds to the Law Courts to receive the King's assent to his election. He rides in the coach shown above, carrying the State Sword and accompanied by his mace-bearer and mace. Lord Mayors used to ride on horseback, but a coach has been employed since one of these dignitaries was thrown from his steed.

TWO LANDMARKS OF LONDON

J. Dixon-Scott.

An exterior view of " Ye Olde Cheshire Cheese," a hostelry in Wine Office Court, on the north side of Fleet Street, London. The cellars are believed to have existed prior to the Great Fire, and the present building has a history of nearly 300 years. Both Goldsmith and Dr. Johnson were visitors at the tavern.

J. Dixon-Scott.

This is an old-world corner of London, to be seen within a few yards of the south-west of Lincoln's Inn Fields. The ancient building is itself of tremendous interest as showing a type of shop with place of residence behind and above. It claims to be the scene of the third book which Charles Dickens wrote, " The Old Curiosity Shop " (the story of " Little Nell ").

THE CHANGING OF THE GUARD

J. Dixon-Scott.

The building in the background is known as the Horse Guards. It stands between St. James's Park and Whitehall, and is surrounded by Government offices. At one time the Horse Guards formed the headquarters of the Commander-in-Chief of the British Army (an office no longer existing), and was originally the guard-house when Whitehall was a royal residence.

J. Dixon-Scott.

Few photographs can afford a better idea than this one of how crowded are the London streets. You will notice what a large number of omnibuses there are mingled with the other vehicles. The view is taken from the north side of Oxford Street, one of the great thoroughfares that link the City with the West End. Oxford Street was named after a former Earl of Oxford,

TO BRITAIN'S GLORIOUS DEAD

Whitehall is the centre of our Government offices, with the Houses of Parliament but a short distance away, and here was erected in 1920 a cenotaph or " empty tomb." The structure was designed by Sir Edwin Lutyens to the memory of those who fell in the Great War and bears the inscription : " To Our Glorious Dead." Every year, on Armistice Day (November 11th), a solemn Service of Remembrance is held at the Cenotaph, and above is a photograph of the scene.

In Westminster Abbey one may see the grave of the Unknown Warrior. Within the grave rest the bones of a British soldier, disinterred from a cemetery in France. No one can say who he was, but to him falls the honour of representing the splendid type to which in life he belonged. Our photograph was taken on an Armistice Day.

globe over as "the Mother of Parliaments." It is the capital of the British Commonwealth of Nations which we call the British Empire.

The London Basin.

London in its local relation is the centre of the "London Basin," which is really the lower basin of the Thames, extending from the gap in the chalk hills west of Reading to the sea, and lying between the chalk ridges of the Chilterns and the North Downs, through both of which roads and railways find their way by gaps in the hills, from the London Basin to the rest of Britain.

Reading is the "biscuit town" of the south. It has iron foundries, too. From it G.W.R. main lines diverge to Oxford and the Midlands, and to the west *viâ* Swindon, the railway engineering town, or *viâ* Hungerford to the west country.

Above Reading, and beyond the gap which the Thames has cut between the Marlborough Downs and the Chilterns, is the Upper Thames Basin, which includes the fertile plain of Oxford, and stretches westward to the beautiful Cotswold Hills, whence flow the "seven springs" that unite to form the young Thames. This Upper Basin is very different from the Lower Basin at whose heart lies the great metropolis— with its busy docks and markets, its factories and business centres, and its Thames, murky with the tide of commerce and clamorous with the voices of ships and men of all trading nations of the world.

The centre of the Upper Basin is the lovely city of Oxford, the ancient

Central Press.

AT TEDDINGTON WEIR

The tide ebbs and flows in the Thames from its broad mouth to Teddington Lock, a suburban part of Middlesex nearly twenty miles by water from London Bridge. If it were not for locks and weirs in its upper reaches, the river would, of course, be unmanageable. In our picture you see winter flood waters rushing over Teddington Weir on their way to the sea. One derivation of the name Teddington is "Tide-end-Town," *i.e.*, where the tide ends. Many people believe, however, that it was called after Tedda, an old-time chieftain.

NEARLY 500 YEARS A SCHOOL

Photochrom.

Here is the main schoolyard and Lupton's Tower, the latter a part of Eton College erected in the sixteenth century. Eton is one of our foremost great public schools for boys, and dates back to the reign of Henry VI. It is situated on the Thames, immediately opposite Windsor, and has upwards of 1,100 scholars. One portion of the red-brick buildings dates back to 1448.

Photochrom.

Eton College has been in existence nearly 500 years, but Windsor Castle, on a hill above the Thames, was founded by William the Conqueror; and there had been a fortress on the spot for an unknown period before his coming. This royal palace, with its grounds, stands upon 12 acres, and we see here Henry VIII.'s Gateway to the Castle, through which the Guard, headed by its band, has just passed. At the top you notice the massive Round Tower or Keep.

CARDINAL WOLSEY'S GREAT KITCHEN

H. J. Shepstone.

Hampton Court Palace, which contains upwards of 1,000 rooms, was built by Cardinal Wolsey and given up by him to Henry VIII., so that it became a royal residence and remained so through many reigns. Above we have a picture of the Tudor kitchen, precisely as it was in Wolsey's time. Note the spits upon which barons of beef and venison were roasted before the open fire, and also the collection of curious implements used in cookery in other days.

Sport & General.

Henley-on-Thames is an ancient and pretty market town in Oxfordshire, known the world over for its annual Regatta, held in July. The Regatta is an amateur fixture, connected with Oxford and Cambridge Universities and with Eton College, and has been instituted upwards of a hundred years. In our photograph one of the heats is illustrated.

THE TOWERS AND SPIRES OF OXFORD

Will F. Taylor.

The University of Oxford is made up of more than twenty colleges, and is governed by a chancellor. Here you see a corner of the quadrangle with a window of the Hall of Oriel College, which dates back to 1326.

Will F. Taylor.

" Tom Tower," Oxford, and the entrance to Christ Church College, whose chapel is the Cathedral of the Diocese. "Tom" is a massive bell within the Tower, and the College was founded by Cardinal Wolsey.

Topical Press.

If you were to fly over the City of Oxford in an aeroplane this is the view that would fix itself upon your mind. The many colleges which collectively form the University are clustered closely together, and one notices mostly the assembly of countless spires, towers, and minarets.

TWO OF ENGLAND'S GREAT DEEP=WATER PORTS

In this remarkable photograph we get a splendid idea of the Docks at Southampton. These docks
Rivers Itchen and Test, and the open sea is reached either by the Solent, to the north-west of the Isle
shelter to shipping in bad weather. Southampton Docks can accommodate the largest

Above we are shown the entrance to the Gladstone Dock at Liverpool. Our great Mersey deep-water
end, you would have to walk nearly thirty miles before you had traversed the entire length. The
journey on the overhead electric railway. Atlantic liners leaving Liverpool reach

IN FRIENDLY RIVALRY FOR ATLANTIC SHIPPING

Central Press.

cover some hundreds of acres and are constantly being enlarged. They stand at the mouths of the
of Wight, or by Spithead, round the Ryde and Bembridge corner, so that the island always affords
vessels. Here one may see not only the biggest, but also the swiftest of Atlantic liners.

Central Press.

port has also docks covering some hundreds of acres, and if all the quay walls could be placed end to
Gladstone is the largest of the docks, most of which one may see to the best advantage by taking a
the ocean either round the north of Ireland or else through the St. George's Channel.

home of culture and learning, rich in history and in art—a city of beautiful towers and spires, set in a green and pastoral countryside, and one of the most famous cities in the world. Every one who can, goes to see Oxford ; and those who go, long to return.

In this pleasant vale, farming is the main business, although remnants of its ancient woollen trade still persist at Witney, and you can go to wonderful old towns and villages in the Cotswolds whose fine churches and monuments tell the story of a once great and flourishing woollen industry, and of the days when Cotswold woollen manufacturers were merchant princes, and Cotswold towns among the most important in the land.

J. Dixon-Scott.

THE ROMAN BATH AT BATH

The waters of Bath have been known for their curative properties since the days of the Ancient Britons, and the bath in the above illustration was actually constructed by the Romans. Bath was a great meeting-place for society and literary people at the height of the coaching times, and is described by Dickens in " Pickwick Papers." Behind the Roman Bath in our photograph is Bath Abbey Church, whose west front shows us in carved stone the story of Jacob's Ladder.

The Bristol Avon.

The Kennet and Avon Canal connects the Thames and Reading with the old Roman city of Bath and the ancient port of Bristol, and one of the main lines of the G.W.R. closely follows its route. The mild winters, and above all the hot springs for which Bath has been famous for centuries, made this a favourite resort of the Roman conquerors, who saw in its genial climate something that reminded them of their home in Italy. To-day Bath, in its amphitheatre of hills, is visited by thousands who come to drink of the healing waters and bathe in its warm pools.

Farther down the Bristol Avon is Bristol, the old port whence the Cabots sailed in Henry VII's reign to discover Newfoundland.

THE GARDEN OF ENGLAND

"The Times."

THE "SEVEN SISTERS" OF SUSSEX DOWNLAND

The Sussex Downs, from Cuckmere Haven to Birling Gap, come sloping to meet the sea in the form of tall chalk cliffs which are known as the " Seven Sisters." They are true " White Walls of Old England," familiar to everyone who passes up or down the English Channel, and extend practically from Seaford to Eastbourne. To prevent these landmarks from being disfigured by buildings they, and the Downs immediately behind, have been purchased for the Nation.

AT least two favoured regions of south-eastern England call themselves " The Garden of England "—one, the fair county of Kent, and the other the Isle of Wight —and both of them have excellent rights to the title ; for both are beautiful and fertile lands in the sunniest quarter of our Homeland, where fruits and flowers come to perfection and where the climate is delightful throughout the greater part of the year.

Both belong to the wonderful Downland region between the Thames and the English Channel. From Salisbury Plain (which is really rolling chalk country, with valleys and hollows in it big enough to conceal large bodies of the troops who use it as a manœuvring ground), two great ridges of chalk hills run eastward, (1) the North Downs with Dover and Shakespeare's Cliff at their seaward end, and (2) the South Downs coming to the sea by way of Hampshire and Sussex at the high cliff of Beachy Head, from whose top Shakespeare says :—

> " The fishermen upon the beach appear like mice."

Castle Towns.

Both of these chalk ridges are cut by streams, many like the Blackwater, Wey and Medway finding their way to the Thames ; and many like the Arun and the Sussex Ouse to the English Channel. In the gaps which these rivers have cut in the chalk ridges, stand old castle towns—Guildford on the Wey, Rochester on the Medway, Canterbury on the Kentish Stour, Arundel on the Arun, and Lewes on the Sussex Ouse, all of which have the ruins of their ancient strongholds. To-day such towns still command the gaps as important route centres on roads and railways. The whole of the south-eastern corner of England is dotted with the ruins of many castles built there, because this was the nearest part of Britain to the Continent.

To this day it plays an important part in our land and sea defences—Chatham (with its suburb, Gillingham) and Sheerness, Dover and Portsmouth are great naval stations ; Canterbury, Winchester and Aldershot are vast military centres.

Canterbury, however, is more famous as the seat of the Primate of All England, and many still go on pilgrimage to visit its wonderful Cathedral, and the ruins of the first Christian Church in England.

Between the Downs.

Between the North and South Downs is the Weald of Sussex and Kent—the Anderida Silva of the Romans and the Andredsweald of the Saxons—with the Forest Ridges in the middle rising to over 800 feet in Crowborough Beacon. The Weald still retains remnants of the ancient forests, and here and there you may yet see traces of the old charcoal burners' fires where the charcoal for smelting the Wealden

iron was made. The British iron industry, however, has long since gone north to the coalfields ; but great new collieries have been opened up in East Kent behind Deal and Dover.

All along the Kentish and Sussex shores are sunny seaside towns, well known to weary Londoners—Herne Bay, Margate and Ramsgate, Deal, Folkestone, Hastings, and Eastbourne ; Brighton—known as " London by the Sea "—Worthing, Littlehampton and Bognor Regis, where His Majesty the King regained his lost health. Important channel ferry towns there are, too ; *Dover*, for Calais and Ostend ; *Folkestone*, for Boulogne, and *Newhaven*, for Dieppe.

The Hampshire Basin.

The Hampshire Basin is almost cut in two by the deep Southampton Water—the estuary of the Itchen and Test, with the great port of Southampton at its head. Southampton has the advantage of double tides—four a

Will F. Taylor.

PLOUGHING IN SURREY

Surrey is one of the most beautiful counties in England, and ploughing a most necessary phase of farming. Notice the patient horses, never hurrying, but pulling steadily and strongly from one end of the straight furrow to the other. The ploughman, who must guide the share and keep it at the proper depth, finds his work hard and exacting, but ploughing precedes sowing, just as sowing comes before harvest—followed by ploughing again when the autumn rains arrive to soften the sunbaked soil.

Will F. Taylor.

IN CANTERBURY CATHEDRAL

For 1,000 years Canterbury has been the centre of our religious teaching, and it was here that Christianity in England first began. In the photograph above we see the door leading from the cloisters into the north transept of the Cathedral. The four knights who murdered Thomas à Becket hurried through this very doorway, meeting the Archbishop just beyond and killing him cruelly to gain favour with their royal master, Henry the Second.

day—which give it practically average high-water conditions most of the time. That is why it is the home port of some of our finest liners, especially those sailing to the Americas and to South Africa.

Two lovely old cathedral cities in the Hampshire Basin are Winchester and Salisbury, the former the ancient capital of England and the city of King Alfred the Great ; the latter near the ancient fortress of Old Sarum.

The Isle of Wight, now separated from the mainland by the Solent (yachting at Cowes) and the Spithead (naval anchorage and reviews), was ages ago part of the mainland ; its chalk backbone is a continuation of the Dorset chalk heights, and the famous Needles at its western end are broken-off fragments. The real busi-

ness centre of the Island is Newport. Much better known, however, are the delightful resorts along its coasts— Ventnor, Shanklin, and Ryde. On the mainland west of the Isle of Wight is the seaside health resort of Bournemouth with its splendid pine woods and sands.

Kentish Fruit and Hops.

A feature of the Dorset coast is Portland Isle, connected to the mainland by the Chesil Beach or Bank, a long natural groyne of shingle that shelters Weymouth and its harbour for naval and channel-ferry purposes. Dorset is mainly a farming county, famous for its milk, cheese and butter, and for its sheep.

South-eastern England—particularly the county of Kent—is noted for its

J. Dixon-Scott.

The county of Kent is, in the main, agricultural, though coal mines are in operation in the vicinity of Dover. We think, indeed, of the "Garden of England" as a district of cornfields, orchards and hop gardens. Here, for instance, is the windmill at Cranbrook. Windmills are mostly used for grinding corn; and the arms, which carry the sails, may be 20 feet in length.

Will F. Taylor.

There are busy times in Kent when the hops are ripe and ready to be harvested. In the country districts there are insufficient people to do the gathering, so men, women and children from the poorer parts of London set out by train or motor lorry for the annual "hopping" expedition.

Will F. Taylor.

Quite a short distance to the west of Eastbourne we find Beachy Head, which rears its great chalk cliff to a height of upwards of 500 feet sheer from the sea. Once upon a time the name given to the British Isles was Albion, from the Latin *albus*, meaning white ; and it is almost certain that the name originated from our glistening white cliffs, of which Beachy Head is a splendid example. You will note the lighthouse at the foot of the cliff, for no ship could live if it struck the rocks in a storm at the base of this towering rampart.

IN THE GLADES OF THE FOREST

Alfieri.

In days gone by one of the chief industries of the New Forest was charcoal burning, and here we see the craftsmen at their work. For upwards of 1,000 years this occupation has been carried on, its knowledge and secrets being handed down from father to son. Now, however, the industry is fast dying out, and very soon there will be no charcoal burners left.

J. Dixon-Scott.

The so-called "New" Forest, which covers a large part of Hampshire between Southampton and Bournemouth, and has its feet on the sea-shore, is believed to have been planted so long ago as the days of William the Conqueror, though it is probably of greater antiquity. In our picture you see the curious twin trees, as well as the Rufus Stone. William Rufus was killed by the shaft of a crossbow at this spot. The King was buried at Winchester.

H. J. Shepstone.

Stonehenge (the actual meaning of the word is "the hanging stones") stands on the edge of Salisbury Plain, and no one can say in what manner the huge blocks were placed there. It is commonly believed that the great circle was a Temple of the Sun, and here we note repairs in progress, one of the upright stones having leaned out of position. On the longest day of the year (June 21st) many people visit Stonehenge to see the sun rise over the stone called the "Friar's Heel."

orchards and its hop-fields. Other famous orchard lands of the south-east are those of Essex, Sussex and Hampshire—all in the south-eastern portion of England.

This part of Britain is so good for fruit growing and hop growing because (1) the soil is rich and well-drained ; (2) there is just the right amount of rain at the right time of the year ; (3) this is the sunniest part of Britain, receiving some hundreds of hours more sunshine than any other part ; (4) it is quite near London and its suburbs, where the fruits find a ready market. Soft fruit must be got quickly to markets and shops, for it has to be sold fresh, or it cannot be sold at all, and this is an important reason why soft fruit growers always have their gardens near regions where large numbers of people live.

Forming a Wind-break.

Hops grow best on well-drained, sunny slopes ; Kent is hilly and sunny, and so grows more hops than any other part of Britain. Tall poles and many lengths of wire and string are necessary to support the plants ; and in fields that have exposed sides, trees are planted to form a wind-break, or an artificial wind-screen of canvas or sacking is put up.

In orchard lands and hop-fields a limited number of men are at work all the year round, for the trees must be tended, the hops must be planted, and the ground must be kept in order. But when the fruit-picking and the hop-picking seasons begin, large numbers of additional workers are required. Many of these are local folk, especially women and children ; but thousands come from the large towns to spend the fruit-picking and the hop-picking season in the country. Train-loads of hop-pickers go to Kent from London during the late summer.

Not all Kent is devoted to orchards and hop-fields ; there are parts which are quite unsuitable for fruit-growing or general agriculture. The high chalk hills (Downs) are mainly covered with grasses, although here and there suitable slopes are cultivated. This rich grassland is used for grazing sheep, which flourish on the crisp downland herbage.

Sheep Farmers and Sheep Lands.

Sheep can find a good living where cattle or horses would not, for sheep can do with less water than cattle or horses, and their small mouths enable them to feed on shorter grasses than those which best suit cattle and horses. Sheep like dry ground ; wet soil may give them disease. Cattle like moister ground, especially dairy cattle, which love the rich low-lying meadow lands.

On the chalky downlands of Kent, Sussex and Hampshire many sheep are fed, because the steep slopes of hard chalk provide quick drainage for rain, and are, therefore, much drier than the clayey lowlands ; the crisp grasses there are just the kind for sheep, and the dew-ponds provide water, and here and there on the Downs where grasses are longer and where water is available, cattle can be profitably grazed.

In the Downland.

The Downs of south-eastern England are not the only important British sheep lands. Wherever hill-slopes are covered with crisp grasses, and are dry enough, sheep are generally reared. Where, however, hillsides become too exposed in winter, or otherwise unsuitable for sheep, the animals are brought down to the lowlands for the winter months.

In a few parts of southern England, however, the reverse is the case ; for some of the lowland marshes (*e.g.*, Romney Marshes) give excellent feed for sheep in summer, when they are dry, but in winter they become too wet, so sheep are driven up to the hillsides just as winter comes on with its cold and wet.

A LIBRARY IN CHAINS

Will F. Taylor.

At one period printed books were so precious and so liable to be stolen that they were secured to their places on the shelves by means of chains. Here is the famous Chained Library of the Minster Church at Wimborne, in Dorset. To read a book one may place it upon the lectern, but the strong chain prevents its removal. This library was formed nearly 250 years ago. Even the Bibles were secured by chains in many of our churches in olden times; and there is another collection of chained books in Hereford Cathedral.

D 2

THE ENGLISH RIVIERA

THE ROCKING STONE ON DARTMOOR

J. Dixon-Scott.

Dartmoor is the largest piece of waste land in the south of England, but it is so wild and rugged, so beautiful and health-giving, that it has become a very popular holiday haunt. Here is the famous logan or rocking stone, to be found near Lustleigh Cleave. How this pile of rocks came to be so delicately balanced it is hard to say, but the stones are sometimes called the " Nut-crackers," because one may crack a nut with them, so perfectly are the granite slabs poised.

WHO has not heard of Devon-shire cream and cider, of Cornish pasties and pilchards, and of the spring flowers of the Scillies ? Some of us, perhaps, have been fortunate enough to spend holidays there, and know what lovely English counties Cornwall and Devon are.

They form a long peninsula that juts out far into the Atlantic, so that no part of it is far from the sea. The west winds from the ocean bring plenty of moisture that keeps the fertile valleys and grassy slopes green for the dairy cattle from whose rich milk Devon-shire butter and Cornish cream are made. These winds bring cool air from the sea in summer ; and in winter, when the sea is much warmer than the land, the westerly breezes make this peninsula milder and warmer than any other part of the British Isles. In the lovely gardens of Penzance and other towns grow palms and bamboos, and beautiful hydrangeas flourish in the open air. No wonder many people who dread cold weather go to Devon and Cornwall to spend the winter, instead of visiting more expensive foreign winter resorts of the Riviera. The winter climate of our English " Riviera " is just as good, and actually less liable to cold spells, for it has no *mistral* to chill one's marrow, and no dust.

The warm moist air of Cornwall and the Scilly Islands makes spring come earlier there than anywhere else in Britain ; that is why we look to these parts of our islands for our first sup-plies of spring flowers and vegetables.

The Moors.

Cornwall and Devon are very hilly, as we see when we go through them in the train. The railway follows the valleys, and avoids the high lands, where the hard old rocks have been raised into the moors for which this western peninsula is famous. *Exmoor*, in Somerset and North Devon, is made of hard sandstone, and stands up sharply in Dunkery Beacon ; *Dartmoor* and *Bodmin Moor* are great bosses of hard old granite, which has been much

CORNWALL'S CURIOUS CHEESEWRING

Will F. Taylor.

The quarrymen of Cornwall and Devon get out fine slate and beautiful granite for use in building, and these counties are both very rocky. Curious, indeed, are some of the rock formations. How, for instance, did this extraordinary pile become assembled in the manner illustrated? They form the "Cheesewring," to be found near Liskeard, in Cornwall, and it is known for certain that the pile existed in this form at least 300 years ago.

china, and some is used in preparing calico in Lancashire, or in glazing paper in Kent, or even in making false teeth in America ! *Fowey* is one of the ports which sends away this china clay in many directions.

A Lovely Coastline.

The coastline of this south-western peninsula is very beautiful, with its rocky cliffs, deep coves and sandy bays, and its water of Mediterranean blue, that sometimes becomes a sea of emerald shot with deep indigo. In former times it extended into the Atlantic, for the Scillies are the up-standing remnants of a sunken land that tradition says was part of King Arthur's lovely land of Lyonnesse. The ruins of Tintagel Castle remind us of the great King and his famous Knights of the Round Table.

Fishing is an important business along this coast. Immense shoals of

Will F. Taylor.

STEEPLE ROCK

If you were to visit the Lizard in Cornwall, you would find a rocky coast of great beauty. The pillar shown above is known as " Steeple Rock," and may be seen at Kynance Cove.

worn by wind and weather, leaving very hard parts upstanding as " tors." Yes Tor (2,028 feet) is the best known, but High Willhays overtops it by nearly a dozen feet. They say that a man who has not tramped over Dartmoor and seen its magic sunsets has yet one of the best things in life to enjoy.

In veins in some of the hard old rocks of Cornwall and Devon there are tin and copper, lead and zinc ; but they have been worked so long ago that there is not much metal left to be easily got. The chief mines are in the neighbourhood of Tavistock, St. Ives, and Camborne. Old workings used by the Romans, and even by people who were in Britain before the Romans came, are still to be seen. The quarry-men of Cornwall and Devon get out fine slate and beautiful granite from the rocks for use in building. From the granite, too, china clay is got ; much of it goes to the Potteries for making

Will F. Taylor.

CHEDDAR GORGE

In Devon and Cornwall you find hard granite rocks, but Somerset contains much limestone. Cheddar Gorge is a deep gape hewn by water out of the Mendip Hills, whose rocks tower above the roadway at Horseshoe Curve.

THE VILLAGE STOCKS

Will F. Taylor.

If we go right back to Saxon times we find that stocks were in use as a form of punishment. Men (and women, too) were held fast by the ankles, the stocks being made to open like a book to receive the unfortunate person's limbs. Here are the well-preserved stocks to be seen in the churchyard at Ottery St. Mary, Devon. Often we can find ancient stocks on village greens as relics of days that have passed ; and, more frequently still, in churchyards. This is because people who failed to attend church regularly were often punished in such a manner.

IN DEVON AND CORNWALL—

J. Dixon-Scott.

This is a scene typical of Devonshire, the well-known forge or blacksmith's shop at Cockington, near Torquay. Notice the narrow, winding lane ; the spreading trees, thatched buildings, and stone walls built without mortar or cement. Drake and Hawkins, Raleigh and Davis, were men of Devon.

Will F. Taylor.

Almost the whole coast of Cornwall is very rocky, and one may see the most curious and fantastic shapes. Here is the cave at Mullion Cove, a very popular Cornish resort. The photographer has arranged his picture so that the top of the cave forms a frame for Mullion Island just out to sea.

LAND OF THE SEA KINGS

J. Dixon-Scott.

Fishing is an important business along the Cornish seaboard. Immense shoals of pilchards and mackerel approach the coast at certain times of the year, and fishing fleets reap rich harvests. Here is a picture of St. Ives, one of the quaintest and best-known fishing towns in Cornwall.

Photochrom.

This weather-beaten cottage claims to be both the first and the last refreshment house in England. It stands very close to the rocky, windswept corner of the coast which we call Land's End. Between Land's End and the Scillies is the sunken territory which tradition says was Lyonnesse.

MAKING DEVONSHIRE CIDER

The rich, pastoral county of Devon is noted not only for its clotted cream, but also for its cider, a most wholesome beverage made from the rosy-cheeked apples with which the countryside abounds at Harvest Home. Here we see workmen preparing the apple pulp for the cider press.

In this picture the press is at work, forcing from the prepared pulp the sweet juices of the fruit. The juice passes then to large open vats, where any solid matter rises to the surface so that it is easily skimmed off. At a later stage the purified juice is allowed to ferment.

CHINA CLAY FROM CORNWALL

Cornwall is the chief source of china clay in the British Isles, and possesses the most extensive mines in the world.   The clay forms in association with granite.   Much of it goes to the Potteries for making china, and some is used in preparing calico in Lancashire, or in glazing paper in Kent. Here we see the settling ponds, where water is evaporated from the clay.

Some of the clay mines are enormously deep. The Southcaudledowns Mine, near Bugle, has workers 300 feet below the surface of the earth.   This photograph gives you an excellent idea of what the mine is like as you look down into it from above.   Note the narrow-gauge railway.

Will F. Taylor.

TINTAGEL CASTLE
These are the ruins of Tintagel Castle, in North Cornwall. The Castle, in legend, is associated with King Arthur, but the stone-work you see here dates from the thirteenth century.

pilchards and mackerel visit the shores at certain times of the year, and fishing fleets from Mevagissey and Penzance, St. Ives and Newlyn, Plymouth and Falmouth, reap rich harvests. From Brixham on the opposite side of Tor Bay to Torquay, the renowned Brixham trawlers go out into the Channel for flounders and plaice, turbot and brill, skate and hake.

The biggest town in south-western England is *Plymouth*, which, with Devonport and Stonehouse, forms the famous "Three Towns" of the West Country. Plymouth is a naval port commanding the Channel approaches, and also a port of call for large liners from which passengers and mails are landed for speedy transit to London by the expresses of the Great Western and Southern Railways. Its harbour is protected by a strong breakwater, and the Eddystone Lighthouse, a few miles off, flashes its welcome and warning to the ships. West of Plymouth the railway

crosses the famous Saltash Bridge on its way to Bodmin, Cornwall's county town, Truro, with its old cathedral, and Penzance.

The English Naples.

Torquay, "the English Naples," on beautiful Tor Bay, is visited yearly by many thousands in successful quest of health, recreation and sunshine. Its counterpart in North Devon is Ilfracombe, twenty miles due west of which is rocky Lundy Island, owned by a London business man, and issuing its own stamps and coinage. Smaller but very beautiful holiday places lie on both coasts of the south-western peninsula.

Exeter, an old Roman city, built where the Britons had a great fortress, stands where many roads and the railways converge to cross the Exe by its bridges. Its cathedral and its castle are well worth seeing, and so is its Elizabethan Guildhall which reminds us of Exeter's powerful guilds in Tudor times.

J. Dixon-Scott.

CLIFTON BRIDGE
The Avon, dividing Somerset from Gloucestershire, is spanned by the Clifton Suspension Bridge, here illustrated, whose carriage-way is nearly 300 feet above the river.

EAST ANGLIA

Central Press.

THE TRAIN FERRY FROM HARWICH

The only train ferry at present in use in the British Isles runs between Harwich and Zeebrugge.
It is employed in goods traffic only. Truckloads of merchandise from the Continent can be
shunted on board the ferry, taken to Harwich, and run off on to the main line of the London and
North-Eastern Railway Company.

EAST ANGLIA got its name from those Angles who, in the sixth century A.D., pushed up the tidal river estuaries in their longships, overcame the Britons, and established their own simple civilisation on the ruins of the Roman-British culture they found there. Originally Norfolk and Suffolk, East Anglia to-day usually includes the county of Essex as well. It is part of the rich agricultural lowland of south-eastern England, and, geologically at any rate, belongs to the London Basin.

In the west is the chalk country of the East Anglian Heights which come to the sea in the steep cliffs of Hunstanton Point. Most of it is the broad gentle slope from those low chalk hills to the North Sea, to which flow sluggish rivers with marshland along their lower courses, and deep estuaries up which the sea-tides make their way. Connected with the lower Yare are the Norfolk Broads, wide sheets of shallow water formed by the barring of the old estuary by sandspits and mudbanks, and to-day a favourite summer resort for those who love sailing and camping and fishing.

The Sunshine Coast.

Orwell and Stour combine their estuaries to form the deep-water harbour of *Harwich*, a naval station guarded by the forts and seaplane base near Felixstowe, and an important ferry-town for the Continent. Mail steamers ply regularly between Harwich and the Hook of Holland, Flushing and Antwerp, and Esbjerg, in Denmark. The only train-ferry at present in use in Britain runs between Harwich and Zeebrugge. It is employed in goods traffic only. Truck-loads of goods from the Continent can be shunted on board the ferry, taken to Harwich and run off to the L.N.E.R. main line to Liverpool Street or the North.

The coast of East Anglia is low and marshy towards the south, but from

Thorpe Ness northwards it has cliffs of firm gravel and sand. The whole coastline has undergone subsidence, and the ruins of several of the old towns and villages now lie beneath the sea. Ancient Dunwich was an important city and port in the Middle Ages, with many churches, monasteries and a king's palace ; to-day all that is left of it is a small fishing village nestling behind a steep cliff on whose brink totter the few ruins of its former greatness. Aldeburgh, now a pleasant but small seaside resort, and once an important port, is another town that has suffered in the past from the inroads of the sea.

This is the drier and sunnier side of Britain, with many more hours of sunshine yearly than the rest, and the whole coastline is studded with popular seaside resorts — Southend, Walton, Clacton - on - Sea, Dovercourt, Felixstowe, Aldeburgh, Southwold, Lowestoft, Yarmouth, Sheringham, Cromer and Hunstanton.

Yarmouth and Lowestoft are the headquarters of great British herring and sprat fisheries in autumn, when Scots lassies come south to deal with the catch, cleaning the fish, grading them and packing them into barrels with salt, with the amazing speed born of long practice. Many other fish, too, are caught and landed at these and many smaller ports along the coast. Colchester oysters from the oyster-beds of the Colne estuary are almost as famous as Yarmouth bloaters and kippers.

A Farming Region.

East Anglia is mainly a farming region, where a good deal of our home supplies of meat, wool, grain, fruit and vegetables, butter and milk are produced. In the Middle Ages East Anglia was the home of flourishing woollen

Will F. Taylor.

HORNING FERRY INN, NORFOLK

In the counties of Norfolk and Suffolk are to be found the Broads, sheets of shallow water that yet afford navigable channels extending at least to 200 miles. Here we see the Ferry Inn at Horning, near which the Rivers Bure and Ant meet. In the foreground you will notice trim bundles of reeds. The Broads are a great centre of the reed industry, reeds being largely used for thatching roofs. From Norfolk skilled thatchers go not only all over England, but abroad as well to ply their craft.

industries; worsted got its name from Worstead, near Norwich, where the Flemish weavers settled in Anglo-Norman times. Great churches, all too large for their villages and small towns, bear witness to ancient days when their population was much larger than it is now.

To-day, the woollen manufactures have gone chiefly to the coalfields of the Midlands and the North, and the old East Anglian woollen towns engage in other business— milling, brewing and distilling, and manufacturing the goods and machinery needed by an agricultural population. Most of them are market towns to which country folk bring their produce, and from which they take home things they need but cannot grow or make for themselves. The very names of some of them—Newmarket (famous for its "Heath" and its horse races), Stowmarket, Needham Market—prove this.

Ipswich has iron foundries and engineering works; it makes agricultural implements and garden tools, and so does *Norwich*, the lovely old Cathedral and castle city on the Wensum, where woollen goods and boots and shoes are made, and also chocolates and confectionery, beer and mineral waters, as well as mustard from local-grown supplies of seed.

In Essex and nearer London, several modern factories have been set up, notably those for making *rayon* (artificial silk). But it is as grainland that East Anglia is most important—field after field of splendid tall strong wheat,

Central Press.

THE SEA TAKES TOLL

The coast line of East Anglia is being gradually beaten back by the sea. Ruins of several of the old towns and villages now lie beneath the water. In this photograph, taken at Corton, near Lowestoft, you see how the coast, battered by heavy seas and undermined by rain, has collapsed, carrying away with it portions of houses. It costs many thousands of pounds every year to wage war against the encroaching sea.

heavy with gold-red ears, especially in the northern half of the region, where beautiful old thatched houses are perhaps commoner than anywhere else in Britain.

Golden Grain.

Why is south-eastern Britain the place where most British wheat is grown?

First of all, the land there is rich enough and the soil stiff enough to grow fine tall heavy wheat. Much of this soil is fine earth made by prehistoric glaciers grinding over the rocks and powdering their surfaces into fine "rock flour," which was left behind when the ancient ice melted and streams washed it down and spread it out over the plains of the east.

But good soil by itself is not enough ; to grow fine wheat the fields must have just the right amount of rain and sunshine at the right time.

Wheat needs rain when it is springing up and sprouting, and when the ears of grain are forming. After that, it requires long bright sunny days to ripen the ears, and then to give the farmer a chance to reap and harvest the grain during fine dry weather.

This is exactly what happens in most years in East Anglia and in other parts of south-eastern Britain. The rains of spring and early summer sprout the wheat, make it grow tall and strong, and swell the ears. The long sunny days of late summer and early autumn ripen the grain and give the farmer a sunshine harvest-time.

Fruit-growing is important in Essex, where rich soil and plenty of sunshine give heavy crops. Poultry farming and market gardening, too, flourish nearer London, whose millions of workers ensure a ready and profitable market. Sugar beet is now cultivated in several districts of East Anglia, and sugar factories have been set up, for sugar beet grows just as well there as on the opposite side of the North Sea.

Rail and Road.

The L.N.E.R. serves this part of England. One main route goes *viâ Chelmsford*, the market centre and county town of Essex, through *Colchester*, once a fine Roman city and now an important military and market centre, to *Ipswich*, whence two main lines branch—one to serve the east coast watering-places, the other to Norwich and the north coast. Another main line cuts north by way of the Lea Valley, Bishop's Stortford, Cambridge and Ely to Norwich and to King's Lynn.

Will F. Taylor.

SPARROWE'S HOUSE AT IPSWICH

We can learn much from ancient buildings and should regard them with the veneration they deserve. This fine house, for example, which stands in the Butter Market at Ipswich, was built in 1567, and shows us the kind of residence in which people formerly lived. The plaster work on the front (of later date) exhibits effigies connected with Europe, Asia, Africa and America. Ipswich has iron foundries and engineering works, and makes agricultural implements and garden tools.

SCOTTISH FISHER LASSIES AT WORK

Sport and General.

At the height of the fishing season and when huge catches of herrings are taken into our great fishery ports of Lowestoft and Great Yarmouth, Scots lassies travel south to deal with the harvest of the sea, cleaning the fish, grading them, and packing them into barrels with salt.

Sport and General.

In the above photograph is shown another group of the women and girls.　The herring is a fish of great value to human beings as food.　When it is salted we call it a "bloater"; and eat it also as a 'kipper,' after it has been smoked.　Herrings travel about in great shoals.

MAKING SUGAR FROM BEETROOT

(1) Sugar beet is now cultivated in several districts in East Anglia, and extensive factories have been set up, for the beetroot grows just as well there as on the opposite side of the North Sea. In this photograph you see truckloads of beet collected in railway sidings adjacent to a factory.

(2) Here we observe the beetroots being passed into a channel along which water flows swiftly.

(3) In this picture the roots are being literally washed out of the railway truck by water.

(4) Some of the intricate machinery employed for extracting sugar from beetroot and separating it from the water and waste.

(5) The finished beet sugar, bagged and ready for transfer to the warehouse. Another lorry load of the roots has arrived as raw material.

BROWN SAILS OF THE BROADS

Will F. Taylor.

Though we are apt to think of the Norfolk and Suffolk Broads as a holiday playground, these sheets of water and the navigable channels by which they are connected are much used for transporting coal, bricks, heavy commodities generally, and countryside produce. Here is a typical Broadland barge, with brown sails, moored adjacent to the Wherry Hotel at Oulton Broad.

THE FENLANDS

OLIVER CROMWELL'S HOUSE

Will F. Taylor.

The so-called " Isle of Ely " was for long the camp of refuge for English freedom, for hereabouts Hereward the Wake had his stronghold. Oliver Cromwell, who was born at Huntingdon, also spent much time in these parts, and you see above the photograph of an old house at Ely which was for a while in the occupation of the Lord Protector. It is a pleasing sight to gaze upon the massive tower of Ely Cathedral, standing sentinel in this flat fenland country.

THIS is the country of Hereward the Wake, who, secure in his Camp of Refuge amid the marshes, long defied Norman William, who in the end went to great lengths to make peace with him. The story of this grand old Anglo-Saxon is told in Charles Kingsley's " Hereward the Wake," where you may read of the fenland, of the men who fought there in Hereward's days, and of those who lived there in Kingsley's time :—

"Such was the Fenland—hard, yet cheerful ; rearing a race of hard and cheerful men, showing their power in old times in valiant fighting, and for many a century since in that valiant industry which has drained and embanked the land, till it has become a very garden of the Lord. And the highlander who may look from the promontory of Peterborough, the ' golden borough ' of old time ; or from that Witham on the Hill which once was a farm of Hereward the Wake's ; or from the heights of that Isle of Ely which was so long the camp of refuge for English freedom—over the maze of dykes and lodes, the squares of rich corn and verdure, will confess that the lowlands, as well as the highlands, can at times breed gallant men."

The English Holland.

The Fen country is the low land round the large inlet of the Wash, into which flow several long slow rivers. At their seaward ends these rivers are filled with tide-water from the sea when the tide is high ; but when the tide is low their water is shallower and their smaller streams flow between wide steep banks of soft mud. For miles they have banks built by men to keep them in their channels when the water is high, or they would overflow the surrounding country, which is at a lower level there.

When there were no banks, these streams overflowed and created great swamps, which were the homes of myriads of water fowl. Reeds and coarse vegetation choked the rivers and overran the swamps. But here and there were patches of higher and firmer

SCENES AND SIGHTS OF CAMBRIDGE

Photochrom.

The beautiful old colleges and their chapels are the chief attractions for visitors to Cambridge. King's College Chapel, illustrated above, is an architectural wonder of the world.

Will F. Taylor.

The River Cam flows placidly through the grounds of many Cambridge colleges. Here we see St. John's, which possesses two bridges, one known as the "Bridge of Sighs."

Will F. Taylor.

Many Cambridge colleges have verdant lawns and beautiful gardens leading right down to the edge of the river Cam, and the ancient buildings thus appear in a setting at once dignified and restful. In this picture we see the grounds of King's College, with Clare College beyond. In the Middle Ages Cambridge was one of the chief distributing centres of England.

land that stood up a little above the marshes, like islands (as indeed they came to be called). In later times towns arose on these fenland "islands"; some of these are important to-day—the cathedral cities of Ely and Peterborough, for example. It was on just such a high and dry spot that Hereward's "Camp of Refuge" was made.

Cambridge.

Other towns grew up on the borders of the Fenland, where higher ground provided good sites. The University town of *Cambridge*, for example, commanded the ridge of downland which in early times formed the only means of communication between East Anglia and the Midlands. To the north lay impassable fenland; to the south impenetrable forest. In the Middle Ages Cambridge was one of the chief distributing centres of England; but when the silting up of the Wash closed its ports, trade declined, and its great annual fair—"Stourbridge Fair"—became but a shadow of itself. It is the University that makes it important to-day; and the beautiful old colleges and their chapels are the chief attraction for visitors. King's College Chapel is one of the architectural wonders of the world. As one would expect in a University town, printing and bookbinding is its chief industry. Its market and corn exchange are still important, however, to the farmers of the surrounding countryside.

The Fertile Fens.

The Fens form "a vast level of black peaty soil 2 feet to 6 feet deep, resting on clay," and stretching into six English counties. This region is kept drained by windmills and steam pumping stations where water is lifted into drainage channels to find a natural way to the rivers and the sea.

A great deal of fenland is now used by farmers, and intersected by "droves" or straight roads that lead from village to field. Much of it is

J. Dixon-Scott.

AT TRINITY COLLEGE, CAMBRIDGE

The charm of old buildings, in a perfect setting, could never be better seen than in this picture of Trinity College, Cambridge. Our view shows the Great Court with its lawn and fountain. As one would expect in a University city, printing and bookbinding form the chief industry of Cambridge.

THE GREAT GATE OF ST. JOHN'S, CAMBRIDGE *J. Dixon-Scott.*
Gateways play a considerable part in all ancient buildings because they were of such importance in more troublous times than those in which we live. Here is the Great Gate of St. John's College, Cambridge. On the site of the College once stood the Hospital of St. John, the conversion being undertaken by Lady Margaret Beaufort, Countess of Richmond, the mother of Henry VII. St. John's " Bridge of Sighs " is comparatively modern, and bears no connection with the famous bridge of the Doge's Palace in Venice.

grazing land for cattle and horses, but in recent years large areas have been turned into fertile fields, orchards and gardens. Cambridgeshire, indeed, has more plough land in proportion to its size than any other English county. The Fen country is famous for its heavy crops of potatoes, its fine celery, and its splendid vegetables, all of which are grown in large quantities for the great markets in London and the English Midlands.

More interesting still are the orchard lands in the Fen country. Acres and acres of strawberries and raspberries, plums and apples, and other fruit pro-vide work for fruit-pickers from June to October. Potato-lifters and pea-pickers, too, find employment there. At some of the towns and villages (*e.g.*, Histon and Shippea Hill) large jam factories, fruit canneries and vegetable canneries have been built, and their goods find their way to shops throughout the Homeland and the British Empire.

The oolite Northampton Heights (whose rich iron deposits feed the blast furnaces of Wellingborough, our second largest iron producer) bound the Fens on the west, and the chalk hills of the Chilterns to the East Anglian Heights bound them on the south and east.

THE HEART OF ENGLAND

Will F. Taylor.

ANNE HATHAWAY'S COTTAGE.

Anne Hathaway became the wife of William Shakespeare, and the delightful cottage above was her girlhood home, for she was the daughter of a farmer. The cottage, which was inhabited by generation after generation of Hathaways, is at Shottery, but a short walk from Stratford-on-Avon. There can scarcely in the whole world be a humble homestead better known than this one. Descendants of Anne Hathaway lived here until 1911.

THE very centre of England, they say, is in Warwickshire, the county of beautiful woods and gardens, through which the Avon flows on its way to the Severn. This is Shakespeare's country, for on the Avon is Stratford, where the greatest poet and dramatist of all time was born in 1564, and where you can visit the house and go into the very room in which the "Bard of Avon" first saw the light. The town is visited by large numbers of people every year; they come from all parts of the civilised world to see the birth-place of Shakespeare, and the wonderful collection of Shakespeare relics in its rooms, the old Grammar School which he is said to have attended, and the cottage at Shottery near-by, where he courted and won Anne Hathaway.

In the neighbourhood are still the remnants of the Forest of Arden, which Shakespeare loved; and in the towns and villages are lovely old Tudor houses that remind us of the days of Good Queen Bess when Shakespeare was doing some of his finest work. Beneath the shadow of Warwick Castle, which is finely preserved, are the beautiful old Tudor houses of Mill Street; and not far away is Kenilworth Castle, where Leicester entertained Queen Elizabeth with splendid hospitality.

The Red Plain.

Warwickshire is part of the English Midlands, which geologists call "The Red Plain." It *is* red—red in the fertile fields when it has been newly turned up by the plough, red in its wayside walls and in the mellow stone of its old cottages, country seats and ancient castles. For the whole of this heart of England is floored with the New Red Sandstone, which is the colour of old-rose; from it the fertile red soil has been formed, and from it the stone for building has been taken. But in places humps of much older and harder rocks have thrust through this New Red Sandstone floor—in Charnwood Forest and in Cannock Chase, for example—and it is in and around such old rocks as these that the great coalfields of the English Midlands lie.

The boundaries of this Midland region are clearly shown on any good map. The oolite (limestone) ridges which can be traced from the Cotswolds through Edge Hill and the North-ampton Heights to Lincoln Edge and the Humber form its southern boun-dary. Its western limits are the Welsh Highlands, along whose edges are the old "Marches" or border lands held in the Middle Ages by the "Lords Marchers"—stout fighters with strong bands of retainers to keep back the Welsh raiders.

In the north the Pennines project far into the plain, above whose floor they stand like a giant promontory of limestone thrust into a sea of sand-stone. From the Pennines, beautiful streams like the Dove and Derwent flow down through their lovely dales to swell their lordly Trent that sweeps on past Burton, the home of the best English ales, past Nottingham, the busy town of the hosiers and boot-makers, past the old castle town of Newark, and through farm lands and factory centres to the deep estuary of the Humber.

The Midland Sea Gates.

The English Midland Plain has three great gateways through which the pro-ducts of its mines and busy factories pour to the wide world. The china and crockery of the Potteries; the boots and shoes of Stafford, Northamp-

Will F. Taylor

INSIDE THE COTTAGE AT SHOTTERY

Here we are shown the interior of Anne Hathaway's cottage, almost exactly as it must have been in the days when she and William Shakespeare sat at the open fireplace. Stratford is in Warwick-shire, which is regarded as being the very centre of England. Through the county flows the Avon on its way to join the Severn.

ton, Nottingham and Leicester; the iron and other metal goods of the Black Country; the motor cars and cycles of Coventry and other centres; and the goods from the engineering shops and electrical works of Rugby and its neighbours all use these gateways. They are sea-gates—one, the Mersey gate at which stands the great city-port of *Liverpool*, with its ship-building sister-town of Birkenhead across the water. Another is the Humber gate, with the important port of *Hull* (or Kingston-upon-Hull as we should rightly call it if we stick to its old name), and its sister-port of Goole farther up the estuary. The third is the Severn gate where are *Newport* and *Cardiff*, which serve not only the Midlands, but also the busy coal and metal businesses of the South Wales coalfield; and on the other side of the estuary, the city-port of *Bristol* on the Bristol Avon with its outport for deep-water ships at Avonmouth.

Ways Across the Red Plain.

South-eastwards, across the oolite ridge and the clay vale on the other side, and then over the chalk Chilterns several great main railways provide highways to *London*, the Imperial Port where gather the ships of the seven seas. L.N.E.R. and L.M.S. main routes cut across the eastern side of the Red Plain, serving Northampton, Nottingham, Leicester and Derby on their way to the north by the eastern flanks of the Pennines. Other main routes, L.N.E.R., L.M.S. and G.W.R. pass through the heart of the plain and serve its western borders, too. The western L.M.S. route to Scotland cuts through the Midland Gate (in which is the great

Will F. Taylor.

SHAKESPEARE'S GARDEN AT STRATFORD

William Shakespeare, the greatest poet and dramatist of all time, was born in 1564 at Stratford-on-Avon. Here is maintained, in New Place, the famous Knot Gardens, designed to reflect a pleasance exactly as it would have been in the lifetime of the Bard of Avon. The very shrubs and plants mentioned in Shakespeare's writings are, where possible, cultivated in his memory.

THE DESK OF THE BARD OF AVON

Our greatest dramatist was born in Henley Street, Stratford-on-Avon, and you can visit the house and go into the very room in which he first saw the light. Adjoining is a museum containing pictures, books, MSS. and other relics, including the time-worn desk shown above. This desk was removed from the Grammar School, where Shakespeare was a pupil.

railway junction and engineering town of Crewe) between the Pennines and Welsh mountains to reach the busy plain of South Lancashire. The G.W.R. crosses the Red Plain by way of the Black Country to Shrewsbury, from whence a main line goes up the Severn Valley into the very heart of Wales.

It is in the Midland Plain, too, that our canals spread their closest network. The main canal routes form a kind of X with Mersey, Humber, Severn and Thames at the extremities of its four arms. Near the crossing of the arms lie the Black Country and the Potteries, where the system of canals is closer than anywhere else in Britain.

Our Canals.

Our canals are not nearly so flourishing as those of the Dutch, the Belgians, the French and the Germans, for many have been allowed to fall into disuse, and some can only admit " monkey-boats " of about 30 tons. On these the canal folk live with their families, every member of which takes a part in the work almost as soon as he or she can run about without fear of falling overboard. Horses are still much used to tow the barges along, but in recent years steam barges and motor barges have become common on most of our leading canals.

On some of the continental canals, barges of a thousand tons and more are in common use. British canals might be made much more valuable if they were deepened and widened and brought under a central control. As it is, the canal route between London and the Mersey is made up of many parts of different sorts and sizes, so that only boats which can pass the smallest locks can get through.

The Red Plain has rich soil, and abundant grasses suitable for cattle and sheep—cattle (especially dairy

Topical Press.

ENGLAND'S WATER GIPSIES

In the Midlands of England our canals spread their closest network. On the canals the barge-folk live with their families, every member of which takes a part in the work almost as soon as he or she can run about without the fear of falling overboard. Horses are still much used to tow the barges along, but in recent years steam barges and motor barges have become common on most of the leading canals. The vessel on the left above is a " monkey-boat " of about 30 tons.

Central Press.

A BUSY SCENE WITH THE BARGES

In the Black Country, the Potteries, Yorkshire, and great manufacturing centres, barges are still largely used for the slow and comparatively cheap transportation of coal and other heavy commodities. Above is illustrated a busy scene on the Aire, in Yorkshire, a river which is closely connected with our main canal system. British canals might be made much more valuable if they were deepened and widened.

cattle) on the plains of Staffordshire and Cheshire (Cheshire cheese!), but sheep on the higher and drier ground of the hills, especially the slopes of the oolite ridge. The hides from its cattle and the wool from its sheep, the clear water and power from its running streams gave rise in early times to the great boot and shoe industries and the woollen industries which have long had their home there, and which grew by leaps and bounds when the rich coalfields of the Midlands were opened up.

In the Coalfields.

The coalfields, as we have already seen, are chiefly on and around the humps of ancient rocks that in past ages forced themselves through the level floor of New Red Sandstone. Each of them has its own particular business, which began in the first place because of special local advantages.

There are, first of all, the coalfields of the Pennine flanks—the South Staffordshire, and the Derby and Nottingham fields. The former is universally known as the " Potteries " because its characteristic manufactures are of china, earthenware and pottery of all kinds. The chief centres are " The Five Towns," of which Hanley, Burslem and Stoke-on-Trent are the chief. The latter is really the extension into the Midlands of the great Yorkshire coalfield, and on it are the iron and steel and engineering works of Derby and Chesterfield, the woollen and cotton hosiery and boot business of Nottingham and Mansfield, and the silk manufactures of Derby and its neighbourhood.

In the very heart of the Red Plain are three coalfields : (1) the " Black Country " or South Staffordshire coalfield ; (2) the Warwickshire coalfield ; (3) the Leicestershire coalfield

The Black Country.

The first gets its name from the " black " industries carried on beneath

Will F. Taylor.

Country cottages are naturally made of the materials that come most readily to hand. Here, for example, we see how timber, bricks and small tiles are used. These cottages are at Tong, in Shropshire, associated with " Little Nell " of " The Old Curiosity Shop."

J. Dixon-Scott.

This cottage may be seen near Fleshwick Bay, in the Isle of Man. It is made of rough stone and the thatch is actually tied to pieces of wood which project from the crude gable end and front and rear walls. Note how the Manx cottage is set in a fold of the ground to give it some protection.

J. Dixon-Scott.

Cottages at Selworthy, Somerset. They have been thatched with straw by a master of the craft. A thatched roof is cool in summer and warm in winter, but is liable to catch fire.

Will F. Taylor.

Surrey has many such cottages as the one depicted above, numbers of them of great age. They are constructed of oak timbering filled in with bricks and the roofs are of stone slabs.

J. Dixon-Scott.

Devonshire is a county of charming cottages, many of which are constructed of nothing but earth rammed first in wooden moulds, which lasts for countless years. Clay or chalk, mixed with cut straw, is also employed. The cottages above are at Thurlestone.

THE CLOSE AT RUGBY SCHOOL

Rugby, one of our foremost public schools for boys, dates back nearly 400 years.   Here the game
Rugby Football was first played, and one always thinks of the classic story "Tom Brown's
Schooldays" in connection with Rugby under its great headmaster, Arnold.   Our illustration shows the Close, with the School beyond.   On the left is the Chapel, with the old buildings
to the right.

a pall of smoke from factory chimneys,
and from its grimy canals and giant
heaps of black and grey waste from the
coal mines or of slag from many blast
furnaces. The great city of Birmingham is near the south-eastern edge of
the coalfield and not on it. It makes
all kinds of metal goods, and is the
business heart of the Black Country.

It has many splendid buildings, and
like most of the big industrial towns
of the Midlands and the North, much
beautiful country around it, and
within easy reach of the city. Other
towns in the Black Country, Wolver-
hampton, Walsall, Wednesbury, Dudley
and West Bromwich, for example,
engage in various branches of the iron
and steel trades and in working in
metals, as well as in engineering and
chemical industries. Each, however,

has its own special business, which is
more important than the several others
carried on there.

We must bear in mind that when we
speak of a certain town as carrying on
a special manufacture, it is the *chief*,
and by no means the only, business
conducted by its workers. Large
factory towns, especially in the Midlands and the North, engage in very
many different industries, because most
of them have been built on or near the
coalfields ; and coal, the source of
power, is all-important in modern
industry in our country, where water-
power is as yet little used.

Yet Other Coalfields.

The Warwick coalfield is near enough
to Coventry and Rugby to be an advantage to both ; Coventry specialises

in motor engineering, and Rugby in the making of electrical apparatus, tramcars and lifts. The Leicestershire coalfield is some few miles from Leicester; it is purely a coalfield, and has no great manufacture which has made its home upon it; it has no large industrial cities like most of the other coalfields, but many mining villages and small towns. Ashby-de-la-Zouch is the most important of them.

On the western borders of the Midland Plain are three other coalfields—the Flint and Denbigh fields, with ironworks at Wrexham, the Shropshire or Mid-Severn coalfields, and the Forest of Dean; which, like the Leicestershire coalfield, is a field pure and simple, and not the home of any great manufacturing industry.

The Forest itself is very beautiful, especially where the Wye comes down from its deep wooded and winding valley past the ruins of Tintern Abbey to Chepstow Castle and the Severn estuary. Tintern Abbey was founded in 1131 by the lord of the castle at Chepstow for Cistercian monks, and was built according to the Cistercian rule: "None of our houses is to be built in cities, in castles, or villages; but in places remote from the conversation of men."

The Salt Towns.

The western side of the Midland Plain, too, has rich salt deposits and

J. Dixon-Scott.

THE RUINS OF TINTERN ABBEY

One of the most entrancing of English rivers is the Wye, and we should all endeavour to make a journey through the lovely Wye Valley. If we do, we shall see the remains of Tintern Abbey, shown in the photograph above, the road from Chepstow to Monmouth affording a delightful view. This ruined building, so perfect in style and proportion, was founded in 1131, so that it has already witnessed the passing of 800 years.

brine springs. In Cheshire, along the line of the Weaver Valley, Nantwich, Middlewich and Northwich are the " salt towns " sending large quantities by the Weaver Navigation Canal to the chemical factories along the Manchester Ship Canal and Merseyside to be utilised in making bleaching powders and other products used in the cotton industry of South Lancashire. Bores are sunk into the rock-salt, water is admitted and afterwards pumped up as brine from which the salt is recovered by evaporation. The subterranean hollows thus created cannot be propped up like workings in a coal mine, and the result is that in places large subsidences have occurred ; houses lean this way and that, and in some cases sink to such a low level that the only means of entrance is by way of the windows !

Topical Press.

A WONDERFUL TRANSPORTER BRIDGE

In the teeming industrial districts, over which a pall of dense smoke seems always to be drifting, the rapid transport of various commodities is essential, and sometimes elaborate methods have to be followed. As a case in point, here is a picture of Middlesbrough, in Yorkshire. The much-used River Tees at this point is bridged by a transporter. Thus a kind of monster cradle, suspended from girders high overhead by wire ropes, is moved from one bank to the other, carrying both passengers and goods. In this way there is no interference with the floating traffic of the river.

THE BUSY NORTH

Topical Press.

WOOL ARRIVING AT BRADFORD, YORKSHIRE

Bradford is the second largest of the great woollen towns of Yorkshire, and specialises in mohair fabrics. Here we see wool in its raw state packed in bales being loaded from trucks to lorries in the station yard of the London, Midland and Scottish Railway. Most of our wool now comes from Australia, New Zealand, South Africa and the Argentine. Yorkshire is the largest of the English counties, and is divided into three Ridings, an old word, meaning " thirds." Bradford is in the West Riding.

NORTHERN ENGLAND is the home of many of Britain's most important industries, for it is well supplied with coal and iron, which are the basis of manufactures, and it has many splendid harbours with large and thriving ports from which the manufactured goods can be exported to all parts of the world, and through which foodstuffs to feed the teeming millions of workers and raw materials to supply the mills and factories can be imported.

Beautiful Scenery.

But we shall make a sad mistake if we suppose that the North of England is a region blighted by endless mines and factory chimneys, and covered with an everlasting pall of smoke. The North of England is a beautiful district. Those who have wandered over the Yorkshire moors, or explored the pretty

dales of Yorkshire, Durham and Northumberland, or tramped over the Pennines, will bear eager witness to that. And linked to the Pennines by the " saddle " of Shap Fell is the English Lake District, which has more real beauty of mountain and dale, lake and fell packed into its small compass than any other region of the same size anywhere on the globe.

There is wonderful scenery within half an hour's ride from many of the big industrial centres ; some, indeed, like Sheffield, have beautiful moorland scenery actually within their boundaries. We have only to go north by train to see green fields, deep woodlands or fine hill scenery separate mines and factory towns.

On the eastern flanks of the Pennines are the three counties of Northumberland, Durham and Yorkshire, well watered by rivers like the Tyne, Wear, Tees and Yorkshire Ouse, which are very beautiful in their upper courses, but become busy industrial rivers near their mouths.

Two great coalfields are there : the Northumberland and Durham, and the Yorkshire coalfield, which sends more coal to London and the south than any other in Britain.

The Coaly Tyne.

Through the very heart of the first runs the "coaly" Tyne, on which stands the great coal-exporting and ship-building port of Newcastle, with its sister town of Gateshead across the river on the southern bank—the two linked by a high railway bridge, carrying the L.N.E.R. trains north for Scot-

land. The banks of the Tyne from Newcastle to the sea are lined with chemical, glass and other factories, iron and steel works, ship-building yards and engineering shops. At the mouth stand Tynemouth, North Shields and South Shields, which share the coal export trade with Blyth farther north, and with Sunderland at the mouth of the Wear, in Durham.

Through the Tyne Gap runs the railway from Newcastle to Carlisle, and following it fairly closely is the old Roman wall of Hadrian, which in places is still sufficiently well-preserved to show what it must have been like during the Roman occupation—walls, turrets and forts and camps can be traced to this day.

Durham, with its ancient castle and

J. F. Corrigan.

BUILT BY THE ROMANS

The railway and also a good motoring road between Newcastle-upon-Tyne and Carlisle follow fairly closely the old Wall of Hadrian, which in places is still sufficiently well-preserved to show what it must have been like during the Roman occupation. The original wall, built to defend England's northern frontier, ran from Solway Firth to the Tyne, and was upwards of 70 miles in length. Can you think of the place where the wall ended on the east ? Why, at Wallsend-on-the-Tyne, of course !

Will F. Taylor.

A ROMAN STATION AS IT IS TO-DAY

The Roman Emperor Hadrian built his marvellous wall in the year 122. It was constructed of freestone blocks with a rubble core. Severus, a Roman Emperor, repaired it in 208, and walls, turrets, forts and camps can be traced to this day. Here is the Roman station of Cilurnum at Chesters, in Northumberland. The ruins are those of barrack-rooms, each accommodating about ten men.

fine cathedral built on high ground in a loop of the Wear, is one of the most beautiful cities of the North.

Cleveland Iron.

At the mouth of the Tees is Middlesbrough, in the North Riding of Yorkshire—the home of Britain's greatest iron and steel industries. Steel from Middlesbrough has gone to make some of the finest ships, the largest steel-frame buildings, and the most wonderful bridges in the world. The great bridge across Sydney Harbour in New South Wales was built by a Middlesbrough firm from Middlesbrough steel.

Good iron from the Cleveland Hills behind the town, good coal from the Durham field to provide the coke for the blast furnaces, and plenty of lime-

stone with which to smelt the ironstone are within easy reach of the industry. Often, indeed, the steel-making firm owns its own ironstone, its own coal mines and its own limestone quarries, as well as its own ships on the deep water of the Tees estuary.

Stockton and Darlington, farther up the Tees Valley, share in the iron and steel business; Darlington specialises in railway plant and is one of the " homes " of the L.N.E.R. engines and trains.

Yorkshire is the largest of the English counties, and is divided into three " Ridings " (an old word, meaning " thirds ")—the West Riding, which is by far the busiest and most thickly populated; the North Riding, which is partly manufacturing and partly agricultural; and the East Riding, which is mainly agricultural. Yorkshire men are proud of their county—and they have every reason to be.

The Busy West Riding.

The West Riding is the home of our biggest woollen industry, which grew up there in the old days because plenty of wool could be got from the sheep grazing on the hillsides; and there was sufficient clear running water to wash it, and many streams to turn the mills. Nowadays, however, most of the wool comes from Australia, New Zealand, South Africa and the Argentine, and it is manufactured into all kinds of woollen goods in great mills and factories, most of which are driven by steam power from coal. The Yorkshire coal has done more than anything else to make the industry so important, but we must bear in mind that the woollen business was already there when the coalfield began to be widely opened up.

As we saw in the Black Country, the towns of the West Riding each produce a special kind of goods, or do some particular branch of the work. *Leeds*, the metropolis of the woollen country, makes more ready-made clothing than any other centre in the world; *Bradford*, the second largest of the woollen towns, specialises in mohair fabrics; *Halifax* has the world's biggest carpet factories; *Dewsbury* is the place for heavy woollens, and *Huddersfield* for worsted cloth and for dyeing. Leeds stands at the meeting-place of many routes that converge upon it to pass through the gap in the Pennines made by the Aire tributary of the Yorkshire Ouse.

Through the Aire gap run L.M.S. expresses on their way to Carlisle and Scotland; and the Leeds and Liverpool Canal, which is the water-link between the woollen towns of the West Riding and the cotton towns of South Lancashire. There are many railways and roads, however, across the Southern Pennines connecting these two leading factory districts of Britain.

"Sheffield Make."

In southern Yorkshire another great industry has long been established—the steel cutlery and plate industry of Sheffield and Rotherham on the Don. All the world recognises the imprint "Made in Sheffield" as the hall-mark of excellence on cutlery. Here, again, we find a great business growing up because of the local advantages of coal and iron, grindstones from the millstone grit of the Pennines, and power from the river; and growing so huge that local iron is not sufficient, and it becomes necessary to import the finest Swedish and Spanish iron ores to make the steel.

The city of *York* (the old Roman *Eboracum*), in the midst of the broad and fertile Vale of York, has a history that reaches back to early British times, and buildings that take its story from Roman times to the present day.

The Humber Ports.

The great port of *Hull* is the sea gate of the busy West Riding, the whole of the basin of the Trent and the English Midlands. It specialises in trade with Australia and New Zealand, but ships from all the great ports of the world enter its spacious docks. *Goole* is a growing port farther up the estuary, and carries on a big business in oilseed and palm-kernel crushing. The vegetable oils thus obtained go to make margarine, or soap and candles.

Grimsby, like Hull, is a huge fishing port and market on the opposite side of the Humber mouth. It is in Lincolnshire. Not far from it are the large docks of Immingham, a port for Baltic Lands. Some few miles inland are the blast furnaces of the iron-smelting centre of Scunthorpe. All derive advantage from being near the Humber; so we mention them here in that connection.

For pleasure and recreation, the

HARVESTING THE PEPPERMINT

Our picture shows a scene on a peppermint farm when the harvest of foliage and stems, made up into bundles by means of woven mats, is being taken from the fields to the drying sheds. Peppermint is used in the making of sweets (" bulls-eyes," for example) ; medicines, perfumes, and a drink called crème-de-menthe, the botanical name of this plant family being *mentha*. Menthol comes from one variety of mint. In our gardens we grow spear-mint, for making mint sauce.

toilers in the mills and factories, ship-yards and chemical works, steel and iron works and engineering shops of the factory towns look to the Pennine dales and moors on the west, or perhaps more often to the many beautiful seaside holiday towns strung like beads upon the coastline. The chief of these are Scarborough and Whitby, where Captain Cook lived as a boy, and whence he first went to sea.

King Cotton.

Now let us look at the other side of the Pennines, which is much wetter than the eastern flanks because it faces the prevailing moist winds from the North Atlantic, and therefore grows potatoes and other root crops rather than grain. The moist air is important even in the manufactures, for it enables cotton to be spun without much risk of the fibres cracking and breaking.

In South Lancashire cotton is king. The cotton manufacture has long been Britain's leading industry. Liverpool, at the sea gate of the Mersey, has always been convenient for the importation of raw cotton from the United States, our chief source of supply ; and since the making of the Manchester Ship Canal, cotton steamers can go right up to the great business heart of the cotton towns. Manchester, indeed, is a first-class *sea* port, with splendid dock equipment, within reach of all the great factory towns of the North and the Midlands. You have not to draw a

EVERYDAY SCENES IN MANCHESTER

Will F. Taylor.

Many small canals run through Manchester, and these waterways are largely used for transporting coal to the numberless factories. Very frequently lumps of the " black diamonds " fall into the water from the heaped-up barges, and here we see girls and boys, and women and men as well, " fishing " for coal from the canal bank. Naturally, one may only witness such scenes as this when coal is very scarce and the weather severe.

Will F. Taylor.

You have not to draw a very large circle round Manchester before you have one big enough to include several millions of people. Much of Manchester's huge growth is due to the fact that she has good coal at her very doors, and here you see the pit-head of one of the collieries.

WHERE COTTON IS KING

Will F. Taylor.

In South Lancashire cotton is king. The cotton manufacture has long been Britain's leading industry. Manchester is the business centre rather than the manufacturing city, and you must go to the near-by towns of Oldham, Bolton or Blackburn to see girls spinning cotton.

Will F. Taylor.

As the natural centre of the roads, railways and canals of the cotton towns Manchester is the place where cotton goods are collected and marketed. This is a view of one of the streets in the very heart of the city, flanked by tall, gloomy warehouses in which bleached cotton is received as it comes from the mills.

very large circle round Manchester before you have one big enough to include several millions of people. All these have to be fed, and both Liverpool and Manchester import huge quantities of meat and grain and fruits, besides other foodstuffs.

The Cotton Towns.

The cotton centres, like the towns of the West Riding and of the Black Country, each have their special business. Wigan is a great coal-mining centre. Manchester is the business rather than a cotton-manufacturing city. As the natural centre of the roads and railways and canals of the cotton towns, it is the place where cotton goods are collected and marketed; it is a port, too, where raw cotton is brought in to be sent to the factory towns and foodstuffs are imported, as we have already discovered.

Some cotton towns, like Oldham, spin chiefly coarse cotton "counts," while places like Bolton spin finer "counts." Blackburn workers are chiefly weavers; the Bolton people specialise in bleaching; the St. Helens and Widnes men do a great deal of the dyeing; and the machinery is made at centres like Oldham and Manchester. Textile machinery made in Lancashire finds its way to all parts of the world where the manufacture of textiles is carried on on a factory scale. We have to think of Manchester and the largest towns not merely as centres of the cotton trade, but as huge manufacturing areas, making many other

Topical Press.

LIVERPOOL FROM THE AIR

We have to think of Liverpool not only as a cotton and foodstuff port, but as a fine city that is the headquarters of many of the leading steamship lines in our Homeland. Liverpool's waterfront, of which the above is an aerial view, is one of the wonders of the world. Large liners can come right alongside its great floating landing-stage.

Topical Press.

ON THE MANCHESTER SHIP CANAL

The United States of America is our chief source of supply for cotton, and since the making of the Manchester Ship Canal cotton steamers can go right up to the great business heart of the cotton towns. Manchester, indeed, is a first-class seaport, though placed so many miles inland. In our illustration you see a view of the No. 9 Dock at the Manchester end of the canal. The photograph was taken from one of the towering granaries at the dock-side.

kinds of goods as well, especially those needed by the millions of people within easy reach of them.

We have to think of Liverpool not only as a cotton and foodstuff port, but as a fine city that is the headquarters of many of the leading steamship lines in our Homeland, especially those running regular services to Canada and the United States, to South America and the West Indies, and to West Africa. Liverpool's water-front is one of the wonders of the world. Large liners can come right alongside its great floating landing-stage. It is a ferry port, too, for Belfast, Dublin and other Irish ports. as well as for the Isle of Man.

Holidays for Lancashire.

Where can Lancashire workers take their holidays ? There is the string of pleasant seaside resorts on the Lancashire coast, *e.g.*, Blackpool and Morecambe ; another in North Wales, *e.g.*, Llandudno and Rhyl ; and there are others like Douglas, in the beautiful Isle of Man. For those who love mountain, moorland, or lake, there are the Pennine Moors, the mountain land of North Wales and the Lake District, part of which is actually in North Lancashire.

Heysham, like Liverpool, is one of the L.M.S. ferry ports for Ireland, especially for Belfast, splendid steamers making the crossing nightly.

THE LAKE DISTRICT

THE LANGDALE PIKES

Will F. Taylor.

The English Lake District is one of the most beautiful parts of our Homeland, and is visited by thousands of tourists every year. In the background of the above landscape we see the famous Langdale Pikes, with Elterwater nearer to us. Elterwater is a beautiful lake because of its setting, and its surface is nearly 200 ft. above sea level. It is only one of nearly a score of lakes in the neighbourhood, of which Windermere is the largest.

THE Lake District is one of the most beautiful parts of our Homeland, and is visited by thousands of tourists who go there to catch glimpses of scenes immortalised in verse by Wordsworth, Southey, Coleridge and others of the "Lake Poets."

William Wordsworth was born there, and lived his boyhood days among the lakes and mountains, wandering over the fells of Windermere and Coniston. You remember his poem about the daffodils? The lake by which he saw "a host of golden daffodils . . . fluttering and dancing in the breeze" was either Grasmere or Rydal Water, near which he lived for many years.

The Lake District has its sterner aspects, too. Its height gives it severe winters and its position on the rainy side of Britain makes it often wet in summer, and swept by snowstorms in winter. Seathwaite, below the Sty Head Pass, is said to have the heaviest rainfall in England. Read Wordsworth's poem "Helvellyn," which paints wonderful word pictures of storm and sunshine, and of the awe-inspiring loneliness of the steep mountain.

Lovely Lakes and Falls.

The lakes themselves are ribbon-lakes in the narrow valleys that radiate like the spokes of a wheel from the central knot of mountains. The largest is Windermere, but there are others which Nature-lovers think more beautiful. Thirlmere, on the western side of Helvellyn, supplies Manchester with pure water.

There are many beautiful waterfalls, most of which are at their best after the rain. The poet Southey thus describes the Cataract of Lodore:

"Gleaming and steaming and streaming and beaming,
  And rushing and flushing and brushing and gushing,

76

And flapping and rapping and
clapping and slapping,
And curling and whirling and
purling and twirling,
Retreating and beating and meeting
and sheeting,
Delaying and straying and playing
and spraying ;
Advancing and prancing and glanc-
ing and dancing,
Recoiling, turmoiling, and toiling
and boiling,
And thumping and flumping and
bumping and jumping,
And dashing and flashing and
splashing and clashing—
And so never ending, but always
descending,
Sound and motions for ever and
ever are blending,
All at once and all o'er, with a
mighty uproar—
And this way the water comes
down at Lodore."

Holidays Among the Mountains.

Scafell Pike (3,210 feet) is the highest
peak in England, and in the same
central knot lie Scafell, Great End
and Bowfell. Helvellyn and the great
slate peak of Skiddaw lie farther north.
To the east of Helvellyn, Ullswater
drains to Penrith and the Eden Valley,
along which is the main L.M.S. line
from St. Pancras to Carlisle, the most
important railway junction of the
north of England.

Keswick is the chief centre for the
northern valleys, but for people coming
from the south, Ambleside is the centre.
Take the L.M.S. express from London
to the north, change at Kendal for
Windermere if your train has not a
" through " carriage, and you are in
the Lake District. Go on by 'bus or
car through Ambleside to Langdale,
and stay in one of the hotels in the
valley below some of the finest of the
mountains. Get up early some morning and make your way up " the

Will F. Taylor.

GRASMERE

Grasmere is not a large lake, being only a
mile in length by half as much in breadth.
The poet William Wordsworth lived by
Grasmere for many years.

J. Dixon-Scott.

DOVEDALE

One must have a conbination of hills and
water for the most impressive scenery, and
here is one of the several charming dales of
Derbyshire, near the old town of Ashbourne.

Band" to the top of Bowfell. Look around you and notice the wonderful golden-green of the fells and deep valleys. All the mountains seem to you to be about the same height. That is because they have been formed by ancient glaciers and streams carving out deep valleys in an old plateau, leaving parts standing out as mountains.

The Cumberland Coalfield.

To the west you can see the Irish Sea, and perhaps catch a glimpse of the high Isle of Man ; to the south-west—almost at your feet, it seems—you see the tall chimneys of the iron and steel works at Barrow and Millom, where the ore got from the mountains is made into all kinds of iron and steel goods.

Barrow-in-Furness, to give it its full name, has large shipbuilding yards and engineering works. Farther north beyond your vision is another and larger strip of " black country "—the Cumberland coalfield along the coast from Maryport to Whitehaven. Some of the workings run far under the sea.

Lake District Folk.

But most of the people of the Lake District are farmers who rear sheep on the fells and cattle in the dales. The sheep are usually of the famous Herdwick breed that can stand the bleak weather of the fells. In such country sheep-dogs are of the utmost importance, for the sheep roam far and often reach spots more or less inaccessible to shepherds, but not to their dogs. The sheep-dogs of the lake country have almost uncanny intelligence ; sheep-dog " trials " are held every year, and draw many farmers to witness them.

Hedges are rare ; pastures and fields are divided by rough stone fences like those which form the boundaries of most of the highways.

J. Dixon-Scott.

THE BOWDER STONE AT KESWICK

If you are ever in the neighbourhood of Keswick you should see the famous Bowder Stone. In some great volcanic upheaval of other times it was probably sundered from the mass of rocks above and came thundering downwards to take up its present amazing position, balanced like a ship upon its keel. The stone is as high as an average cottage and believed to weigh nearly 2,000 tons.

Photochrom.

STOCK GHYLL FORCE.

In the English Lake District waterfalls are termed "forces," and here we see Stock Ghyll Force, which comes leaping down from a height of 70 ft., "curling and whirling and purling and twirling" through its tree and fern-lined pathway, scattering spray in its track. The Force is to be found but a short walk from the pleasant town of Ambleside, through which its waters pass to the Rothay.

The land as a rule is too wet for successful agriculture, and the small amount of plough-land makes this branch of farming the exception and not the rule.

Some of the people are quarrymen, getting out the fine slates and building stones ; or miners working in the iron mines, or winning the few lead and other metal ores from veins in the hard old rocks.

THE POET OF HELVELLYN

G. P. Abraham.

The rugged, stone-built "Dove Cottage" at Grasmere is practically the same to-day as when William Wordsworth took up his residence within its humble walls so long ago as 1799. There are many relics of the poet to be seen at Dove Cottage, including first editions of his works.

J. Dixon-Scott.

Rydal Water is one of the smallest of the English Lakes. A short distance on the Keswick side you may see the rock pictured above, which is known as Wordsworth's Seat. You should read Wordsworth's poem "Helvellyn," in which he describes so wonderfully the storm and sunshine and the awe-inspiring loneliness of the steep mountain.

The Story
of the
World and
its Peoples

Great Britain
and Ireland—
the Fortunate
Isles

CONWAY CASTLE

J. Dixon-Scott.

The ways into Wales, by the river valleys, like those by the northern and southern coast plains,
were commanded in mediæval times by strong castles. Some, such as Conway Castle, still remain
externally in a good state of preservation. This romantic building was commenced in the
reign of Edward I., and could tell stories of bitter siege. Its mighty walls stand firm upon
foundations of solid rock.

THE PRINCIPALITY OF WALES

AT first sight a population map is a very dull thing. But when we read it with knowledge and use our imagination a little, it springs to sudden life, and becomes an interesting human record of the country it represents.

Look at the population map of Wales, for instance. Two facts catch your eye at once : (1) the very densely peopled region of South Wales ; (2) the large patches of very thinly populated country in the middle and north.

Why are there so many people in South Wales ? The county of Glamorgan alone contains nearly half the people in Wales ; and if we examine the population figures for Welsh counties and towns we make the surprising discovery that the city of Cardiff has a bigger population than any Welsh county, except the one in which Cardiff is situated. Evidently, then, there must be special opportunities for people in South Wales to get a living.

The South Wales Coalfield.

The secret of it all is that in this part of the Principality lies the rich South Wales coalfield, which covers at least a thousand square miles and extends into the counties of Glamorgan, Brecon, Monmouth, Carmarthen and Pembroke. It has steam coal for ships, any amount of bituminous coal for homes and factories, and the best anthracite ("smokeless" coal) in the world. In places the sea has cut deep inlets into the coalfield (*e.g.*, at Swansea, the second city in Wales), making it easy for coal export; and the richest part of the coalfield is deeply seamed by streams whose valleys provide easy ways for the coal-trains to the great ports of Cardiff, Newport, Swansea and Barry.

Workers in Metal.

When the coal exporting business is good, there is prosperity in South Wales, for it gives employment to miners and other workers, numbering hundreds of thousands. For Cardiff leads in Britain's coal export trade, and Newport and Swansea come next. At all of these ports expensive and wonderful coal-handling machinery has been set up to deal with huge quantities of coal in a short time.

Such a rich coalfield is bound to become the home of great manufactures, especially if it has iron as well. There is iron in the South Wales field, but nowadays Welsh ironmasters prefer to import high-grade but cheap iron ores from Spain and Sweden rather than spend more money in getting the local iron. The iron and steel industry of South Wales is enormous; the chief centres are Merthyr Tydvil, Cardiff, Dowlais, Ebbw Vale, Tredegar, Aberdare and Blaenavon.

This has attracted other great metal industries. The tin-plate business—manufacturing thin steel sheets and coating them with tin to prevent rust—is the biggest in the world. The tin is imported chiefly from Burma, the Straits Settlements, Bolivia and Nigeria. Even the United States, itself a great metal-working country, buys Welsh tin-plate. The huge increase in the use of "tinned" and "canned" meats, fish, fruits and vegetables, has resulted in demands for tin-plate from every important part of the globe.

Sport and General.

A WELSH NATIONAL FESTIVAL

Once a year there is a national gathering of Welsh people where prizes are awarded for poetical compositions, singing, choral renderings and similar exhibitions in the real Welsh spirit. The festival takes place alternately in North and South Wales, and is known by the name Eisteddfod, pronounced i-steth-vod. Our photograph shows the herald opening the ceremonies, and the crowning of the bard is one of the features of the occasion. The clothing worn is of Druidical origin, and it is said that these sessions took place before the Romans came to Britain.

" 'TIS DISTANCE ...... ROBES THE MOUNTAIN "

CAMPBELL

J. Dixon-Scott.

The finest scenery in the Welsh Highlands is perhaps in Snowdonia, where Snowdon, the highest peak south of the Tweed, rears his head 3,560 feet above the sea. The photograph shows the mountain from one of the many lakes in the vicinity of Llanberis. The bards and poets of Wales have never ceased to sing the glories of her mountains and valleys, and to tell of the wonders of her changing skies above the high and broken horizon.

83

G 2

Swansea, Llanelly, Port Talbot and Pontypool lead in the tin-plate industry.

There are besides large copper, zinc and nickel works, factories in which fire bricks are made for furnaces, or where patent fuel is made, or where the coal by-products are extracted and used. All these industries help one another in some way, and each depends upon *coal*. Cardiff is one of the most important ship-repairers in the world, largely because of the advantages offered by the industries of South Wales in providing the necessary materials.

How South Wales is Fed.

Food must be brought to this dense population in enormous quantities— and it should be remembered that Cardiff and Newport are gates to the industrial Midlands as well for food products. This helps to explain the

J. Dixon-Scott.

LIKE A DOLL'S HOUSE

What is claimed to be the smallest house in Great Britain is illustrated above. It is to be found in Conway, the ancient fortified town on the Conway River in Carnarvonshire.

gigantic flour mills at the four leading ports of South Wales. Oil and timber also come in large quantities from overseas.

All these industries, and the transport by railways and roads, by inland waterways and the sea, which keeps them alive, employ large numbers of people. That is why South Wales supports more than five-eighths of the Welsh people.

The Real Wales.

But this is not the Wales of the bards and poets, who have never ceased to sing the glories of her mountains and valleys, and to tell of the wonders of her changing skies above the high and broken horizon. If we wish to see the real Wales of poetry, song, and story, we must visit those regions which show up on the population map as being of little account to busy modern industries and the question of employment. These quiet places are, in fact, the spots more visited by those who go to enjoy the beauties of Welsh scenery, or to recover their lost health in some site of mineral springs and the towering hills.

The mountains of Wales have played a very important part in Welsh history. To the mountain fortresses of the west fled the Britons when wave after wave of invaders conquered the eastern plain lands. From them are descended the Welsh, who lived among their hills and crags apart from the English who for centuries did no more than penetrate the wide southern plain. But those same mountains which bred love of liberty and independence proved in the end the undoing of the Welsh, for they so barred off tribe from tribe and valley from valley, that strong united action against the invading forces of Edward I. was impossible.

In spite of long-continued guerilla warfare, the English conquered Wales piecemeal and set their castles in strong places to control the ways.

The Welsh spirit, however, still lives

AFTER FIVE HUNDRED YEARS!

Will F. Taylor.

Known as "The Aberconwy," the extremely interesting residence pictured above is not only the oldest house in Conway, but also in the whole Principality, as the sign now swinging at the entrance up the rugged steps proclaims. The house stands at the corner of High Street and Castle Street, and we should understand that its sturdy framework and beams of oak, long ago blackened with age, stood in the same positions five hundred years ago.

THE CASTLE OF CARNARVON

Will F. Taylor.

Carnarvon Castle, like that at Conway, was begun in the reign of Edward I., and was not only a fortress, but also a place of royal residence.   In olden days there was long-continued guerilla warfare ; and, when the English conquered a portion of Wales, they set a castle in some strong place to control the ways.   Edward II., our very first Prince of Wales, was born in the stronghold illustrated above, which stands on the Menai Strait.

and so does the Welsh language, which is taught in Welsh schools, and spoken by many of the people of the Principality.

Amidst Welsh Mountains.

The Welsh Highlands, like those of Scotland and the Lake District, have been formed by streams and prehistoric glaciers carving out deep valleys in an ancient plateau, leaving other parts standing as mountains.   The finest scenery perhaps is in Snowdonia, where Snowdon, the highest peak south of the Tweed, rears his head 3,560 feet above the sea.   Eighty per cent. of the slate quarried in Wales comes from this region, especially from the famous quarries of Bethesda, Llanberis and

Blaenau Festiniog.   The slate is exported in coasting craft from Bangor and Carnarvon.

The lovely Vale of Conway cuts a deep cleft opening towards Conway and the sea.   Near its head is Bettwys-y-Coed, a famous beauty spot.   On its western side is the great power station and aluminium works of Dolgarrog. To the east and parallel with the Vale of Conway is another beautiful valley, the Vale of Clwyd, at whose sea end is Rhyl.

Separated from the Welsh mainland by Menai Strait, which is crossed by two bridges, the Britannia Tubular Bridge and the Menai Suspension Bridge, is the low island-country of Anglesey, famous in ancient days as the granary of Wales.   Connected with

WHERE HAVE THE SLATES ALL GONE?

Will F. Taylor.

Some eighty per cent. of the slate quarried in Wales comes from the region of Snowdon, especially from the famous quarries of Bethesda, Llanberis, Blaenau Festiniog and Penrhyn, the last-named shown in our photograph above. The slate is exported in coasting vessels from Bangor, Carnarvon and other small ports. Roofing slates, according to their size, are known by the curious names of Important Ladies, Countesses and Duchesses.

Anglesey by a causeway bearing the L.M.S. line and the motor road is Holyhead Island, on whose northern side is the port of Holyhead, the L.M.S. ferry town for Dublin.

The Welsh Valleys.

The deep valley of the Upper Dee (the Vale of Bala) separates the Berwyn Mountains from the northern masses, giving a route from Chester and Wrexham by way of Llangollen and Lake Bala to Barmouth and other pleasant seaside resorts on Cardigan Bay.

The Vale of Powys (Upper Severn) affords a route for road and railway from Shrewsbury through the very heart of Wales to Aberystwyth, and separates the Berwyn mass from Mynydd Bach and Clun Forest. In this valley are Newtown and Welshpool, both old centres of the Welsh woollen industry.

Another valley giving entrance to Wales from England is the Wye Valley from the Plain of Hereford, an ancient castle town in the midst of beautiful scenery.

These ways into Wales, by the river valleys, like those by the northern and southern coast plains, were commanded in mediæval times by strong castles, the ruins of many of which still remain. Some, like Conway Castle, are yet in a good state of preservation.

Wales supplies two great English cities with pure water that is conveyed many miles in iron pipes. Liverpool gets its water from Lake Vyrnwy; Birmingham from the two lake-reservoirs of the Elan Valley.

Topical Press.

THE BUTE EAST DOCK AT CARDIFF

Cardiff is the first city in Wales, and a most important centre in the coal export trade. Like Swansea and Newport, it has expensive and wonderful coal-handling machinery set up to deal with huge quantities of coal in a short time. South Wales, because of its industries, supports more than five-eighths of the Welsh people. In addition to its coal interests, Swansea leads in the tin-plate industry, manufacturing steel sheets and coating them with tin to prevent rust.

The Story
of the
World and
its Peoples

Great Britain
and Ireland—
the Fortunate
Isles

The Times.

THE ROYAL TWEED BRIDGE AT BERWICK

Old Berwick Bridge, built in the reign of James I. of England and still preserved, had no fewer than sixteen arches, but the new ferro-concrete structure which carries the traffic between England and Scotland has but three arches over the water. Berwick is in the County of Northumberland only for local government purposes. It forms a county by itself and Royal Proclamations are to this day addressed to the Kingdoms of Great Britain and Ireland, and the town of Berwick-on-Tweed.

THE LAND OF MOUNTAIN AND GLEN

TWO great main natural ways lead from London and the English Midlands into Scotland, the East Coast route by way of Doncaster, York, Newcastle and Berwick-on-Tweed, and the West Coast route by way of the Plain of Lancashire, Shap Fell and Carlisle. Between these natural routes rise the long Pennines.

The L.N.E.R. follows the eastern route, which is by far the easier from the point of view of the railway engineer. The L.M.S. follows the western route by way of Crewe, Wigan, Preston, Lancaster and Penrith. A second L.M.S. main line first reaches Leeds on the eastern side of the Pennines, and then cuts through the Aire Gap to Settle and the Shap, thus meeting more natural obstacles than either of the other two.

The Southern Uplands.

The border between England and Scotland is difficult country for roads and railways. The actual boundary runs from Solway Firth and along the crest line of the Cheviots to the Lower Tweed, which enters the North Sea near Berwick-on-Tweed. It is easy for roads and railways to avoid the Cheviots by following the coast plains at their seaward ends; but beyond the Cheviots and the boundary lie the

WHERE FLODDEN WAS FOUGHT   *Will F. Taylor.*

The Battle of Flodden (1513) was fought on a hill near Coldstream and a short distance on the English side of the Border. Our photograph shows the view when looking north from the hill upon which the Scots were encamped prior to the battle. This spot is called the " King's Chair," because King James is said to have studied the country round from this position. The fight was a most unequal one, in which the English were the victors.

Southern Uplands of Scotland, which must be passed before travellers can reach the Scottish Midland Valley— the busiest and richest part of Scotland.

Border Forays.

These Southern Uplands rise in places to over 2,000 feet, and the hills that go to form them are made of hard old rocks, some harsh and gritty, some slaty. Their slopes are covered chiefly with the short, crisp grass that sheep love; their valleys are floored with rich soil formed of rock-meal made by the grinding of the ancient glaciers over the rocks, or of fine silt washed down by the mountain streams. In some places among the hills there are wide areas of peatland, and bogs that will probably in time become peat beds.

The country on both sides of the border is thickly sown with ancient battlefields, and the approaches to it on both sides are marked by the ruins of many an old-time castle, tower and fortress. But even these could not prevent the border forays frequent in the old days when raiding and fighting were common and profitable amusements for the sturdy warrior-lords of the borderlands—and by no means dishonourable occupations. Many an old ballad still lingers to tell the tale of border warfare and sing the praises of the proud chieftains and border earls to whom battle and pillage were the spice of life.

The Southern Uplands were once an old high plateau, which for ages has been cut up by many streams into deep valleys, leaving parts upstanding as the hills and mountains of to-day.

The highest point is Mount Merrick (2,764 feet) in the west. But it is the valleys that are most important to the road-makers and railway-builders, for they provide the only easy ways across this difficult country, except for those along the coastal plains. Fortunately, the Southern Uplands lie so that a number of streams run south and a number run north. These roads and railways can use valleys up the southern slopes and then descend the northern slopes by the valleys leading down to the Scottish Midland Valley.

Ways North From Carlisle.

From Carlisle three main railways pass northwards: (1) by the "Waverley" route up Liddesdale down to the valley of the Tweed, up the Gala Valley and down to Waverley Station at Edinburgh; (2), by the Caledonian route up the valley of the Annan and down the valley of the Clyde to Glasgow and Edinburgh; (3), by the south-western route up the valley of the Nith and by a long journey over the plain of Ayrshire to Glasgow. The last two are L.M.S. routes; the first is followed by the L.N.E.R., and is called the "Waverley" route because it passes through country where Sir Walter Scott lived and wrote his novels.

As we cross the Southern Uplands in the train we notice that towns and villages are few, and that, on the whole, there are not many people living in

Central Press.

THE SMITHY AT GRETNA GREEN

Travelling north by road from Carlisle one enters Scotland on passing over the little River Sark. A short distance further is Gretna Green, in Dumfriesshire, a place made notable for runaway marriages. Above we see the Gretna Green smithy and the anvil over which the couples to be wedded clasp hands. The blacksmith officiates at the weddings, which are made possible by a difference between English marriage laws and those of the sister country. In the Great War, Gretna was an important centre for the making of munitions.

Photochrom.

In this picture we see Abbotsford, as viewed from the Tweed. This magnificent pile, built more than a hundred years ago, was the residence of Sir Walter Scott and is a place of pilgrimage for numerous visitors to Scotland. It was originally a cottage, but was transformed into a castle.

Will F. Taylor.

This homely cottage is to be seen at Alloway. It was the birthplace of Robert Burns, on January 25th, 1759, and is much the same to-day as it was in the time of Scotland's National Poet. The counties of Ayrshire and Dumfriesshire are the ones most associated with Burns. Near Alloway are the " banks and braes o' bonnie Doon." Burns died at Dumfries.

FOR VISITORS TO SCOTLAND

Will F. Taylor.

Melrose Abbey, illustrated above, is in the heart of the " Scott Country," and the sacred ruins attract pilgrims from all parts of the world. A monastery existed here as far back as the seventh century and the present Abbey was founded in 1136 and endowed by David I. Near the eastern side of the Abbey is buried the heart of Robert the Bruce.

McBain.

Here is a photograph of the sinister Loch Neldricken, to be found amidst the Kells Hills in the Galloway district of Southern Scotland. S. R. Crockett in " The Raiders " laid some of his finest scenes hereabouts and the circular stretch of water is the " Murder Hole." Here, according to Crockett, the smugglers and gipsies of the hills concealed the bodies of their victims.

GLASGOW UNIVERSITY

Photochrom.

Both Edinburgh and Glasgow have great universities and above is seen the one at Glasgow, designed by Sir Gilbert Scott in 1868.   Glasgow is our second largest city, and the Clyde Estuary as far as Greenock is lined with large shipbuilding yards and engineering works.   Glasgow has a wide variety of industries, many based on raw materials from the Americas.

this part of Britain. Those who do make their homes there are chiefly farmers, who keep large flocks of sheep on the grassy hillslopes, or grow grain, roots and vegetables in the rich soil of the valleys in which most of the farmsteads lie.

Wool from the sheep of the Southern Uplands goes to make the tweeds ("twills") manufactured at Hawick, Selkirk, Galashiels and Peebles.

Lead is mined in the Southern Uplands at the villages of Leadhills and Wanlockhead, a little to the west of the Caledonian route. They are said to be the highest villages in Scotland, and stand on open grassy moors amid the hills.

The Heart of Scotland.

Eight-tenths of the people of Scotland live in the Midland Valley, which has only one-tenth of Scotland's total area. For there is the most fertile land, and there also are the great Scottish coalfields which support many busy industries. The rest of Scotland is largely filled with moun-tains (except for the eastern coastal plain, whose old red sandstone floor has given rise to rich soil), and therefore cannot support a very large population.

How is it that Scotland's coal and most of her richest plough-land lie in the Midland Valley instead of being scattered in various places over the country ?

Geological Accidents.

It is due to what we may call a series of geological accidents which caused two great lines of faults or cracks in the earth-crust to develop—one along a line joining Stonehaven on the east to the Firth of Clyde, and the other from St. Abb's Head on the east to a point south of Ayr on the west. Along both of these lines are multi-tudes of more or less parallel faults penetrating to great depths.

In past ages, and long before Britain was ready for the coming of the first men, the stretch of earth-crust between these two great lines of faulting sank, and in the rift valley thus created other rock material gathered, covering up the coal measures. When the moving glaciers of the Ice Age ground heavily over most parts of Scotland, planing off the upper rocks and among them most of the coal, the coal measures of the Midland Valley lay snug and untouched beneath their covering of younger rocks, to prove real hidden treasure for the enterprising people who, ages afterwards, were destined to dwell there.

Beauty of the Lowlands.

We must not imagine the Midland Valley, however, as a more or less continuous "Black Country" with belching factory chimneys, grimy canals and a landscape everywhere blighted by monster heaps of waste from mines and blast furnaces and with every green thing seared by the hot breath of chemical works. There *are* spots like this, of course, for they are part of the price men must pay for the profits and advantages of mining and manufacture. But most of the Midland Valley is pleasant country with a quiet beauty all its own, and half an hour's ride by car or train from the biggest city will take you to spots as delightful as any lover of the real countryside could wish to see.

The Midland Valley is often called "The Lowlands," and that gives some of us the impression that it is more or less flat. Nothing could be farther from the truth, as we can see if we look

Valentine & Sons, Ltd.

PRINCES STREET, EDINBURGH

Princes Street, the pride of Scotland's Capital, is regarded as being one of the finest thoroughfares in the world. The monument in the centre was erected to the memory of Sir Walter Scott. Edinburgh is known all over the universe as the "British Athens," and there are few finer views than the one you obtain from Castle Rock. Leith is virtually a part of Edinburgh.

at a good map showing the height of the land

Across the middle of the Midland Valley runs a line of volcanic hills, with here and there wide, deep breaks, through which the rivers have cut their way. The Sidlaws overlook the long Firth of Tay, along whose northern shores, sheltered by the Sidlaws from cold north winds, stretches the fertile Carse of Gowrie, famous for its grain and its fruits.

To the south-west of the Sidlaws rise the crests of the Ochils; and between the two the lordly Tay has made its way, giving a gap through which approach to the Highlands is easy. In that gap sits the fair city of Perth, near which is Scone, the ancient coronation-place of the Kings of Scotland.

Look south-west again from the tops of the Ochils, and you see another hill-mass—the Campsie Fells, with the winding Forth making its way between the Ochils and the distant hills. In that wide and fertile gap is Stirling, with its grand old castle high-perched on an isolated rock which was once the lava-plug that sealed the throat of a prehistoric volcano, after its last dying eruption. Stirling is another important gateway to the Highlands; and many a stern fight contested the passage of its famous bridge over the Forth, whose multitudinous windings are known as " the Links of Forth."

From Earl's Seat.

Now climb to Earl's Seat on the top of the Campsie Fells, and look south to where the great city of Glasgow, with its busy shipyards, factories and engineering works—the home of more than a million people—stands on its wide valley at the head of the estuary of the Clyde. Far away to the south-west across the Clyde estuary rise the outlines of another hill-mass; and westward is lovely Loch Lomond and its majestic encircling peaks, of which Ben Lomond is perhaps the best known. Glasgow and its neighbours, Greenock and Dumbarton (another ship-building town with an ancient castle perched upon just such a rock as that upon which Stirling Castle is built), are also well-known gateways by which approach to the Highlands is fairly easy.

North of this central line of hills is

Photochrom.

HOLYROOD PALACE, EDINBURGH

The way from Edinburgh Castle, perched on top of the famous Castle Rock, to the old Royal Palace of Holyrood at its foot is known as the " Royal Mile." Many a regal personage passed along it in the days of Scotland's glory as an independent kingdom. Holyrood has been used by our Sovereigns since George IV on their visits to the Scottish Capital.

J. Dixon-Scott.

ON THE FIELD OF BANNOCKBURN

Bannockburn was fought near Stirling, in 1314, and ended in the defeat of the English. On the site, depicted above, is the Bore Stone, upon which Robert Bruce planted his standard. Stirling is a very important gateway to the Highlands and in many a stern fight was contested the passage of its famous bridge over the Forth.

the broad and fertile Plain of Strathmore—the " great valley "—between the Highland edge to the north and the volcanic hills to the south. On the southern side of these hills there is not so much plain land, for the ground rises more or less gradually to the Southern Uplands—the Border Lands of the old ballads famous in Scottish song and story. Edinburgh, the capital of Scotland, with the port of Leith, is on the coastal plain of the Forth. The Pentlands, the Moorfoot Hills, and the Lammer Moors rise in a semicircle to the south, broken here and there by gaps used by the roads and the railways. All are within easy reach of the capital.

The British Athens.

Edinburgh grew up on and around its famous Castle Rock, which is yet another old volcanic stump. The way from the Castle at its summit down the long slope to the old royal palace of Holyrood at its foot is known as the " Royal Mile," for many a royal personage passed along it in the days of Scotland's glory as an independent kingdom. There are other noble hills, too, within the precincts of the city. So splendid is Edinburgh that it is known all over the world as the " British Athens." You must go far indeed before you find a nobler thoroughfare than Princes Street, or a finer view than you can get from the Castle Rock. Leith nowadays is virtually part of Edinburgh; busy streets connect the two, making them one continuous city. The fine docks at Leith and Granton are the sea gates of Scotland's capital, and give harbour and wharfage accommodation to

Valentine & Sons, Ltd.

JOHN KNOX'S HOUSE AT EDINBURGH

John Knox was a great Scottish Reformer who lived in the sixteenth century and frequently preached in St. Giles Cathedral. His house in High Street, shown in the centre of the picture, is sought out by most visitors to the capital of Scotland. Few cities have more objects of deep historical interest to show the traveller.

vessels from all the leading sea-trading countries of the world. Through these ports and others on the deep long inlet of the Firth of Forth come much of the foodstuffs and the raw materials to feed the workers and the mills and factories of the Scottish Midland Valley.

Glasgow and the Clyde.

On the western side of the Midland Valley is another deep estuary—that of the Clyde, which is even more important as a sea gate, because it faces the Atlantic and the New World, from which Britain gets vast amounts of foodstuffs of all kinds, as well as raw materials for her manufactures.

Not far west of Edinburgh is the famous Forth Bridge, which carries the L.N.E.R. expresses over the estuary on their way to the north.

The Clyde estuary from Glasgow to Greenock is lined with large ship-building yards and engineering works. The estuary is carefully buoyed, so that large vessels can reach the docks; for, like Liverpool, Glasgow is the headquarters of famous steamship lines and vessels from all parts of the world unload and load cargoes there. Like other large ports in Britain, Glasgow has a wide variety of industries, many based on raw materials from the Americas, for trade with which this port is exceptionally well placed. This fine city is very largely the growth of the past century, although it has always been an important centre at the meeting-place of several routes. It was trade with the Americas which caused a sudden and great increase in its population; for when the Glasgow people realised its possibilities, they enlisted the services of the most prominent engineers of the day and deepened the Clyde to admit large ships. There are still living people whose grandfathers waded across the Clyde, where now some of the biggest vessels can lie in safety.

West of Glasgow and not many miles from its boundaries are Renfrew and Paisley, in which the cotton manufacture is the leading business. Like the textile industry of South Lancashire and the West Riding of Yorkshire, those in this neighbourhood are of many kinds, utilising different raw materials. Where one textile industry is firmly established, others are likely to follow it.

Scotland's busy Heart.

The Midland Valley has three great coalfields : (1) the Lanark coalfield, chiefly in the valley of the Clyde, with Glasgow as its outlet, but with other outlets on the Firth of Forth, for it extends really into Clackmannan on the other side of the river ; (2) the Ayr coalfield, with the coal shipping ports of Troon and Ardrossan on the west coast ; and (3) the coalfields of the Firth of Forth—the Fife coalfield in the north, and the Lothian coalfield on the south of the estuary, beneath which they are doubtless connected.

The Lanark field is by far the largest and the most important. Its iron gave rise to the iron and steel industries, the engineering works, and other great businesses which grew amazingly when imported iron and raw materials from the Americas were brought in large quantities to supplement the local supplies. Many large towns have grown up on this coalfield—Lanark, Coatbridge, Airdrie, Motherwell and Falkirk, for example, to say nothing of Glasgow, the second largest town in the Homeland.

BUILDING A LINER ON THE CLYDE

This photograph gives you a splendid idea of what a modern shipbuilding yard is like. The picture was taken from the air and shows a 40,000-ton ocean liner nearing that stage in her construction when she can be launched into her proper element. Starting with the keel-plate, the monster ship is built girder by girder and plate by plate with the aid of giant cranes.

F. C. Inglis.

In the Great War deep tunnelling under the ground or the laying of mines and other military operations necessitated the use of canaries and white mice, mainly to test the purity of the air. These humble creatures are not forgotten in the Scottish War Memorial at Edinburgh.

FOR SCOTLAND'S FALLEN

F. C. Inglis.

In Edinburgh Castle, as befits the Capital, is the Scottish National War Memorial, erected to the memory of Scots men and women who lost their lives in the conflict. Above is a picture of the Shrine with seven stained-glass windows and a Casket containing the names of the Fallen. In the Hall of Honour all the Scottish Regiments are mentioned.

The Ayr coalfield supports the smelters of Irvine and the manufacturers of Kilmarnock. The Fife coalfield, with its coal port of Methil, supports the linen mills of Dunfermline and the linoleum and oilcloth industries of Kirkcaldy, as well as the linen, marmalade and jam business of Dundee and neighbouring towns. The Lothian coalfield is convenient for ships using the ports of Leith and Granton, and for the city of Edinburgh's big paper, printing and biscuit industries.

The Forth and Clyde Canal provides a narrow waterway between the two great estuaries, but a proposal for deepening and widening it to form a ship canal from the North Sea to the Atlantic has been abandoned.

Famous Scottish Universities.

Edinburgh and Glasgow have great universities. The ancient town of St. Andrews on the coast of Fife has a famous university, too, and picturesque ruins of its former greatness on a rocky platform almost entirely sea-girt on which the old city grew up as a stronghold.

Farmers of the Lowlands.

The main routes to the north from Edinburgh and the Forth Bridge cut across Fifeshire, one crossing the Tay by the Tay Bridge, another triumph of British engineering, and going *via* Dundee and Montrose to Aberdeen, the " Granite City," the home of another famous Scottish university and of Scotland's leading fishing and fish-exporting business. The other crosses the Tay at Perth, the lowest bridge-point on the river, and the centre of important dyeworks.

Many people of the Midland Valley get their living by farming. In the

THE PALACE AT LINLITHGOW

Photochrom.

Linlithgow is about 17 miles from Edinburgh and is a most picturesque and ancient town standing on a loch or lake and famous for the ruined Palace of the Scottish Sovereigns. In this Palace that tragic figure of history Mary Queen of Scots was born and here Parliaments were held.

Will F. Taylor.

HIGHLAND CATTLE

Highland cattle, with their shaggy coats, are known everywhere as a type by themselves. Their beef is greatly valued and is always in evidence at the Christmas Fat Stock Shows. The animals are exceptionally hardy. Some of them are black and others cream-coloured, touched with reddish-brown.

wetter west root-crops are more frequent than grain; the best grain country is in the drier and sunnier east.

Cattle are more numerous than sheep on the western pastures, but sheep are more numerous than cattle on the eastern pastures, which have less rain than those of the west.

Farming in this part of Scotland is very thorough, and the fertile soil is made by diligent and careful attention to yield richer crops than most other parts of the British Isles.

The Scottish Highlands and the Hebrides.

The most beautiful part of Scotland lies north of the Midland Valley in the Scottish Highlands, which fill the greater part of the country north of a line drawn from the Firth of Clyde to Stonehaven on the east coast.

When you enter the Highlands at Dunkeld or at Callander you feel that you are entering a new country, so different is it from the great valley you have just left. From Dunkeld (on the Highland Railway from Perth) you can follow the route through the famous Pass of Killiecrankie up Glen Garry past Dalnaspidal, the highest railway station in the British Isles, and over the Drumochter Pass (1,484 feet)—(the highest railway summit) to the valley of the Spey at Kingussie, and on *via* Aviemore to Culloden Moor and Inverness.

All the time you have travelled through magnificent highland scenery unrivalled anywhere else in the Homeland.

The Beautiful Trossachs.

From Callander, on the railway from Stirling, a visit can be paid to the Trossachs and lovely Loch Katrine, which Sir Walter Scott describes in " The Lady of the Lake." King James V. has climbed to a high viewpoint :—

" Where, gleaming with the setting sun,
  One burnished sheet of living gold,
  Loch Katrine lay beneath him rolled

A GEM OF THE HIGHLANDS

Will F. Taylor.

Hard by Loch Leven in the shire of Argyll is Glencoe, illustrated above, one of the typical valleys and passes of the lovely Highlands. It is notorious in history for the massacre of the Macdonalds in 1692, following upon an insurrection of supporters of the Jacobite cause.

Photochrom.

This great cairn stands where raged the centre of the fight at the Battle of Culloden (1746). The Jacobites fought under Prince Charles Edward, over whom Flora Macdonald and the Highlanders watched whilst he slept. Here the Scottish rising of 1745 was shattered in defeat. The battlefield is near Inverness.

WHERE THE CLANSMEN GATHERED

Will F. Taylor.

Banavie Bridge, which crosses the River Lochy in the neighbourhood of Fort William. In the distance, framed by the archway, is the huge bulk of Ben Nevis.

Will F. Taylor.

Fort William is a famous holiday resort, one of the chief attractions being that King of Mountains, Ben Nevis. In the distance is General Wade's bridge over the Spean.

Will F. Taylor.

Loch Shiel is encircled by mountains and typical wild Scottish scenery. Here Prince Charlie called his followers together and unfurled his banner in 1745. This monument, standing lonely and most impressive, marks the historic spot.

In her all length far winding lay,
With promontory, creek, and bay,
And islands that, empurpled bright,
Floated amid the livelier light ;
And mountains, that like giants
    stand,
To sentinel enchanted land.
High on the south, huge Ben Venue
Down on the lake in masses threw
Crags, knolls, and mounds, con-
    fusedly hurled
The fragments of an earlier world ;
A wildering forest feathered o'er
His ruined sides and summit hoar,
While on the north, through middle
    air,
Ben An heaved high his forehead
    bare."

From Loch Katrine the tourist can go by motor coach to the shores of island-studded Loch Lomond, the largest lake in Scotland, where a lake steamer will take him southwards past lofty Ben Lomond to Balloch at the end of the lake, within a short train journey of Glasgow.

" Caledonia, Stern and Wild."

Bolder scenery is to be found in the Grampians, where Ben Macdhui and at least three other peaks rise above 4,000 feet, and where splendid pine forests are to be seen in the valley of the Spey. These are in the Central Highlands. The Northern Highlands, lonely and desolate, with wilder and sterner scenery than anywhere south, lie to the north of Glen More, a deep trench created by faulting in the rocks.

In the bottom of Glen More lie Loch Lochy and Loch Ness with their rivers ; and sea, lakes and rivers have

Will F. Taylor.

ON THE CRINAN CANAL

In Argyllshire, Scotland, is the Crinan Canal, which is some nine miles in length and along whose course are no fewer than fifteen locks. The above view is at Crinan, at the northern end of the canal. The small vessel is the " Linnet," which conveys passengers and mails. This canal saves a circuit round the Mull of Kintyre.

ABERDEEN, THE GRANITE CITY

Aberdeen is a great port, a fishing centre and also a holiday resort, but we think of it most as the " Granite City," for it is one of the largest producers of granite in the world. Its stone is sent to almost every other country, and we see here a mason cutting "setts" for road-surfacing.

In this picture a huge mass of granite has been torn by explosives from the rock-face of a quarry near Aberdeen, and is now being cut into pieces of the required shape and size by a powerful pneumatic drill. Many of the buildings in Aberdeen are constructed of granite. Granite is immensely hard and strong and therefore costly to work.

At certain places in Scotland, notably at Aboyne and Braemar, Highland Gatherings are held during diminishes, and they draw together clansmen and their womenfolk to take part in the Games, which

Sport and General.

Throwing the Hammer is always one of the events of Highland Games and also figures in field athletics in other countries. The so-called "Hammer" weighs 16 lbs. and its handle must not exceed 4 feet in length. The hammer has been thrown upwards of 170 feet.

GATHERING BY THE CAIRNGORMS

the late summer. The gatherings are of ancient origin, though their interest increases rather than consist mainly of sports and dances. Above is a panoramic view of the Braemar Gathering.

In this photograph we see two helpers returning the caber. It takes two men to retrieve the caber, but only one to toss it.

In the Putting the Weight event a ball weighing 16 lbs. has to be hurled through the air to the greatest distance.

109

been joined by the cutting of the Caledonian Canal from Inverness to Fort William beneath the great hump of Ben Nevis, the highest peak in the United Kingdom. The canal is used chiefly in summer for tourist traffic. At the Falls of Foyers on the southern side of Loch Ness, and farther to the south-west at Kinlochleven, water-power has been utilised for large aluminium works.

The Scottish Crofters.

Not many people live in the High-lands, especially in the lonely west and north where plough-land is scarce, and mountain and heathery moors are everywhere. The few crofters or farmers live in their small "crofts"

in sheltered glens, more or less cut off from the rest of all the world, growing oats and potatoes, rearing a few cows for milk, butter and cheese, and poultry for eggs, and perhaps sheep on the hillside to provide the wool which is spun, woven and dyed for cloth by their wives and daughters. In the west and by the sea, and on the lonely isles of the Inner and Outer Hebrides, crofters are fishermen and farmers too, living on the joint harvests of the sea and the land. They depend upon the small steamers that call periodically for their flour and groceries, and their newspapers and the mails. Their small homes are built of stone from the hills, thatched with heather, or with straw

Photochrom.

ON THE ISLAND OF IONA

Among the islands to the west of Scotland is the holy isle of Iona. Here St. Columba built his church and monastery in the sixth century A.D. and began his work of spreading Christianity throughout our sister country. Iona lies just off the Isle of Mull and upon it are the ruins of its ancient cathedral, with tombs of old-time kings.

Will F. Taylor.

ONCE A HOUSE OF THE PICTS

The Orkney Islands form one of the counties of Scotland and embrace nearly one hundred
separate isles, though only thirty of them are inhabited. In the long-ago the Orkneys belonged
to Norway and at some remote period were occupied by the Picts. These were the people who
so strongly opposed the Roman occupation, and here we see a present-day ruin of what was once
a Pictish dwelling house.

from their small crofts, and timbered
perhaps with driftwood picked up on
the beaches.

In the north are wide, open heathery
moorlands which are let out to wealthy
folk as deer forests or grouse moors,
to be visited for deer-stalking and
grouse-shooting by gay parties at
certain seasons of the year.

Oban, on the coast of Argyll, is a
favourite tourist and yachting centre
in summer; and many visitors from

all parts of Britain go to see the
wonderful Fingal's Cave in the island
of Staffa, and the holy isle of Iona
where St. Columba built his church
and monastery in the sixth century
A.D. and began his work of spreading
Christianity in Scotland.

The Lonely Isle.

Far out in the Atlantic is the lonely
isle of Saint Kilda now denuded of
its population.

MAKING WOOLLEN HOMESPUN

Central Press.

The Isle of Skye, situated off the north-west coast of Scotland, is both romantic and picturesque, with most inspiring coastal scenery. Here some of the crofter women still weave from native wool.

Central Press.

They also dye the wool by the same primitive, but wholly satisfactory methods that have prevailed for countless years. Above you see one of the housewives occupied in this particular task.

Central Press.

In this picture the same deft worker is engaged in spinning wool upon a simple spinning wheel. There is much demand for homespuns from the Scottish Islands, for the simple reason that the raw materials are so excellent and the craftsmanship skilful and thorough.

TRANSPORT IN OTHER LANDS

Will F. Taylor

We are so accustomed to our railway trains, motor cars and lorries, horse-drawn vehicles, cycles, boats, steamers, aeroplanes and other forms of transport that it is difficult to imagine parts of the world where both people and heavy loads are moved from place to place by other means. This section, however, will prove that many very strange methods are still employed. Here, for example, a scene in Rangoon is depicted.

IN MADEIRA'S SUN-KISSED HIGHWAYS

Keystone View Co.

The Island of Madeira, which is becoming increasingly popular as a holiday resort for people from the British Isles, has innumerable steep and narrow streets, many of them paved with small pebbles of kidney shape. For such peculiar conditions of transport what could be better than this strange type of sledge, drawn by bullocks?

James's Press Agency

Though the coming of the motor lorry has considerably altered the outlook, we must remember that this form of transport is useless unless there are first-class roads and substantial bridges. In the picture above you see wool being removed from the back blocks of Australia to the point of shipment or else the first station on the railway.

Will F. Taylor

How would you like to ride in a native Indian cart, such as the vehicle above, which was photographed near Delhi? You would sit cross-legged upon cushions with a shell-like canopy over your head, this part of the carriage decorated in the brightest colours. You could not expect to make great speed, of course, and your progress would be accompanied by the cheery tinkle of bells worn by the patient beasts of burden.

"ALL ALIVE-O!" IN FAR-AWAY JAPAN

James's Press Agency

"All Alive-o!" might well be written as a title for this picture. It shows two happy, lissom Japanese fish-hawkers setting off on their round through the streets of Tokyo. Most of the wares are kept in tanks of water, but the dealer makes light of his loads.

Record Press

Though the method of travel is to some extent dying out in the course of social progress, you might still see in some parts of Japan a lady making a journey in this peculiar manner, suspended in a kind of hammock from a pole carried by two sturdy bearers.

THE WHEELBARROW MEN AT REST

Will F. Taylor

This is a picture from China. It shows a group of wheelbarrow labourers, evidently enjoying a brief rest, possibly just after their mid-day meal. Many of the streets of Peking are narrow and a great deal of the moving of heavy merchandise is done by means of these barrows. Both the vehicles and the men who propel them are immensely strong.

Keystone View Co.

In some parts of the Mystic East water is actually more precious and costly than wine, and many strange devices are pressed into service for transporting the life-giving fluid. Above we see the method used for delivering water at Aden.

A SHIP THAT FORSAKES THE WATER

Will F. Taylor

These curious circular boats are known as "rufas" and are employed on the River Tigris in Mesopotamia. The ancient Britons also used round boats which were called "coracles."

Will F. Taylor

Another interesting form of water transport, contrasting strangely with the railway train seen in the background, are the boats of straw used for passengers and goods on Lake Titicaca in Bolivia, South America.

James's Press Agency

Here you are shown a ship ready to proceed over land. The scene is one which you might encounter in Prussia. The small steamer, used for merchandise as well as for passengers, has reached a point where there comes a break in the canal. It is therefore floated on to a wheeled framework, surmounted by a strong iron cradle, and is so hauled along rails.

WAITING FOR HIS PASSENGER

Will F. Taylor

We have all heard of rickshaws, and those who have not travelled far from home have seen them on the stage in plays and at summer exhibitions. Here is one of these extremely comfortable and well-sprung carriages, which has a hood for protection against sun and rain. The man is, in the East, called a "rickshaw wallah," and can trot for considerable distances at quite a good speed, seemingly utterly tireless.

DOGS WHO WORK FOR THEIR LIVING

Will F. Taylor

In the snow-lands of the Far North wheeled vehicles are impracticable and the natives must fall back upon sledges. Here is a sledge and dog-team as used in Labrador. Six good dogs draw a man comfortably, but nine sound "huskies" make a more satisfactory team, especially when the ice is rough or the snow deep.

Will F. Taylor

If you travel on the Continent of Europe you will find in many countries small carts drawn by one or more dogs. Probably you will see the morning milk being delivered by dog, and much transport of vegetable and farm produce is carried out by this means. Here you observe a motherly Dutch woman going shopping.

The Story
of the
World and
its Peoples

Great Britain
and Ireland--
The Fortunate
Isles

Will F. Taylor.

THE GIANT'S CAUSEWAY, NEAR PORTRUSH

One of the most interesting formations of old Mother Nature is that to be seen at the Giant's Causeway in the extreme north of Ireland. It is one of the show places of Ulster and is formed of thousands of stone pillars, mostly five-sided or three-sided, standing up right out to sea, so that their tops form a rough platform. The curious formation is believed to be due to some strange effect in the cooling of the lava in earth's earliest ages. The portion depicted above is known as the "Wishing Chair."

BEAUTIFUL IRELAND

THE Green Isle of Erin is a little larger than Scotland, but has rather fewer people. It lies right in the track of the prevailing westerly winds of the Atlantic, which keep it ever fresh and verdant, so that it is known all the world over as "The Emerald Isle."

Ireland has two separate political divisions : (1) Northern Ireland, which is still part of the United Kingdom, and consists of the five counties around Lough Neagh and the county of Fermanagh ; and (2) the Irish Free State (Saorstat Eireann), which is the rest of Ireland, and a self-governing Dominion of the British Empire. Of the two divisions, Northern Ireland, which has several flourishing manufactures, is the more densely populated ; the Irish Free State is mainly a farming country, with a more evenly distributed population, whose great business is dairy-farming and the export of foodstuffs, mainly to the sister island of Great Britain.

The Making of Erin.

Ireland's mountains lie mainly in the great detached masses around its rim. The middle of the island is largely the great Central Plain through which flows the slow, deep Shannon, linked with Dublin by the Royal Canal and by the Grand Canal.

The Central Plain was once covered by other layers of rock among which were the coal measures; but these have nearly all been planed off by the ancient ice and by the work of running water, leaving the old limestone floor with here and there steep isolated hills and mountains of millstone grit like that of the Pennines. Ireland has little coal, and this partly explains why she is not a manufacturing island. But in recent years the mighty Shannon has been harnessed to provide electricity at the great power houses of Ardnacrusha, above which is an eight-mile canal bringing water from the river. The Shannon Power Scheme, it is hoped, will bring electric light, heat and power within the reach of every large town, and enable the Irish Free State to develop manufactures on an important scale.

Peat instead of Coal.

Bogs are common on the Central Plain—soft, swampy and treacherous; others solid and full of the peat, that is much more used than coal in Irish homes. The largest is the Bog of Allen. These bogs have been formed by the age-long decay of marsh plants and sphagnum moss in the water-filled hollows of the limestone, where boulder clay from the ancient glaciers has given them a waterproof bottom. There are bogs, too, in Connemara to the west, and in other low-lying spots among the Irish hills. They are by no means without natural beauty. As the year rolls on, "the bare brown bog turns

ON THE RUGGED ANTRIM COAST

Will F. Taylor.

Here we see the rugged coast of Antrim and obtain another view of the Giant's Causeway. Some of the rocks hereabouts have curious names, such as the Giant's Granny; the Giant's Horse-shoe, and the Giant's Coffin, and the formation is a miracle in stone. The Antrim coast road hugs the marvellous scenery of the seaboard and is thought to be one of the most majestic highways in the British Isles.

THE SHANNON IN HARNESS

Topical Press.

The Shannon, the longest river in the British Isles, which unites the whole four provinces of the Emerald Isle, has now been put in harness, and by means of the huge weir illustrated above is made to operate machinery that will produce electric power for a large part of Ireland, a country that yields very little coal. Already electrical current passes from the wonderful hydro-electric power plant at Ardnacrusha to Dublin, a distance exceeding 100 miles.

gradually warmer in tone till it becomes a bright orange, a pale red, and then in October a vivid crimson as the grass and the bog-plants turn scarlet."

Colours, indeed, are nowhere brighter and fresher than in the clear rain-washed atmosphere of Erin. To appreciate this we have only to visit the lovely Wicklow Hills with their " sweet vale of Avoca," or the beautiful Lakes of Killarney amid their encircling peaks, or wild Connemara with its marble mountains and its deep lakes, Corrib and Mask.

Ireland's highest peak is Carrantuohill (3,414 feet) in Macgillycuddy Reeks amid the mountainous region

of south-western Ireland, whose coast-line is cut up by long deep inlets called *rias*.

Northern Ireland.

Northern Ireland has important manufacturing industries, the chief of which are the linen industry and ship-building. The headquarters of both are at Belfast, which contains about a third of all the people in Northern Ireland.

The linen industry grew up there because it is a flax-growing region, although to-day large quantities of flax from Belgium and Holland, Germany and the Baltic lands have to be imported to meet the needs of the linen mills of Belfast and Londonderry, Larne and Coleraine, Lurgan and Portadown, Armagh and Monaghan.

Ship-building is mainly centred at Belfast at the head of the deep Belfast Lough, where are the famous ship-yards of Harland & Wolff, which have launched many of our finest ocean liners. Although a little coal and iron can be got near Belfast, the main supplies come from Britain—coal from the Ayr coalfield and iron and steel plates from Northern England.

Belfast has also flourishing tobacco factories, the biggest rope works in the world, and mineral water factories. Londonderry also—generally known as " Derry "—has a number of thriving industries besides its main business of linen manufacture. It stands at the head of Lough Foyle, near whose sea-ward end is Moville, a port of call for Atlantic liners.

Northern Ireland is a rich agricultural and stock-breeding country, too. The basin of the River Lagan is remark-ably fertile and grows many kinds of crops ; dairy-farming and pig-rearing being profitable occupations for many people.

The Giant's Causeway.

An interesting spot which every one who can makes a point of seeing is the Giant's Causeway, near Portrush, on the northern coast. It is formed of thousands of basaltic pillars, mostly five-sided or three-sided, standing up right out to sea, so that their tops form a rough platform. The cliffs near by have a similar formation. The famous " organ pipes " of Fingal's Cave in the island of Staffa are of the same structure, and are probably due to a similar great upheaval of ancient lava.

IN THE SHIPYARDS OF BELFAST

Central Press.

At the head of the deep Belfast Lough are famous shipyards, from whose " slipways " have been launched many of our finest ocean liners. Above is a scene at one of the yards on the " Island," as the shipbuilding district is called. Here the ceaseless clangour of metal meeting metal is the only music, and men in their thousands are simply dwarfed by their monstrous surroundings.

ALL READY FOR THE PLUNGE

Central Press.

The largest shipbuilding yards in Belfast are those owned by Messrs. Harland & Wolff, and here we see a liner, the motor-propelled vessel "Highland Princess," at the moment when she is about to be launched into the waters of the River Lagan. It is an inspiring sight to watch a great ship go sliding and plunging into the element for which she was constructed.

The Irish Free State.

Saorstat Eireann is mainly a farming country whose real wealth lies in its dairy produce, and in its cattle and horses, pigs and poultry.

Potatoes, said to have been introduced from the Americas by Sir Walter Raleigh in the sixteenth century, grow well almost anywhere, and to this day form the chief food of a large number of the Irish country folk. So much, in fact, have the Irish depended upon potatoes in past years, that the failure of the potato crop has meant widespread distress.

The dairy industry of Ireland has been greatly helped by the building of central creameries, run by co-operation among the farmers. The milk is brought to the creamery from farms great and small in all sorts of vehicles, from humble donkey carts to large motor lorries. Here the cream is separated from it by machinery to be made into the famous Irish butter, and the " skim milk " that is left is given back to the farmers to use at home or to feed the pigs. There are some hundreds of co-operative dairy societies worked in this way, which gives the big farmers and the poor peasants alike the chance of getting good prices for their cream in a ready market.

Bacon factories and ham factories are run on much the same lines. Poultry kept on the dairy farms yield additional income to their owners. Most of this dairy produce goes to the busy towns and manufacturing regions of Britain, through ports like Dublin, Wexford, Waterford and Cork. Store cattle —cattle reared on the Central Plain and sent to the eastern pastures or even to Britain for fattening—are exported also in large numbers.

Every true Irishman is a lover of fine horses, for some of the finest horses in the world are bred in the Emerald Isle, and horse racing is one of the most popular sports.

Will F. Taylor.

ON A SWINGING BRIDGE

Carrick-a-Rede is a small place on the Antrim coast, and here a great chasm between two high walls of rock is spanned by a crazy-looking rope bridge for the use of fishermen. Another curious bridge is one made of oval girders which spans a cleft in the rocks at the Gobbins, in the neighbourhood of Larne.

Beautiful Connemara.

Much of Ireland, however, is poor

F. Deaville Walker.

A CELTIC CROSS

Monasterboice is a village in the neighbourhood of Drogheda, famous for its ancient ruins. The High Cross seen above was carved from a single block of granite. It stands 27 feet in height and is ascribed to the tenth century. To the left is the base of one of the characteristic Round Towers.

F. Deaville Walker.

ARDMORE'S ROUND TOWER

Ireland possesses a great many Round Towers, believed to have been used as belfries and strongholds for church valuables. The one illustrated belongs to the twelfth century. It is 95 feet in height and in perfect condition, being probably the last erected. Ardmore is in County Waterford.

country for supporting the people who live upon it. In the far west—in Connemara, for instance, where the soil is poor and thin, and the climate wet and raw—the peasants in their little cabins of turves and stones live in the direst poverty, depending upon their small potato and cabbage patches and upon their pigs, if they are lucky enough to have them.

But Connemara is a beautiful region of lake and mountain, visited by more and more people every year for its scenery and its quiet, whilst its trout and salmon fishing attracts sportsmen from all quarters of the British Isles. The gate to it is Galway.

The eastern half of the Irish Free State is much more densely populated, and some manufactures are carried on in the towns and cities.

Dublin.

Dublin (Baile Atha Cliath), the capital, shelters within its city boundaries quite one-eighth of all the people in the Irish Free State. Its port is Kingstown, which is now called *Dun Laoghaire,* and is in daily communication with Holyhead and Liverpool. The River Liffey cuts the city in two, and is lined with busy wharves and warehouses, for Dublin is the main entrance into the Free State. Saint Patrick's Cathedral, founded in the twelfth century, and restored in 1865, and Christchurch Cathedral, stand not far from the Castle in the heart of the city. St. Patrick's Cathedral has a monument to Jonathan Swift, dear to schoolboys and schoolgirls as the author of " Gulliver's Travels."

BY KILLARNEY'S LAKES

F. Deaville Walker.

In Tipperary you may find the famous Rock of Cashel, illustrated above. Upon the Rock are the remains of a castle, palace, cathedral, chapel and round tower. The place is associated with the former kings of Munster. On the Cross of Cashel is carved an effigy of St. Patrick.

Photochrom.

A splendour associated with wild country in a true state of nature is that which belongs to the lakes of Killarney. Here is a photograph of the lovely Upper Lake, which is broken by many fairy-like islands, most of them covered with magnificent trees and shrubs.

The Story
of the
World and
its Peoples

The Empire
on which
the Sun
Never Sets

Col. F. D. Fayrer.

A WONDERFUL BUILDING AT RAGNAGAR

Ragnagar is a remote place in Rajputana, a district made up of several States each ruled by its native prince, and here we see a structure of singular beauty whose pillars and ceiling give evidence of most exquisite carving and workmanship. This building is of great antiquity, but so far from the beaten track that few people can visit it.

THE INDIAN EMPIRE

THE British Overseas Dominions and the smaller outposts of the Empire are inhabited by our fellow-citizens, who with ourselves form what we may justly call the British Commonwealth of Nations.

Some parts of the British Empire are self-governing Dominions which manage their own affairs, but have their share in matters that concern the Empire as a whole. They are the homes of people of the British race who have settled there, or who are the descendants of those who emigrated there long ago. The Dominion of Canada, the Commonwealth of Australia, the Dominion of New Zealand, the Union of South Africa, and the Irish Free State belong to this class.

In other parts the native peoples are not advanced enough to be able to undertake the responsibility of governing themselves. These are parts which must be ruled by white men for the good of the natives, who without proper control and leadership would fight and quarrel among themselves, or remain more or less in their original condition of savagery. British East Africa is a good example.

India and Its People.

India is different from all other parts of the Empire because it is the home of a civilisation much older than our own, and because its 320 millions of people do not belong to one, but to many nations. In India there are

SHIPPING AT PORT SAID

Will F. Taylor.

Port Said is at the entrance to the Suez Canal, a place made fascinating by the strange colour and movement of the people and the ships. High in a domed cabin sits a man who controls the passage of all vessels through the canal. Every movement of craft in the Suez is recorded automatically on a wonderful chart, so that the officials in charge can regulate the traffic.

people of different races, different languages, different religions and very different manners and customs, with smouldering and bitter hatreds that would long ago have burst into flame of war if they had not been kept in check by a strong central government.

Under British Rule.

The British " Raj " (rule), as the people of India call it, has prevented quarrels among the different races, put down injustice with a strong hand, brought education and medical science to the aid of the Indian citizens of the Empire and shown them how to make the best of the rich land that is their home.

India is fast moving towards self-government, and when the people have shown that they are capable of ruling themselves, India will doubtless become another of the British Dominions beyond the seas. A great deal of it even now is ruled by native princes

with the advice and assistance of the British Raj. Many of India's people are well educated and fitted for exercising the duties and carrying the responsibilities of citizenship ; some, indeed, hold responsible offices in the Indian Government, but the greater number are still uneducated and unable as yet to take a share in the government of their country, like other people in the self-governing Dominions of the Empire.

The Rainy Season.

The best time to visit India is during the cool season, which extends from about the middle of October to the end of February ; for in March the hot season begins, and the climate becomes more and more unbearable to Europeans until June, when the south-west monsoon brings heavy rains of the rainy season, which lasts until October. India has no winter as we understand the term, except on the high mountains of the

Topical Press.

Aden is a great coaling base in the East and an important shipping junction. One of the chief objects of interest are no fewer than nine tanks or reservoirs for holding water. These tanks, one of which is illustrated above, are believed to have been built before the time of Christ to catch rain water from the towering hillside. The tanks, however, scarcely ever hold water, for rain falls very seldom, and Aden depends for its water supply upon wells, upon condensation, and also upon an aqueduct seven miles in length.

north and in the lands in the extreme north-west, where winter snows are common.

By the Suez Route.

A good time to start from Britain is about the middle of November, so that you may have the best part of the cool season before you. Even in January, the greater part of India has an average temperature of over 60° F., and the southern half of the peninsula over 70° F. Ceylon, much nearer the Equator, is never cold, and has temperatures round about 90° F. all the year round, except in the hill country, where people find it chilly in comparison with the lowlands.

You will probably take the Suez route to India (unless you prefer the air route which takes you there in a week), and your first port will be either Bombay, or Colombo, the capital and port of Ceylon. You will be wise to visit Ceylon first for two reasons : first, that Ceylon and Southern India begin to get very hot sooner than India ; and second, that the great cities of the plains of India will be at their best in the latter end of December and early January. You can conclude your Indian tour before the end of February and reach home just in time for the first beginnings of the English spring.

The Suez Canal.

By the time you reach Port Said, at the entrance to the Suez Canal, you have caught up summer sunshine again, and think now and then of friends in England shivering in chilly blasts or making the best of a raw fog. The Canal offices are even more fascinating than the strange colour and movement of the people and the ships ; for up there in his cabin in the dome sits the man who controls the passage of all vessels through the canal, and who has made your ship drop anchor ahead of a red mooring buoy patiently to await her turn.

Across the Arabian Sea.

In the hall every movement of the ships is recorded automatically on a wonderful chart of many colours, so that the men in charge can use their telephones and telegraphs to regulate the canal traffic by means of signals placed at intervals along the canal. They decide which ships are to go ahead, and which shall enter *gares* or stations in order to allow other ships to pass.

The next call is at *Aden*, where passengers for Bombay transfer luggage and themselves to the mail steamer for that port ; then your ship steams off for Colombo across the Arabian Sea.

Sport and General.

THE HARBOUR AT ADEN

Aden is the port and harbour that stands at the southern entrance to the Red Sea, and is a place of call for ocean liners to and from the East. It is a coaling station and also a centre in the cable and wireless services.

SUNNY CEYLON

COIN-DIVERS OF COLOMBO

The Singhalese natives seen in the above photograph earn their living by diving for coins thrown from passing ships into the waters of the harbour. The native boats are called catamarans, and within the great breakwaters of Colombo are moored vessels of all seafaring nations. At this seaport are no disreputable or ugly water-side slums.

FIVE days' run from Aden brings us to Colombo, and a different world. Lithe brown fishermen in their strange catamarans have prepared us for a host of new experiences. Within the shelter of the great breakwaters are moored ships of all seafaring nations, it seems. Unlike many of the world's great seaports, Colombo has no disreputable or ugly water-side slums ; as soon as we land we pass through the Fort district, where the Government Offices are, into a region of fine streets lined with shady trees, shops and business offices. New things that attract us are the lines of rickshaws awaiting fares, skirted natives, each with the inevitable black umbrella, and now and then lumbering *ekkas* with their matting hoods sheltering market produce or a party of country folk, and drawn by sleek bullocks.

Colombo, Capital of Ceylon.

Prince Street is Colombo's principal thoroughfare and chief shopping centre, running parallel to the sea. Here we are almost as much in Europe as in Asia, were it not for the climate. But if we go down to the Pettah or native town we are very definitely in the East, although even the Pettah is changing. Two Buddhist temples still remain, however, covered with strange and intricate carvings and multitudes of figures. They are the first we have ever seen, and perhaps we give them more attention than they deserve. The people interest us, too—Singhalese and Moormen, Tamils and Burghers, with representatives of other Eastern races as well as Europeans, crowd the streets.

Our first trip up-country is to the ancient capital of Kandy, among the hills. We can go by train, but decide that a run by car along the fine Colombo-Kandy motor road will give us a better general idea of the country.

Will F. Taylor.

ON A TEA PLANTATION

The row upon row of neatly-pruned bushes here depicted are those from whose leaves we obtain tea. There are busy times on the plantation during the picking season, after which work is transferred to factory buildings on the estate. Here the prepared tea must be packed for transport to the coast.

The Road to Kandy.

Almost at once the road plunges into the midst of luxuriant tropical vegetation. Coco-nut palms by the million grow on both sides of it ; and here and there the Singhalese are busy breaking open the nuts, to get the white kernels which will be dried and exported as copra. The stout husks will be shredded up and spun into coir rope and sennet, or made into net-bags or matting, or one or other of the many things that come from coco-nut fibre

Villages are frequen —most of them two lines of low, palm-thatched buildings on either side of the way —with their rice fields and their water buffaloes with monstrous horns and lumbering carcases. The rice on this side of the island is sown during March, April and May, and reaped in July, August and September ; but on the other side of the island, facing the northeast monsoon of the cooler months, the sowing begins in July and the harvesting in January. The rice fields here are being prepared for the coming of the rain ; those on the other side of Ceylon are almost ready for harvest.

The village schools interest us mightily, for as we speed past their low walls we can see the dark heads of the children at their work, and the village teacher at the blackboard. Two elephants stand at the place where a small road branches off ; except that they sway their huge trunks rhythmically from side to side, and occasionally flap their large ears, they might be carven in stone.

Tea Plantations.

All the time the road is winding up into the hills, and at every bend a new and astonishing landscape unfolds itself now that we have left the lowlands behind. Presently, on both sides are rows upon rows of neatly - pruned bushes, which we know, without being told, are tea bushes. Here and there in the hollows are the white buildings of the tea factories. Few people are at work in the gardens, for picking ceased for the time-being a month ago ; but the factories are busy enough, no doubt, packing the prepared tea for transport to the coast.

Rubber plantations claim our attention next, each tree with its trunk carved in V-shaped patterns by the incisions made to get the white latex or milk, which is regularly collected and sent to the factory on the estate to be turned into rubber.

At last we reach Kandy, the old capital of Ceylon, some 1,600 feet above sea level, but in a basin among the hills, which are covered with verdure where they are not cut into marvellous terraces for paddy cultivation, and supplied with water in all sorts of ingenious ways through channels and pipes of stones, bamboo, or even mud. Kandy itself stands by a beautiful lake, which, it is said, was made artificially by the last Kandyan King very early in the nineteenth century.

The Temple of the Tooth.

The most interesting thing to us in Kandy is the famous " Temple of the Tooth." This old Buddhist temple has its moat, in which live the sacred tortoises. Within the shrine behind the finely-carved doors is a yellow piece of ivory mounted on a stand. This is the

Will F. Taylor.

PREPARING THE " PADDY " FIELDS

Fields for growing rice are prepared by natives aided by water buffaloes with monstrous horns. Rice seed is sown at different times of year, according to the situation of the fields and when rainy weather may be expected, and harvest follows in from four months to six months.

famous " tooth " reputed to be the tooth of Buddha, and visited as such by pious pilgrims from distant parts of Asia. As an act of devotion, these pilgrims place gold leaf upon the stone pillars surrounding the shrine, much as the pious in Burma gild the pagodas.

The highest part of Ceylon's mountain knot is Pidurutallagalla (Pedrotallagalla), which reaches an altitude of over 8,000 feet. Much better known, however, is Adam's Peak, whose cone-

IN CEYLON'S OLD=TIME CAPITAL

Kandy is the ancient capital of Ceylon, standing some 1,600 feet above sea level in a basin among the hills. Here we are shown the beautiful lake, upon the shores of which the city encroaches. The lake is not a natural one, but was made artificially by the last Kandyan King very early in the nineteenth century.

Here is a picturesque group of " Devil Dancers." These men, in their amazing attire, perform different ceremonies which are believed by the native demon-worshippers to be a cure for sickness and disease. The photograph was taken at Kandy, and the masks form one of the most curious features of this quaint group.

THE TEMPLE OF THE TOOTH

F. Deaville Walker.

One of the most interesting sights of Kandy is the famous "Temple of the Tooth," depicted above. It is an ancient Buddhist temple with a moat, in which live the sacred tortoises. Here you see the entrance to the temple, with the library on the right.

F. Deaville Walker.

This is another view of the celebrated temple, showing the actual shrine. Behind the finely-carved door is a piece of yellow ivory mounted on a stand. This is reputed to be the tooth of Buddha. As an act of devotion pilgrims place gold-leaf upon the stone pillars surrounding the shrine, much as the pious in Burma gild the pagodas.

like summit is about 1,000 feet less—for this is sacred ground. Up there is a strange depression in the earth, about 2¾ feet wide and from 3 to 5 inches deep, which is regarded with reverence by Buddhists, Hindus and Moslems alike. Buddhists say it is the foot-print of Buddha; Hindus say that it is Shiva's footmark; and the Moslems aver that it is neither of these, but in very truth the foot-print of Adam, who came to this precise spot on his expulsion from Eden.

Not far from Adam's Peak is the lovely hill-station of Nuwara Eliya (Neuralia), which is very popular in the hot season. In December and January, however, the air is distinctly chilly, for the town is some 6,000 feet above sea level, and overcoats and fires are quite in order.

The Buried Cities.

The visit to Kandy makes us all the more eager to see something of the " Buried Cities of Ceylon "—cities which were the capitals of mighty kings hundreds of years before the birth of Christ, and the centres of early and wonderful civilisations. Their glory passed and the jungle swept over them as if they had never been. In recent years, however, much time and money have been spent in clearing away the jungle growths sufficiently to reveal the main features of these ancient cities, palaces and temples.

The oldest remains are at Anuradhapura in the central part of the island, where an image of Buddha sits in lofty contemplation regardless of time and change, where temples and *dagobas*, *wiharas* (image houses), and

F. Deaville Walker.

AMONG THE " BURIED CITIES OF CEYLON "

The colossal structure in this photograph is an ancient dagoba to be found at Anuradhapura, in the central part of Ceylon. Here temples, image-houses, priests' houses and other buildings of a religious character peep out unexpectedly from the jungle. This dagoba is built entirely of bricks and is believed to contain sufficient material to erect a city as large as Coventry.

pansalas (priests' houses) peep unexpectedly from the jungle, and where Buddhist priests to-day still keep watch and ward over temples that have been restored to something like their original beauty. At Anuradhapura, too, is the sacred *bo-tree*, sprung from a branch of that same tree of Gaya in the Valley of the Ganges, beneath which Gautama Buddha sat in contemplation.

Farther south are the famous ruins at Polonna-ruwa—a capital of later date, and in much better preservation than those of Anuradhapura. Its walls, 10 feet high and 10 feet thick, built of brickwork over 800 years ago, ex-tended for twelve miles round the ancient city. Even to-day you can trace them in a series of irregular grassy humps, with great masses of brickwork ex-posed here and there.

The Jungle.

Glimpses of forest and jungle give us but a faint idea of Ceylon's glorious trees and marvellous flowers, and none at all of the jungle folk. To discover the real secrets of the wilds, one must penetrate deeply into the little-visited parts of the islands, where herds of wild elephant a d the bison (*tsaing*) live, where the fierce leopards stalk deer, and where birds of gay plumage flutter among the branches, or sip honey from the flowers. Myriads of fire-flies flit amid the velvet gloom of jungle nights, and those who seek care-fully may find those strange stick in-sects and leaf insects, which evade their foes by successfully pretending to be what they are not.

F. Deaville Walker.

IN LOFTY CONTEMPLATION

Here is an image of Buddha, to be found among Ceylon's "Buried Cities" at Anuradhapura. It sits in lofty con-templation regardless of time and change and is the symbol of the religious faith of the Singhalese. Near by is the sacred bo-tree, sprung from the branch of a tree beneath which Gautama Buddha sat.

But our time will not permit of hunting expeditions in Ceylon; we must catch the express from Colombo northwards for Southern India. This fine train will carry us north to Mannar, whence a comfortable passage of twenty-two miles in the South India Railway ferry steamers will bring us to Danushkodi, the gateway to Southern India from Ceylon.

The ferry here carries one across a gap known as "Adam's Bridge." At one time it was thought that Ceylon and India were joined in bygone ages, but modern scientists have disproved this theory.

L 2

E. N. A.

THE ELEPHANT TEMPLE AT MADURA

Madura is one of the most wonderful old cities of Southern India, and here we see the famous Elephant Temple. Elephants were often carved out of solid rock, and we should remember that Ganesh is the elephant-headed god of wisdom and good fortune—one of the sons of Siva the Destroyer. Visitors to some of the temples of Madura have bestowed upon them garlands of marigolds at the time of the Hindu festival held at the January full moon.

FROM the sea and sand at Danush-kodi, where we disembarked from the steamer that brought us from Ceylon, we take train across a low-lying country with clumps of cabbage palm and clusters of mud huts, thatched with palm leaf, to the richer land where peasants clad only in waist cloths are busy in the paddy fields, watering the land by the ancient method of raising water from the wells and pouring it into little channels of the fields. Patient bullocks work all day long up and down the little slopes by the wells, lowering the big hide buckets into the water as they go up, and lifting them filled as animals strain down again Then comes a pause for the buckets to be emptied by the peasants as soon as they reach the top, with a pleasant gurgling as the cool water slips down the conduits.

Madura and Its Temple.

Our first stop is at Madura, one of the most wonderful old cities of Southern India, containing a great temple which is reckoned to be the finest of its kind in the Indian Empire. It covers twenty-five acres. Like most temples of Southern India, it stands within a number of squared walled enclosures, pierced by magnificent tall gateways called *gopurams*, which rise storey upon storey on a rectangular base to a high crowning ridge. Each storey is carved into thousands of sculptured figures of gods and heroes, with an effect that is staggering to the Western mind bewildered by the over-richness of detail. To understand the meaning of the figures one must be well-versed in the Hindu religion, and know at least the chief of the hundreds of shapes and forms assumed by the two great gods—Vishnu the Preserver,

BY THE GOLDEN LILY POOL

Bourne and Shepherd.

If you were travelling in Southern India you could see this wonderful gopuram or gate to the Great Temple of Madura. The gopuram rears its stone head to a height exceeding 150 feet. It is shaped something like a pyramid, and in what looks to be a maze of sculpture are figures of gods, heroes, bulls, elephants and many other gilded or brightly-coloured forms. There are thousands of these sculptured figures, some of them representing Vishnu the Preserver and Siva the Destroyer in hundreds of shapes and forms.

and Shiva or Siva the Destroyer and Re-creator.

Within the walled enclosures are the priests' dwellings, and the temple itself, which rises tier upon tier, each crowded with sculptures. Within the temple is the sacred place where the figure of the god is kept. At Madura there is the image of Ganesh, the elephant-headed god of wisdom and good fortune—one of the sons of Siva the Destroyer. We give a present of money to the priests and go into the temple to wander for an hour or so through its mysterious interior and among its thousands of carven pillars.

A Hindu Festival.

As we come out a priest bestows upon each of us a garland of marigolds,

Col. F. D. Fayrer.

FROM CENTRAL INDIA

A typical fakir, a kind of beggar, though really a religious mendicant. Fakirs belong to many different religious orders; and, whilst many of them are devout, a few are merely quacks and charlatans. Note the holy symbols which the man carries and his dish for alms.

Col. F. D. Fayrer.

A HINDU BRIDE

This young Hindu girl is clad in her wedding finery and wears the marks of her rank. Hindus bear upon their foreheads signs that indicate the particular religious sects to which they belong. Further, the Hindus are divided into many castes or classes, each of which keeps strictly to itself.

for this is the time of the Hindu festival that is held at Madura at the January full moon. The streets of the city are thronged with pilgrims gathered together for this solemn occasion from all parts. The chief ceremony will be the passage of the gods on richly-ornamented rafts round the sacred tank, which is a vast sheet of water two miles in circumference.

Millions of fairy lamps will glow from the terraces round the tank, and the procession of the gods will be illuminated with coloured fires and heralded by the booming of gongs and the beat of drums. Elephants will clear the road round the tank so that the priests and their helpers, pulling on the huge hawsers, will have clear space in which to manœuvre their

Sport and General.

BOULDER-PERCHED TEMPLE AND FORTRESS

At Trichinopoly is a great rock-fortress which towers above the town roofs from its high perch
on the rock that heaves its shoulders above the palm trees. The rocks are picturesquely sculptured by nature, and on the very summit is a temple. This is one of the most impressive sights
of Southern India, and the rock-mass rises to a height of more than 270 feet.

unwieldy rafts to the landing-places
whence the gods will be borne high to
the temple from which they were
brought, there to rest until next year's
festival.

Hindu Castes.

This visit to Madura brings us into
sudden contact with Hinduism, the
great Indian religion. We cannot pre-
tend to understand it, and we are far
too wise to smile at what we do not
understand. What to us is a meaning-
less jumble of gods and goddesses, and
a number of festivals attended by
crowds of excited people, is a very
different thing to the Hindus themselves.

We learn, for the first time, that
the coloured marks we notice on
the foreheads of many Indians are
marks that indicate the particular
religious sects to which they belong.

These marks are not caste-marks, as
some people suppose. Caste, again, is
another matter which we find difficult to understand. The Hindus are
divided into many castes or " classes,"
each of which keeps strictly to itself ;
a man of one caste may not marry a
woman of another—he may not eat
with people of another ; even the
shadow of a lower caste person falling
upon his food will prevent a high-
caste man partaking of it. Long ago
the castes were only four — the
Brahmins, of priestly descent ; the
Kshattruyas, of military descent ; the
Vaishiyas, or merchant class ; and the
Sudras or workers, builders, farmers
and labourers. To-day, however, there
are many divisions and subdivisions
of these ; and there are the " un-
touchables," with whom none but
themselves may have any dealings
whatsoever.

Trichinopoly and the Carnatic.

From Madura we take train again for Trichinopoly, not forgetting to buy a bunch of small plantains to give to the monkeys that come down from their playgrounds on the roofs of wayside stations to beg at the carriage windows. The sight to see at Trichinopoly is the great roof-fortress, which towers above the town roofs from its high perch on the rock that heaves its shoulders above the palm trees. Facing it is the sacred tank, in the midst of which is a small shrine; the temple itself is carved out of the rock. The great plain which stretches around Trichinopoly in a sea of chequered tints of growing crops is the part of the Carnatic about which we read in our history books at those pages which tell of the exploits of Clive in the early days of British interest in India. The Fort of Arcot is only 100 miles away to the north.

Madras.

Madras is our next objective. Like all India's great sea gates, it has a part that is distinctly European, with fine modern buildings, and a portion that is even more distinctly native. The bazaars interest us more than the European quarters of the city; but we find the splendid Law Courts worth a special visit. The great banyan tree —a tree which we see in Madras for the first time in reality—commands our attention; its branches drop to the ground suckers which take root and become new trunks, so that a single tree looks like a grove of trees.

Col. F. D. Fayrer.

THE PERFORMING BEARS

Whilst travelling in India you might by chance come upon a wayside scene such as that shown above. The bears are trained to perform many interesting tricks, but they are so jealous of one another and so pugnacious by nature that they would quickly commence to fight if the attendants did not keep a firm hold over them.

Ewing Galloway, N.Y.

PEACOCKS ON THEIR TRAVELLING PERCH

This photograph was taken at Bombay, a city which is the gate to the whole of India. It shows a native salesman of peacocks, and you will observe that the birds are carried on a roosting-perch, and also that each of them is blindfolded to prevent it from flying away. Could you possibly imagine a more novel method of transporting goods for sale?

In the hot weather, the Europeans who can afford it forsake Madras for Ootacamund—" Ooty " they call it—a hill station in the midst of the beautiful Nilgiri Hills, where tea plantations and cinchona plantations flourish, and where tiger as well as sambhur and other deer roam in the thick forests that clothe the wetter slopes. These forests are the homes of the primitive Toda people, who speak their strange language that has never been written down, and live their lives in the same way as their forefathers did 2,000 years ago and more.

FROM BOMBAY TO THE CAPITAL

A HIGHWAY IN THE BOMBAY PRESIDENCY

F. Deaville Walker.

From this illustration you can gain a very realistic idea of what travelling by road is like in a
country district round Bombay. Here you see native carts, two of them drawn by bullocks;
whilst wiry horses are harnessed to the one in the foreground. Motor propelled vehicles are,
of course, being more and more used on the Indian highways.

RAILWAY travel in India is very
different from a journey by rail
in Britain. The distances, to
begin with, are much greater, and the
trains are specially adapted to give
passengers as much comfort as possible
over long journeys in a climate which is
distinctly hot for the greater part of
the year.

Every traveller who intends to see
more of India than he can from the
windows of his express train will
engage a native servant or " bearer "
to take a good many of his little worries
from his shoulders and to smooth out
the way, so that everything runs
without a hitch. If he plans to go any
distance from the main routes, the
traveller also takes care that a " cook "
goes too.

As long as you are in one of the fine
trains of the Indian State Railways,
or located at one of the many excellent hotels in the cities, you are
quite able to fend for yourself ; but
directly you strike out into less beaten
tracks, you will be sadly at a disadvan-

tage without your " boy " or bearer.
For it is he who books your seat in
the trains, packs and looks after your
luggage ; he sees that your meals are
forthcoming at the proper time, whether
you are on the train or staying for the
night at one of the " rest-houses "
provided at convenient places along
the roads away from the towns ; he
makes your bed for you, valets you,
tips the right people (with *your* coins,
of course) and sees that you get your
money's worth everywhere.

You might think that such a jewel of
a man-servant is a rare one : but if you
have quite ordinary luck, you will find
just such a " bearer " awaiting your
arrival at your port of entry into India,
if you have taken the precaution to have
one engaged for you, either by some
friend in India or some big banking or
business firm which has branches there.

Indian Trains.

The carriages on the Indian express
trains are so arranged that the seats,
which lie in line with the length of the

train, can be converted into comfortable beds for the night—a job which your bearer does for you. The white carriages are fitted with electric fans and dust-proof windows ; and there is a comfortable restaurant car as well as a bath-room. You can, if you wish, have one of the splendidly-equipped tourist cars, with your own private dining-room, sitting-room and bedroom, and with your own kitchen and your own servants' quarters ; but that is for wealthy people who like to travel in luxury !

Suppose you have landed at Bombay instead of visiting Ceylon first, as we suggested. Bombay is the gate to the whole of India. You have your choice of at least five mail trains and three main line expresses a day on the G.I.P. (Great Indian Peninsula) route —to the Punjab by way of Delhi and Lahore ; to Calcutta *viâ* Jubbulpore and *viâ* Nagpur ; to Cawnpore, Lucknow and the cities of the Ganges ; or to Madras and the wonderful city-temples of Southern India, by way of Poona and Raichur.

Railway Routes from Calcutta.

If, however, you have made Calcutta your starting-point, you have the choice of an even greater variety of routes and fast trains. From Howrah terminus of the E.I.R. (East Indian Railway) two mail trains and seven

IN THE DOCKLAND OF BOMBAY

H. J. Shepstone.

The Presidency of Bombay comes on the westernmost side of the Empire of India, and the island city of the same name is the chief port on the western seaboard. Here is a picture of a portion of the docks and the Ballard Pier station, where fine railway trains are brought alongside ocean liners. It is said that upwards of sixty dialects are spoken in this vast city.

expresses run daily to Benares, Cawn-pore, Lucknow, Agra, Delhi, the Punjab and Bombay. From Sealdah terminus the Eastern Bengal line has four or five good trains every day to Darjeeling, the beautiful hill station which is the refuge of many Europeans during the hot season, to the tea plantations of Assam, and to Chitta-gong and the farthest east of India.

Using the railways alone, it is pos-sible to visit all India's finest cities and to learn a great deal of the country with-out departing very far from the beaten track. But if you want to see the real India, you must forsake the tourist routes, strike out into less-known high-ways, and live in India long enough to understand her people and their ways.

Let us take such a journey, starting from Victoria Station at Bombay, and climbing over the Western Ghats on to the Dekkan by the pass. Four hours' journey brings us to the sacred city of Nasik, which is the holiest of all Indian cities, save Benares. It stands at an altitude of nearly 2,000 feet above sea level, near the source of the sacred Godavari, by whose waters gather millions of pilgrims from all parts of India to perform the one essential duty which ensures them salvation. Nasik is a city of Hindu temples where, at certain times of the year, great religious festivals are held.

The Ellora Caves.

Stranger still are the cave-temples of

THE CAVE-TEMPLES OF ELLORA

H. J. Shepstone.

The temples of Ellora, believed to date from the eighth century, have been carved out of the solid hillside—great pillars, images of gods and goddesses, life-size elephants and a profusion of intricate ornamentation all cut with patient perfection from the rock itself. Above we see the Kailas Temple, and there are in the same neighbourhood caves of great antiquity hewn in the rock.

Col. F. D. Fayrer.

A COTTON-SPINNER AT WORK

This is a picture of a wayside scene in Central India. The dusky, bearded native is spinning cotton upon a primitive appliance known as the Persian or gandhi wheel. In effect, the raw cotton must pass through a somewhat similar though far more rapid process in a modern power mill.

Ellora. These we can visit by car from Aurangabad, which is not on the main line, but on a narrow-gauge railway from Manmad. If we elect to stay at Ellora for the night, there is a good rest-house or dak bungalow where we can put up. The temples of Ellora have been carved out of the solid hillside—great pillars, images of gods and goddesses, life-size elephants, and a profusion of intricate ornament all cut with patient perfection from the rock itself.

Monasteries, too, with numerous rooms and windows and staircases for the monks of old, have been similarly excavated from the solid rock with infinite care and labour. At least three religions have played a part in the work: Buddhist, Hindu and Jain. The Buddhist temple has great seated figures of Buddha, and a marvellously-carven roof; the Jain caves are filled with perfect statues, each in its niche, storey upon storey. The Jains have their finest temples at Mount Abu, which is visited by many tourists during the season; their faith is very much like that of the Buddhists, for they believe that after this life a man's soul may pass into the body of an animal, and therefore look upon ill-treatment and slaughter of animals as utterly hateful.

Cotton on the Dekkan.

Up here on the Dekkan is the wonderful black soil in which cotton grows best. It was formed by the breaking up of the lava which covers the north-western part of the Dekkan. It does not powder into dust as most other soils do in the hot season, but retains a great deal of moisture, although it cracks widely. The cotton seed is sown when the big rains are over, and the tenacious lava soil forms a sort of clod round the roots of the growing plant, so that it flourishes without irrigation and without much rain, and the cotton is ready to pick when the hot season begins in March. Indian cotton is grown also in the Upper Ganges basin and in the Punjab, but under very different conditions.

We saw at Bombay how the people of India engage in the cotton manufacture themselves, employing the most up-to-date machinery in large cotton mills that bear comparison with those of Lancashire. We shall see the same thing at Delhi, Lucknow, Cawnpore, and other Indian cities, where the tall fingers of factory chimneys break the beautiful skyline of ancient temples and palaces. The people of India, however, still use cotton in the ancient way, weaving it on their primitive looms and dyeing it perhaps with the old vegetable dyes, producing really fine fabrics.

Famous Strongholds.

Back at Aurangabad, we are reminded of the great Moghul Emperor, Aurangzeb, who gave his name to the city, for we can go to see the stronghold of Daulatabad which he built for himself long years ago. Farther north, another stronghold perched bravely on a great hill overlooks the city and the palaces and gardens belonging to the Nawab—the native Prince of Bhopal. From Bhopal, visitors go to see the strange domelike monuments on the hill at Sanchi. They are called stupas or topes, which the ancient Buddhists erected over sacred relics or holy spots. The most wonderful things at Sanchi, however, are the beautifully-carved gateways, stone rails and steps, which are covered with elaborate sculptures that tell the story of the life of Buddha. They are the Buddhist scriptures written in stone by the sculptor-artists of the sixth century before Christ, at the command of the great Indian Emperor, Asoka. Some of the stupas have been opened and found to contain the bones of famous disciples of the great teacher, Gautama Buddha.

Gwalior's Castled Crag.

Going north, the train takes us to Gwalior, dominated by the "castled crag of Gwalior," flat-topped, with steep sides that actually overhang in places, and approached by a single road guarded by six great gates. Here the mutineers of 1857 took refuge, and held out until two young British officers with a small force, including a clever blacksmith among its number, crept up and picked the locks of the first five gates before they were discovered by the defenders.

Now we are on the way to Agra and Delhi, the two great Indian cities that recall most vividly the splendour of the Moghul Emperors who from the time of our good Queen Bess to the days of Queen Anne ruled over the greater part of India—sometimes from Agra, sometimes from Delhi. Their names are more than memories, for they stand also for mosques, palaces and monuments that to this day are among the wonders of the world—the Emperors Humayan and Akbar, Jehangir, Shah Jehan and Aurangzeb.

The Great Moghuls.

It was Babar, descendant of the great Mongol conqueror, Jenghiz Khan, who swept down into the plains of the Ganges and Jumna with his twelve thousand wild hillmen and desert warriors, met Lodi, the last of the Afghan kings of Agra, and completely routed his hundred thousand men and their thousand armoured elephants, in 1526.

Both Agra and Delhi became the prizes of the conqueror, whose son, Humayan, was the second of the Moghuls to rule an empire in India.

"CROWN OF THE PALACE"

Will F. Taylor.

The Taj Mahal near Agra is known throughout the world as the loveliest specimen of Indian architecture. It was built by the Shah Jehan in memory of his beloved queen, Mumtaz Mahal, whose sepulchre it forms. Twenty thousand men worked upon this beautiful building.

It was Humayan who began to build Agra's great fortress of red sandstone that still sprawls along the banks of the Jumna, at which people of to-day may marvel. Its walls were 70 feet high and a mile and a half long; within them still remain enough of the palaces, mosques, marble baths and terraces to testify to the splendours of the place when Humayan and his successors lived there. There are the balconies and balustrades of exquisitely-carved stone built by Akbar, and the pearl mosque built by his grandson, Shah Jehan.

The Taj Mahal.

Most marvellous of all Agra's monuments is the peerless Taj, which is known throughout the world as the loveliest specimen of Indian architecture—some say the most beautiful the world has ever seen. It was built by the Shah Jehan in memory of his beloved Queen, Mumtaz Mahal, whose sepulchre it forms. Taj Mahal is a modern corruption of her name.

Mumtaz Mahal—" Crown of the Palace "—was famous throughout the land for her charity and wisdom as well as for her beauty. She was married to Shah Jehan in 1622, and died in 1631, four years after her Lord became Emperor. Shah Jehan's grief was so poignant that he wished to give up his throne. He was persuaded to remain, however, and resolved to build for his beloved the most beautiful building in all the world. Twenty thousand men worked upon it for twenty-two years; twenty precious kinds of stone were used in its fabric, and its design was chosen from among those submitted by all the master architects in the Moghul Empire.

The Taj Mahal stands on its marble terrace by the Jumna, with a beautiful mosque at each side, the whole set in wonderful gardens.

F. Deaville Walker.

THE SAS BAHN TEMPLE, GWALIOR

Here we are shown one of the many wonderful buildings of Gwalior. This state, and more particularly the city of the same name, is dominated by the "castled crag of Gwalior," flat-topped, with steep sides that actually overhang in places and approached by a single road guarded by six great gates.

DELHI TO-DAY AND YESTERDAY

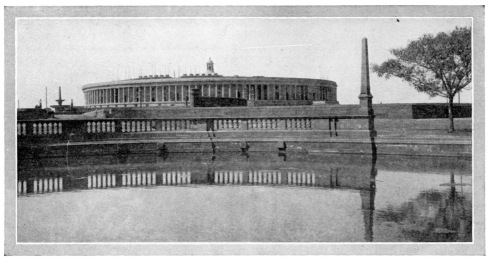

NEW DELHI'S COUNCIL HALL

H. J. Shepstone.

On the northern side of modern Delhi a New Delhi is arising at Raisina, some three or four miles from the city walls. Most of the buildings are white, but the Secretariat, Government House and the Rotunda are built of red sandstone. New Delhi is the centre of the Indian Government and is ideally placed, for it is the meeting-place of the nations.

FOUR hours from Agra by train is Delhi, the capital of the Indian Empire. Seven cities, all capitals at one time or another, have arisen on or near this spot since the eleventh century, although the name " Delhi " is as old as the first century before Christ. The present city is a strange medley of old and new, of the tawdry and the magnificent. There are the high-balconied houses and the crooked narrow streets of its bazaars ; there is the great fort and its halls, its wonderful palaces, and its mosques that tell of the vanished splendour of the Great Moghuls.

Delhi proper is known as Shah-jehanabad—the city of Shah Jehan. It is surrounded by a great wall of red sandstone pierced by seven glorious gates. In the centre of the city stand the beautiful Jama Masjid (great mosque) and the palace built by Shah Jehan in 1638. The palace is mainly of white marble with inside work of mosaic in beautiful stones of many colours, and its ceilings were once covered with paintings and ornamented with gold.

Visitors to the great Hall of Public Audience (the *Diwan-i-Am*) are shown the recess in which once stood the famous " Peacock Throne " of Aurangzeb, made of solid gold, encrusted with diamonds, rubies and emeralds, and ornamented at the back with two peacocks ablaze with gems. Between the peacocks was a parrot carved from a single magnificent emerald. Above all rose a golden canopy upheld by twelve pillars rich with jewels and fringed with precious pearls.

The Wonder of the East.

This wonder of the East was carried off by Persian invaders in 1739. It is said it was worth nearly seven million pounds sterling.

The innermost court of the palace is the Hall of Private Audience (*Diwan-i-Khas*), which bears over its outer arches a Persian text which runs : " If there be a Paradise upon the face of the earth, it is this, oh ! it is this ! "

Within the precincts of this marvellous palace-fort there are also beautiful

ROADSIDE TYPES OF INDIA

Will F. Taylor.

In the characteristic roadside scene here depicted we see Hindu dancing girls in their picturesque costume. The music is produced from a fiddle of curious type and a native drum.

Col. F. D. Fayrer.

Here is the Indian equivalent of a pedlar. This woman, with her brown but chubby infant, has spread her wares on the footpath, and we see that she sells chiefly spectacles of many types, in addition to razors, penknives and similar small articles.

THE BOYISH HINDU BRIDEGROOM

Col. F. D. Fayrer.

On a previous page we saw a Hindu bride in all her wedding finery. Here is a bridegroom, wearing his gorgeous head-dress. Hindu boys marry at the age of ten years.

J. Horrell.

Among the types of Indian tradespeople and craftsmen here is one of the strangest, for our picture shows a fisherwoman engaged in spinning line from the fibres of a palm tree.

Col. F. D. Fayrer.

We have all heard of Indian snake-charmers, and here is a trio of these men following the calling which gains for them a frugal livelihood. The snakes used in this instance are cobras, who respond to the music of the curious native instruments.

gardens, and the three domes of the perfect Moti Masjid, the Pearl Mosque built by Aurangzeb of marble. The Jama Masjid is built of red sand-stone and flanked by two tall minars or towers 130 feet high, ornamented with vertical stripes of white marble and red sandstone. It is one of the largest mosques in the world, and is regarded as particularly sacred because it con-tains precious relics of the Prophet— one of them a hair from his beard.

Leave Delhi by the Delhi Gate or by the Ajmer Gate and you come to old Delhi—Firozabad; and beyond that the ruins of six former Delhis stretching over a distance of some twelve miles. Among the most interesting of these ancient monuments are the Tomb of Emperor Humayan, beneath whose marble dome repose the bones of the Moghul in their coffin of pure white marble; and the Kutb Minar that points its tall tower of red and cream-coloured stone 238 feet into the air. Close by is the famous iron pillar—a solid shaft of plain wrought iron, at whose base is the inscription: "Whilst I stand, shall the Hindu Kingdom endure."

On the northern side of modern Delhi a New Delhi is arising at Raisina, some three or four miles from the city walls. Most of the buildings are white, but the Secretariat, Government House, and the Rotunda are built of the same red sandstone which the architects of the Moghul emperors used for much of their finest work. New Delhi is the centre of the Indian Government.

What is there about this spot that has made it the site of seven Delhis— and of the new one that is being created in our own time? The choice of the ancient rulers of a suitable spot for their seven capitals has been endorsed by the British as the best that can be made. A glance at a good map of India will answer this question for us.

Delhi stands between the Ridge that is the north-easternmost spur of the Aravalli Hills and the Jumna, and in the narrowing of the gap between the Himalayas and the Dekkan; so that it is ideally placed for commanding both the Ganges and the Indus Basins. This central position has always made Delhi the meeting place of the nations, and to this day you will see in its crowded streets representatives not only of most of the people of India, but of the nations of the East. Where the tall houses lean towards each other across the narrow ways, buffalo carts, ekkas drawn by sleek bullocks, camels with bulging loads, tall narrow camel carts, asses bearing incredible burdens, and mules with tails like frayed-out steel rope dispute the passage with a crowd of people dressed in many colours—and all apparently with time to spare. Indeed, there is not such a thing as "time" in the East—or if there is, it is quite unimportant.

The Holi-puja.

Visit the bazaar during a festival— the Holi-puja, for example, which comes in spring at the time of full moon in the month of Phalgoon. That is the time when the mango trees are loaded with blossom, and the sweet-scented flowers cover the asoka trees. All the world is abroad, enjoying the festival. Boys and girls bombard passers-by with powder which stains the white garments with red that looks like blood. They will tell you it is the sand of the Jumna stained with the gore of the evil spirits and demons whom Krishna slew.

Within the bazaar you find each trade in its own particular quarter, where it has been established from the beginning of Delhi. The vegetable sellers squat cross-legged by their heaps of produce, some of which we recognise and some of which are new and strange; the rice-seller, not far away, has his stall in the same old spot, where he sits, balance in hand, and with his image of Ganesh near by to bring him luck in the days of trading. Ganesh is the elephant-headed god—

A CHARMER OF SNAKES

Col. F. D. Fayrer.

This is a portrait of a typical Indian sampiah or snake-charmer. He heralds his approach by a few notes upon a weird musical instrument ; and, when he has gathered a modest audience, commences operations at the roadside. Meanwhile the snakes are carried in baskets contained in a sack slung, with a staff, across their master's shoulder. Snake-charmers are found in Egypt as well as in India.

A "PARADISE ON EARTH"

Will F. Taylor.

The Kashmir Gate of Delhi, in whose crowded streets you may meet representatives not only of most of the people of India, but of all the nations of the East. Buffalo carts, ekkas drawn by sleek bullocks—and also motor vehicles—pass through this gateway.

F. Deaville Walker.

The interior of the innermost court of the Palace at Delhi is here illustrated. It is known as the Hall of Private Audience, and bears over its outer arches a Persian text which runs : " If there be a Paradise upon the face of the earth, it is this, Oh ! it is this ! "

H. J. Shepstone.

In Old Delhi you may see the Kutb Minar, here illustrated. This tall tower of red and cream-coloured stone rears its head 238 feet into the air. Close by is the famous iron pillar—a solid shaft of plain wrought iron, at whose base is the inscription : "Whilst I stand, shall the Hindu Kingdom endure."

benign, and the bringer of good fortune.

In the Bazaar.

The *haloai* and his wife sell strange and sticky sweetmeats, or fry over an absurdly tiny charcoal fire the twisted rings of *jelabi* which all Indian boys and girls love. Over there, down another alley, is the fisherwives' quarter, as you can hear by their shrill cries. They sit by their baskets of plaited bamboo, in which are the fish caught by husbands and brothers. Strong women they are, and tremendous talkers. They are keen bargainers, and eye you with reproach if you offer too little, following this up by proving volubly that the fish they sell are the best in the world and descended from the gods themselves.

Coppersmiths, goldsmiths, silver-smiths—all have their corners in the bazaar. So do the perfumers, whose attar of roses, musk and sandalwood fill their quarter with fragrant odours.

The barber shaves the heads of his patrons, telling all the latest news to an interested group of hangers-on and prospective customers. The story-teller sits cross-legged on his box-like platform holding his audience spell-bound with his tales of the old heroes and their adventures. The letter-writer plies his trade in public. A holy man or *yogi* plucks plaintively at his one-stringed instrument, and gives advice and comfort to those who seek his aid.

News travels fast in the bazaars. What the newspapers do not tell, you can always hear from your native servant if you have won his heart—for he has heard it in the bazaar.

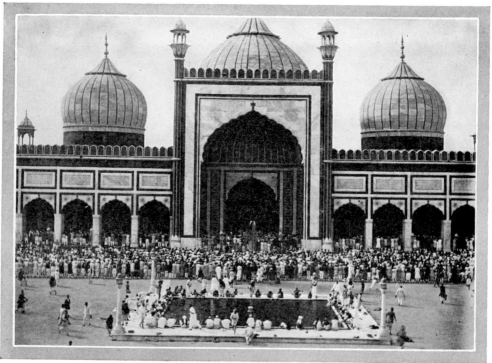

F. Deaville Walker.

THE GREAT MOSQUE OF DELHI

Here is the beautiful Jama Masjid, where on Fridays there may be as many as 10,000 wor-shippers. It is regarded as being perhaps the finest mosque in the world and was built by Shah Jehan 300 years ago. It stands near a wonderful palace of white marble.

THE NORTH-WEST FRONTIER

Will F. Taylor.

A MEMORY OF THE INDIAN MUTINY

This old gun is a relic of the Indian Mutiny. It may be seen at Lahore, capital of the Punjab, and visitors are always specially interested in the cannon because it is the one upon which " Kim " is discovered sitting in the opening chapter of Rudyard Kipling's book.

THE hill station for Delhi is Simla, where the Government of India has its headquarters during the hot weather, and where lesser officials and fashionable folk of all sorts follow its example. Although Simla is only about 7,000 feet above sea level, there is a great difference between its genial climate and the baking heat of the plains.

You go up to Kalka by the single-line 5 feet 6 inches gauge railway, and there you take the narrow-gauge Kalka-Simla line which winds up and up through deep cuttings and round perilous-looking loops and bends to the forested hills, among which stands Simla, with magnificent views of the far-distant snowy ranges of Tibet.

Our next journey, however, is in a different direction, through the country of the Sikhs to the far north-western gateway of the Khyber, through which wave after wave of invasion has, in past ages, descended to the fertile plains and rich cities of India.

Amritsar, some 300 miles from Delhi, is the most holy city of the Sikhs, and a great market and caravan centre for the whole of central Asia. Here, in the caravanserais, you may see merchants from Persia and Bokhara, slant-eyed Tibetans and Mongols from the interior plateaux, Kashmiris and Afghans, Baluchis and Turkomans, and sturdy Gurkhas and lean tribesmen from the frontiers.

The Golden Temple.

Its chief glory is the Golden Temple —the " Darbar Sahib "—whose white marble walls, adorned with patterns in precious stones, and surmounted by a roof of gilded copper, rise from a stone platform that rests island-like in the Pool of Immortality, whose glassy mirror reflects every tiny detail of this holy of holies of the Sikh religion. Around the Pool the *bungahs* of great chiefs are built. The temple is approached by a beautiful causeway and gate of marble ; within, beneath a canopy lies the holy Granth, the Sikh "bible," in which are recorded the wisdom and teaching of the Gurus, the first of whom, and the founder of the Sikh religion, was Nanak, who was born in 1469. This great book is wrapped in rich silk coverings, and is constantly guarded by an official of the temple. Pilgrims from afar make offerings of flowers and grain, as well as things that appear strangely tawdry to European eyes, but which must have meant much work and self-denial on the part of those who bestowed them.

Visitors to the temple must remove their shoes as a mark of respect; and when they go upon the roof to view the city they must, above all things, avoid the holy circle that has been drawn above the spot where the Granth—the holy book—lies on its silken cushions in the temple below.

Among the Sikhs.

The Sikhs themselves, bearded and handsome, are men of splendid physique. Their religion forbids the cutting of hair and beard; their hair is curled up under the conical peak in the midst of their voluminous turbans, set off by quoit-like steel ornaments. The women-folk plait their hair into a peak at the back of the head and load their ears with rings and precious stones.

The chief industry of Amritsar is the weaving of fine carpets on the primitive looms, some of which have done duty for centuries. At each is the master weaver with six or eight boy workers who weave in the colours as their master calls out the patterns.

The Punjab.

Lahore, capital of the Punjab, is our next stop. Those of us who have read Kipling's "Kim" naturally go to see the old gun under the tree—the Zamzamah—on which Kim is discovered sitting in the first chapter. The Jama Masjid of Lahore was built by the Moghul emperor Aurangzeb.

From Lahore we go by way of Rawalpindi, where people start for Kashmir, into the North-west Frontier Province and on to its capital, Peshawar, the most important centre on the great caravan road, linking up Samarkand, Bokhara, Teheran and Kabul with Lahore, Amritsar and Delhi. In the bazaar are people from all the markets of Asia, but notably the tall,

W. Bosshard.

THE BARRIER AT THE FRONTIER

Here is a picture of the boundary between India and Afghanistan, with a sign which sternly forbids the traveller to cross the frontier. This is a portion of the famous Khyber Pass, one of the most important of all the frontier gates. The forces of Alexander the Great entered India by this gateway before the birth of Christ.

THE GOLDEN TEMPLE OF AMRITSAR

Will F. Taylor.

Amritsar, some 300 miles from Delhi, is the most holy city of the Sikhs, and its chief glory, the Golden Temple, is illustrated above, with some fakirs and the sacred pool. This impressive building has white marble walls, adorned with patterns in precious stones and surmounted by a roof of gilded copper. Visitors to the temple must remove their shoes as a mark of respect.

lean, hook-nosed tribesmen from the frontier hills—grim fellows in white, with callouses on their cheeks made by the stocks of their rifles in frequent recoil.

The Khyber Pass.

The Khyber Pass begins near Jamrud, about ten miles from Peshawar ; at Ali Masjid it plunges into a deep gorge, through which the road and the railway reach Landi Kotal at the highest point of the pass, but only about 3,500 feet above sea level. This pass is low, and it has sure water supplies. It is on the direct route between Kabul and Peshawar, and is consequently the most important of all the frontier gates from the west. The others— the Malakand, the Tochi, the Gomal Valley and the Bolan—were none of them so convenient for the old commerce that flowed into India from South-western Asia.

The forces of Alexander the Great entered India by this gate in 326 B.C. ; the Moghuls Babar and Humayan came this way to found Empires in India, and so in later days did the Persians.

At Landi Kotal, the summit of the Khyber, is the well-laid-out modern " fort " town, with tribal villages of the natives within sight of it, each with its wall and its fortified look-out tower, where the villagers can take refuge in case of a raid. The barren hills offer little to support the tribesmen ; their lean sheep and goats find coarse herbage in places that look as arid as the barren rock, but beyond these the people of this frontier region have no resources and no supplies save those they can get by trading or plunder. The frontier is less lawless and much safer for caravans than it formerly was, thanks to the British forces stationed at its control points.

If you could take a journey through the Khyber Pass you would be amazed at this great highway, which has been used in all the ages of history. On the Indian side at all events the road is so well maintained that motor traffic is now quite common, jostling perhaps with various trade caravans whose wares are carried on the backs of beasts of burden.

In any country of towering mountains travellers can only proceed through passes, and the Khyber is largely the bed of a stream. In length the actual defile is about 33 miles. Sometimes it is a broad highway with desert waste on either side, but at one point it narrows to 15 feet.

Will F. Taylor.

AN OUTPOST OF EMPIRE

The sentinel here shown, seeming to peer challengingly over boundless space, is stationed at Landi Kotal, the summit of the Kyber Pass. Thanks to British forces, the frontier is now much safer for caravans than was formerly the case.

THE WARRIOR RAJPUTS

INDIA'S "CITY OF SUNRISE"

Col. F. D. Fayrer.

In this captivating picture we see the beautiful Lake Peshola at Udaipur, in Rajputana. Mirrored in the lake, as it were, is the island palace of the reigning prince. During the Indian Mutiny British refugees found shelter in the pavilion of white marble depicted above.

IN the middle of North - western India is the land of the Rajputs, "sons of princes" and a warrior race who held sway over most of the upper Ganges until the Moghul conquerors came down into the plains from the Khyber gate. To-day their country is known as Rajputana—a collection of several States, each ruled by its native prince—a dry region, but with wonderfully fertile spots here and there, and with beautiful cities containing the palaces and the strongholds of their rulers. A large part of it is the Thar or Indian Desert, which for ages protected the Rajputs from attacks by way of the south-west.

Rajput history is full of heroic stories that are equal in their romance and fineness to the best we know of the days of Chivalry in Western Europe. Many of them deal with the exploits of Rajput heroes in the stirring times of the Moslem invasions. The very names of the cities recall great deeds of heroism and sacrifice. There is *Chitore*, whose ruined fortress and towers remind us of the three times it was taken and sacked by the invaders, despite the brave resistance of its defenders, and of the devoted self-sacrifice of the people of the city who made a vast funeral pyre in the caverns beneath the rock and threw themselves upon it—clad in their finest garments and singing as they did so. When the city was taken —but only when its defenders had been slaughtered to a man—the conqueror entered it to find its streets and houses deserted. It was in very truth a city of the dead.

The City of Sunrise.

Udaipur, the "City of Sunrise" and the capital of Mewar, is one of India's most lovely cities, with its palaces and ghats mirrored in its beautiful lake Peshola, amid which, like a fairy palace floating upon the water, is an island bearing the Jag Mandir ("World Minster") of the reigning Prince. This lovely water palace was built in the first quarter of the seventeenth century by the Maharana Karasinghji. During the Indian Mutiny the Maharana supported the British and lent his water palace as a home for Mutiny refugees who sought shelter in Udaipur.

The water palace of the Maharana is hardly less wonderful than his great high palace with its three-arched gateway and its domes and spires, that stands on a ridge above the lake.

In the city, tall men of fine physique and martial bearing, with black beards, parted in the middle and drawn aside to curled ends, and the graceful women closely veiled against the curious eyes of strangers, decked with ornaments of silver or gold, and clad in robes of every hue, tell plainly that here are people of a splendid race—the descendants of warriors who 700 years ago were masters of Upper India.

Jaipur.

Jaipur is another fine city—the capital of the Maharajah of Jaipur—with wide streets and a busy market. You can see here the ancient observatory of the Indian astronomers; the instruments are of stone. One of them is a giant sundial—Samrat Yantra—whose gnomon is nearly 80 feet high.

The old capital of Jaipur State was Amber, whose ruins lie some few miles from the present capital.

If we wish to visit the drier part of Rajputana we cannot do better than go to *Bikanir*, which stands in its oasis in the Thar Desert. Here camels are as common as are elephants in the cities farther east, and the water carrier is one of the most welcome of all the traders in the city.

Mount Abu.

At the end of Rajputana, and far away to the south, is Mount Abu—a granite island set in an ocean of sand, with forests and beautiful lakes upon it, and a town that to-day is the headquarters of the Government in this part of India, where the British Agent for Rajputana lives. Over 4,000 feet above sea level, Mount Abu is a pleasant place in the hot weather, and is a favourite spot for many Europeans.

People come to Mount Abu especially to see the famous temples built by the Jains at

Col. F. D. Fayrer.

A RAJPUT SERGEANT

This tanned and bearded non-commissioned officer was photographed at Udaipur. The word "Rajput" means "a prince's son," and members of this tribe are great warriors. Such men as the one illustrated above fought in France in the Great War.

about the same time as William of Normandy was setting about his conquest of England. These are at Dilwara among the green hills, their multitudes of marble columns, their lovely arches linking the columns together, and their marvellously carved shrines, roofs and pillars make the Dilwara temples a sight to astonish the beholder. Strange legends arrest his ear—he hears how Siva in the days of the gods thrust his foot through the earth from his shrine at Benares to steady Mount Abu when it quaked, and how the mark of Siva's toes is still to be seen in a hole, whose depth has never been plumbed. "It goes down," say those who tell the tale, "even unto Patal," which every one knows is the very lowest part of the earth.

Why a Throne was Lost.

There was a prince who doubted this tale and swore that he would fill the hole with water. He gave orders to his masons to build a great aqueduct, through which water was allowed to flow for six months, but without avail. The anger of Siva at his unbelief cost the prince his throne, for his people revolted and cast him forth.

The Jains who built these marvellous temples were members of a religious sect that arose 500 years before the birth of Christ, and was founded by men who did not agree with all the beliefs and ceremonies of the Hindu religion. In many ways the teaching of the Jain *tirthankars* (holy teachers) was like that of Gautama Buddha.

The Lower Indus.

West of Rajputana is the lower Indus valley, that comes to the Arabian Sea in the Indus delta and the Province of Sind. *Karachi*, the port of the Indus Basin, and the first air-port in the Indian Empire, is here; it exports a great deal of Punjab wheat and cotton, and is important, as the terminus of the great railway that runs north into

Will F. Taylor.

A JAIN TOWER AT CHITOR

Chitor is a town in Rajputana, inhabited mostly by Hindus, and here we see the famous Tower of Victory, built by the Jains at about the same time as Queen Elizabeth ruled in England.

Col. F. D. Fayrer.

.IN THE HEART OF THE JUNGLE

Ragnagar, in Rajputana, is so remote that few travellers are able to pay it a visit. Yet in the very heart of the dense jungle are wonderful sacred places of which the above is an example. This temple, with its marvellous carvings and elaborate decorative work, is almost fairy-like in its conception and wealth of artistic detail.

the " Land of the Five Rivers," with branch lines to the passes through the western mountain barriers. *Hyderabad* is the chief native city.

By the Sukkur Dam.

Sind is a dry country, where water is the most precious thing on earth. But, thanks to great irrigation works, large crops of cotton and other produce are grown. The most famous of all these irrigation works is the Sukkur Dam, which gives life to millions of acres that would be barren desert without it. The Sukkur Dam is the greatest work of its kind in the world.

THE VICTORIA MEMORIAL, CALCUTTA

Indian State Railways.

Calcutta stands some eighty miles from the mouth of the Hugli River. It was long the capital and is still the leading seaport of India. Its population exceeds a million, among which are represented nearly four hundred separate races and castes of men. Above is illustrated the Victoria Memorial Hall, but one of a great many fine buildings in the city.

THOSE who enter India by the Calcutta sea-gate are following the old way of the East Indiamen, who in the days of " John Company " thronged the Hugli and made Calcutta the chief seaport and the capital of India. For as long as British interests in India had to be backed by a show of armed force, the capital was bound to be a sea-gate, since Britain's lines of communications with India in those days were sea-ways.

The Treacherous Hugli.

The Hugli is only one of the many mouths of the Ganges. Among sailor-men it has an evil reputation; its swift and dangerous currents and its shifting mud-banks make it extremely difficult to navigate, and the job of a Hugli pilot is one not to be envied. He must be more than a knowledgeable man ; he has to be ever on the alert, ever learning the new positions of the shifting banks, and ever resourceful.

If the ship but touches the tail end of one of the banks, the current may quickly swing her broadside on, heeling her on to the bank and at the same time scooping out a steep hollow on the downstream side of her, with the inevitable result that she tumbles sideways. The tons of silt swept down upon her by the currents soon bury her in the graveyard that holds the bones of the ships of all the centuries since the navigation of the Hugli began.

Sundarbans of the Ganges.

The lowlands of the Ganges delta are known as the Sundarbans. They are covered with low and malaria-smitten jungle, and are the haunts of the crocodile, whose log-like stillness awakens to sudden and vigorous life when a shot sends him scuttling into the water. The tiger, too, inhabits the drier parts of these jungle lands, although he is very seldom seen by those who pass up and down the water-way in the ships.

Man disputes with the tiger and the crocodile the right of living in the delta lowlands, for he has planted jute in the rich wet soil, and toils amid fever-haunted waterways to reap his jute harvest and to prepare it for sale to the jute factories.

All About Jute.

Jute grows to a height of 11 feet or 12 feet. If you penetrate up one of the narrow creeks to the jute planta-tions you may see thin, brown men clad only in waist-cloths, cutting down the tall jute stems, trimming them and making them into bundles to be carted away by buffalo waggons or taken off in square-ended punts to the pools,

where the stems will be steeped for many days in order that their juicy, fleshy parts may rot. Later you may see men standing up to the waist in murky brown water beating the stems with flat-ended mallets to get rid of the waste material, while on the higher ground other workers are hanging up the long silky, pliant fibres to dry in the hot sunshine.

The sequel to all this you may see at the great jute mills of Howrah, across the Hugli from Calcutta, where the jute is made into bgas and sacks, rope and mats. Jute, indeed, is a flourishing crop in North-eastern India, where plenty of heat and moisture favour its tall growth. Bengal, Bihar and Orissa, and Assam all grow it, but 85 per cent. of it is produced in the

Bourne & Shepherd.

BALING JUTE IN THE INTENSE HEAT

At Howrah, which faces Calcutta across the river, are the great mills where jute is made into bags and sacks, rope and mats. Here you see this useful commodity being baled under tremendous pressure and in terrific heat for transport overseas. Jute is a plant used after the manner of flax, but its fibres are tougher than those of flax. Near Calcutta jute grows to a height of 11 feet or more, the moist heat favouring its rapid development.

ABOVE THE BLACK HOLE OF CALCUTTA   *Topical Press.*

The marble pavement shown in this photograph, surrounded by ornamental railings, marks the site of the prison in old Fort William known as the Black Hole. Here 146 British inhabitants were confined, only twenty-three of them being taken out alive. The monumental pavement was placed here by Lord Curzon, Viceroy and Governor-General of India, in 1902. A tablet on the building records details.

Bengal delta lowlands. Jute is the cheapest fibre in the world ; it is cultivated on a large scale only in India, where abundant rain and moist heat favour its quick growth. All over the world where grain, seeds, and other dry foodstuffs and raw materials are produced there is a demand for the " gunny bags " made from jute, which to-day forms more than a quarter of the total export of India.

Calcutta.

Eighty miles up the Hugli is Calcutta, long the capital and still the leading seaport of India. Mills and factories announce to the new arrival by sea that industry is carried on here on a European scale, and ships of all the seafaring nations in the world testify to its greatness as a port. You can still see old Fort William on the eastern bank of the river, where the British built it in 1702, and on three sides of it—north, east and south— stretches the wide plain of the Maidan, east of which is the European part of the city with fine hotels, public buildings and houses that tell of the British people who live and work there. The native city lies away to the north, with its crowded bazaars, its narrow streets and its jostling crowds buying and selling, gossiping and gaping at shows and sights, as crowds do all the world over.

Those interested in the history of British India will make a point of visiting the " Black Hole " monument at the corner of Dalhousie Square, set up by Lord Curzon in 1902 to mark the spot where 146 unfortunate prisoners were shut up by Suraj-ud-Dowlah in a tiny cell, 22 feet by 14 feet, when Fort William fell in 1756, in the days of Clive and the East India Company.

Nothing in Calcutta is more wonderful than the crowd which flows endlessly across the great Howrah Bridge from dawn to dusk—a moving throng which seems to have in it representatives of every nation under the sun. The middle part of the bridge can be swung aside to allow ships to pass up and down the Hugli. Across the bridge is Howrah with its great jute mills and steel works.

Up to Darjeeling.

Calcutta people who can afford it go up to the beautiful hill-station of Darjeeling during the hot weather, a lovely spot with pretty villas and bungalows among forests of pines and firs seven thousand feet above the bed of the Testa River, and with the grandest mountain scenery in all the world as a background. Lofty peaks crowned with eternal snows occupy two-thirds of Darjeeling's horizon. Everest, the giant that overtops all, cannot be seen from Darjeeling itself, but all who long for a glimpse of this peak that so far has defied every effort to scale it, can see it on a fine day from Tiger's Hill, which can be reached on pony back, by rickshaw, or by *palki*—a chair carried by four sturdy bearers. Kanchenjanga, however, can be seen from Darjeeling, and so can other mighty peaks all over 22,000 feet in height.

The journey from Calcutta to Darjeeling is made by one of the most wonderful railways in the world, and one of the most costly ever constructed.

The first stage is across the lowlands of the Ganges plain dotted with many villages amid rice fields and jute fields, waving palms and big-leafed plantains, and clumps of feathery bamboos. The Ganges is crossed by the great Hardinge Bridge, which the natives know as the Sara Bridge ; it is nearly a mile and a quarter in length, and cost over two and a half million pounds.

Across the Terai.

The next stage takes us into the tea country of the Dooars, and on to Sukna, where the real difficulties which the railway builders had to face begin to show themselves. The train suddenly enters dense forest of tall sal and giant bamboo, and other quick-growing vegetation which seems woven into an impenetrable mass by great creepers that throw curtains of blossom sunwards. This is the jungle of the Terai, the home of the tiger and the Indian rhinoceros, the sambhur and the wild buffalo, where even experienced *shikaris* go with caution.

Up and up the line twists and turns, boring into tunnels, skirting giddy precipices, crossing deep gorges by slender bridges, and now and again stopping to reverse because of the impossibility of negotiating the steep gradient by loops or hairpin bends. Soon the increased altitude begins to be evident in the change of vegetation —oaks and mulberries, peach trees and almonds are common at 4,000 feet ; another thousand feet takes the traveller to the region of tree ferns ; then come the pine forests and glimpses of the far-away Himalayan snow peaks ; and at last Darjeeling, which means " the place of the thunderbolt."

Heroes of Everest.

No man with British blood in his veins can arrive at Darjeeling without a proud memory of those heroes of his race who gave their lives in the attempt to scale the highest mountain on earth —of Mallory and Irvine, who were last

A TEMPLE OF THE JAINS

A. Schalek.

The Jains form a very ancient religious sect in India, and this is a picture of the famous Badri Das Temple which they built in Calcutta. The Jains number to-day about a million followers. They will never kill an animal, however insignificant, because they believe that after death human beings enter the kingdom of four-footed creatures.

seen by anxious watchers from Camp VI. within 800 feet of Everest's snowy summit.

> " Climbing in air too thin for mortal breath
> These men stood poised on the world's parapet ;
> Watched by the stars, on the last height they met,
> Content in Victory, the Kiss of Death."—
>
> DOUGLAS FRESHFIELD.

Will F. Taylor.

A SCENE IN KASHMIR

Kashmir is an important native Indian state to the north of the Punjab. At one point along its frontier, India, China and Afghanistan have their boundaries. The country is one of winding rivers, clear blue lakes and Lombardy poplar trees and has a background of lofty snow peaks.

Will F. Taylor.

TRAVELLING BY DONGA

Though the motor car is becoming more in evidence, much of the travelling in Kashmir is still done in boats, such as those pictured above. These vessels, flat-bottomed and of shallow draft, are called dongas. The boatman and his family dwell at one end of the donga.

For the three great Mount Everest expeditions—1921, 1922 and 1924—started from Darjeeling, making their way by the Chumbi valley on to the plateau of Tibet, and launching their attacks upon the giant peak from their base camp on the Rongbuk glacier. All failed ;   the old gods

CROWNED WITH ETERNAL SNOWS

H. J. Shepstone.

Lofty peaks, crowned with eternal snows, occupy two-thirds of the horizon of Darjeeling, and visitors are taken to points of vantage to view the scenery in *palkis* or chairs, each of which is carried by four sturdy bearers. Darjeeling is a most important tea-growing district.

painted on the walls of the Rongbuk Monastery—guardians of sacred Everest—seem to have defended their charge all too well, and Everest remains unconquered, unless, as most of us believe, those two devoted climbers who vanished into the swirling mists a few hundred feet below the crest actually set foot on its summit at the price of their lives.

It is at Darjeeling that the traveller meets for the first time the hill people who are in every way different from the inhabitants of the plains. Darjeeling stands at the gate of Sikkim, and between Nepal, the mountain land of the sturdy Gurkhas, and Bhutan, the home of the Bhutia mountaineers; and it is near enough to the Tibetan frontier to have many people of Tibetan stock in its neighbourhood. Buddhist temples, like those of Tibet, can be visited from Darjeeling; there are several monasteries where the strange Tibetan "Devil Dances" are performed by the lamas, dressed in their frightful masks and gorgeous costumes, and gyrating to the horrific music of gongs and cymbals, and the blare of mighty trumpets ten or twelve feet long. Great prayer wheels turn, reiterating the mystic Buddhist text, "Om Mane Padme Hum"; fluttering prayer-flags from little forests of poles carry on them other prayers and symbols.

Lt.-Col. P. T. Etherton.

A PILLAR-BOX IN THE WILDS

This strange receptacle, suspended beside the track, is actually a pillar-box in which letters may be posted. It is to be seen among the Himalayas, not far from the frontier of Tibet. Only once in a month is this pillar-box of the wilds cleared.

ELEPHANTS IN PROCESSION

Elephants are very largely used in India for ceremonial purposes and play an important part in official parades and processions. Most of the Indian princes keep elephants for state ceremonies. Previous to such an event, the animals are thoroughly washed and scrubbed and have their hoofs trimmed. The next day their hides are painted with traditional designs and devices. On the day itself wonderful trappings and gorgeous howdahs are placed upon the elephants, precious silks and brocades and even gold and silver ornaments.

IN THE LAND OF THE LAMAS

Will. F. Taylor.

Tibet is situated between India and China, and is known as the " Forbidden Land " because of the decree that foreigners should be kept outside the boundary. This rule is far less strictly observed than was formerly the case. Tibetans are spoken of as being " cheery folk," and the beggars at the roadside, pictured above, dance and sing most light-heartedly.

Will F. Taylor.

Tibet is also referred to as the " Land of the Lamas," the lamas being priests who rule the people not only in religious matters, but in their every-day lives as well. The chief industry of Tibetans is farming, and they are great breeders of sheep, whose wool is here shown being carried to India by patient donkeys. The lake seen in the photograph is Hram Tso.

MOTHER GANGES

THE HOLY CITY OF BENARES

H. J. Shepstone.

The old-time name of Benares is Varanasi, the " bright-robed daughter of Ganga," and the city
is visited by hundreds of thousands of pilgrims every year from all parts of India. For four
miles the high northern bank of the Ganges is crowded with palaces and temples. The flights
of stone steps are known as " ghats," from which the sacred river is worshipped every day by
her followers. Crowds of bathers throng these steps.

MOTHER GANGES is the greatest
river of India, and the most
sacred. Her waters from their
sources to the sea are holy to the
Hindus, and her banks are lined with
wonderful temples and stately cities
which have arisen through the ages to
bear witness to the might of Hinduism
and the sacredness of the Ganges
flood.

For 1,500 miles Ganga Mai traverses
the most densely-peopled plain in the
world, spreading abroad her great fan
of tributaries and their associated
networks of irrigation canals. She
comes down from the cold Himalayan
snows to holy Hardwar and the plains,
and flows on to the jungles and marshes
of the Sundarbans to empty her waters
into the sea. On her bosom she bears
craft strange to European eyes—rice-
boats, boats laden with pilgrims journey-
ing to one of her many shrines, and

hosts of smaller craft with wide curved
awnings of matting amidships to give
shelter from the hot sun.

Benares, a Holy City.

The most holy of her cities is *Benares*,
whose proper name is Varanasi—
" bright-robed daughter of Ganga,"
and which is visited by hundreds of
thousands of pilgrims every year from
all parts of India.

Benares can be reached from Calcutta
by following the main Calcutta-Bombay
railway route as far as Moghal Serai
junction, whence a short run of ten
miles takes us across the Dufferin
Bridge over the Ganges to the Holy
City, whose splendid temples and
palaces are mirrored in the face of
" Ganga Mai " herself—Ganga Mai who
appeared at the god Siva's wedding,
they say, clad in many-coloured robes,
" when the rivers and the Seven Seas,

as well as the Sacred Places of Pilgrimage assembled together, with the Sun and the Moon and many other notabilities."

For four miles the high northern bank of the Ganges at Benares is crowded with palaces and temples, most of them built of reddish-yellow sandstone, looking across the river to a low and sparsely-inhabited shore. Leading from the temples on this high bank to the river are the great flights of stone steps known as the "ghats," from which the Ganges is worshipped every day by her followers, who bring offerings of rice, milk and flowers, and bathe in the holy waters.

The Ghats.

At the Dasasanedh Ghat—"the ghat of the Ten Horse sacrifice"—all the chief roads of Benares meet. It is one of the five sacred places to be visited by the Hindus who come to the city to take part in the great religious festivals. Crowds of bathers throng the steps ; processions of men, women and children swell the number as the day wears on, bearing the brass or copper vessels used in pouring the sacred water over their bodies and garlands of flowers and sacred leaves to cast into the stream. Men pilgrims throw off their outer garments before entering the river, but the women, clad in their brightly-coloured *saris*, wade in slowly until they can dip their heads below

the surface. Thrice immersing themselves in the sacred flood, the pilgrims emerge, dry themselves, and go to the *yogis* or wise elders seated beneath the shade of great mushroom-like umbrellas of woven cane to receive the mark upon their foreheads that shows to all who know what it means that they have washed away all their offences in the purifying waters of Ganga Mai.

Festivals.

In the month Kartik (October-November) there is a great festival at this ghat, in honour of Kali the black goddess of darkness, whose strange

Will F. Taylor.

ON THE RIVER GANGES, BENARES

This picture shows us one of the burning ghats beside the sacred Ganges. On such a ghat pious Hindus cause their dead to be cremated, and one may often see thin smoke arising from the funeral pyres. The word ghat means "a path of descent," and these flights of steps are found in every city upon the banks of the Ganges.

SOME TYPES OF NATIVE CRAFTSMEN—

Col. F. D. Fayrer.

Wonderfully clever craftsmen are the Indian natives, many of them following closely a routine that has remained unchanged for countless years. In the picturesque scene above a man is printing upon cloth. He is using dyes purely of vegetable origin and impressing the simple pattern by means of primitive printing blocks.

Col. F. D. Fayrer.

This photograph comes from Rajputana and shows us a native potter at his work. He is using a form of potter's wheel, a device so old that no one knows for certain when it was first employed. By his side is a piece of elaborate ornamental design, such as the Indian potter delights to fashion.

AS SEEN 'NEATH INDIAN SKIES

The water carrier. This man takes holy water from the sacred River Ganges and tramps with it across the burning plains of Central India.

The plume and tassel maker. In almost every Hindu festival, plumes and tassels plentifully adorned with tinsel play a part, and here is a craftsman making them.

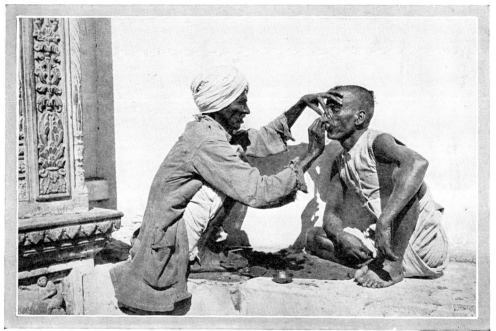

In the bazaar in the native quarter of any Indian city you would find the narrow, winding streets so crowded that only foot passengers could pass. Almost certainly you would see the barber plying his calling just outside one of the open-fronted shops. He is illustrated above.

image with protruding tongue is taken in procession from its shrine and accompanied by throngs of pilgrims on foot, on elephants and camels, or in carriages to the river, where at sunset it is immersed. Hundreds of smaller images of Kali are thrown in by the pilgrims. Then as night falls begins the feast of Lakshmi, the goddess of Fortune, when little lighted lamps are set afloat upon the waters to be watched until they fade into the darkness. Should a lamp go out, its owner need expect no good fortune in the coming year.

Below the temples, shrines and palaces farther along the river, their clusters of domes and spires stained deep red and tipped with gold, are other ghats; some crowded with wor-shippers, among whom sacred bulls garlanded with marigolds wander in and out as they please, while monkeys clamber on the cornices and brightly-plumaged birds dart here and there among the temple domes. Wise old pandits, garlanded with flowers, sit like cross-legged statues, now and then reciting in dignified tones the sacred texts.

At the burning ghats thin smoke arises from the funeral pyres on which pious Hindus are burning their dead. The Scindhia Ghat is the haunt of *sadhus*, strange wandering mystics who beg their way from shrine to shrine, smeared with ashes and marked with the coloured sect-mark upon their foreheads. Some torture themselves in strange ways to show

H. J. Shepstone.

THE RESIDENCY AND MEMORIAL AT LUCKNOW

Lucknow is in population the fifth city of India. It was the scene of a historic siege in the Indian Mutiny (1857). The Residency was strengthened so that it could afford shelter for Europeans and some faithful Sepoys and was beset by the mutineers for more than eighty days before it was relieved. Our picture shows the ruined British Residency, over which the Flag always flies, together with the runic cross of memory. The heroic defence of Lucknow is an undying memory in our British history and literature.

their devotion ; some gather funds to pay for the repair of a temple ; some are learned men who have renounced the world and given themselves up to a life of self-denial.

Within Benares.

Within the city the narrow winding streets are so crowded that only foot passengers can pass. Beneath the tall houses on both sides of the way are the open shops — mere recesses in the walls—some crammed with figures of gods and goddesses ; some hung with prayer bags, embroidered with bright colours ; and some full of sweetmeats and s t i c k y cakes. Stalls heavy with marigolds and other flowers stand at every available spot, so that the pilgrims may buy garlands for their *puja* (worship) on the ghats, or for hanging on the necks of sacred bulls and *yogis*, or to adorn the images and symbols of the gods.

Blue-throated Siva, father of the gods, has his shrine covered with sculptured figures. There you can see Nandi, the sacred bull on which he rides, and Kali the terrible, wearing her necklace of skulls and her girdle of cobras, with her four hands— one bearing the head of a demon, and another her keen sword.

The Golden Temple has two of its domes plated with real gold. No European may cross its holy threshold. But every man, be he Hindu or Christian, may visit the " Well of Knowledge," where a Brahmin sits with his metal ladle to pour into the palm of everyone's right hand a few

H. J. Shepstone.

THE GUARD GATE, LUCKNOW

Thoughts of Lucknow bring to mind the gallant Sir Colin Campbell, who rescued the besieged garrison. The remains of the Residency are carefully preserved precisely as they were at the termination of the siege, surrounded by beautiful gardens of remembrance. Above we see the Guard Gate at Lucknow.

drops of the precious water in return for a small offering of copper coins as his reward.

In the Gothic Style.

There is another part of Benares which is very different from the native city and its crooked streets thronged with folk clad in many-coloured robes. That is the European quarter, where there are many fine modern buildings, among them Queen's College, which is said to be the finest example of Gothic architecture in all India.

Cawnpore and Lucknow.

At *Cawnpore*, easily reached by train from Benares, we are in the "Manchester of India," where there are large modern cotton and woollen mills, leather industries and clothing factories. Evil days in Indian history are brought to our memory here by the beautiful monument that stands over the well into which the bodies of those slain during the Mutiny were cast by the followers of the rebel Nana Dundhu Panth ("Nana Sahib") in 1857.

Lucknow, too, has its reminders of those perilous times. Its heroic defence has passed into both our history and our literature in undying memory. It has many temples and palaces, but none to compare either in age or beauty with those of Benares. We can see here, as at Cawnpore, evidences of changing India in the application of modern methods of manufacture. But the goldsmiths, silversmiths and jewellers of the bazaar still maintain their honoured reputation of the cleverest in the Indian Empire.

One of the stories of Lucknow concerns Jessie Brown, wife of an English corporal. She cheered up her despondent companions by recounting details of a dream in which she had heard bagpipes playing, which she believed to be those of a relief party.

SUTTEE CHOWRA GHAT   *Indian State Railways.*

Cawnpore is often spoken of as the "Manchester of India." It has large cotton and woollen mills, leather industries and clothing factories and is also an important railway junction. The ghat illustrated above was the scene of the massacre of the Europeans who surrendered to Nana Sahib at the time of the Indian Mutiny. It stands on a bank of the River Ganges.

THE LAND OF PAGODAS

A SAMPAN ROWER OF BURMA

Topical Press.

The dusky toiler seen above is characteristic of the great River Irrawaddy, which runs from north to south almost throughout the whole length of Burma, forming a water highway a thousand miles in length. Sampans are the native boats, often elaborately carved, and this rower handles his oars in a manner that seems very strange to western eyes.

DIRECTLY we land in Burma we know that we have come to a country whose people are followers of Buddha, the great teacher. Wherever we go, be it in city or village, we always find three things that are constant reminders of Buddhism— the *pagodas* or temples, the *pongyis* or monks, and the *monasteries* where the monks live, and where the Burmese boys go to school. Buddhist teaching, Buddhist law and Buddhist religion seem to govern everything in the lives of the people.

Perhaps the most wonderful natural feature in Burma is the Irrawaddy, the great river which runs from north to south almost throughout the whole length of the country—a water highway for 1,000 miles that has served the Burmese since the beginning of their history and is still, with its regular service of river steamers, a very important and cheap means of getting about in Burma. There is the railway too, but that is dearer ; besides, it cannot call at all the villages on the way north as the river steamers do.

Great parallel ranges of high mountains, thickly covered with forests, shut in the deep valleys of the Irrawaddy, the Salwen, its smaller sister-river, and their tributaries. The forests, which are still the haunts of the tiger, the leopard and the wild elephant, come down to the rivers in thick jungles or deep elephant grass, or marshes, except where Burmese farmers have made their paddy fields around their little villages of brown houses on stilts. Towards the south and in the wider valleys the country is more open and the people more in touch with European people and European ideas, which enter Burma, as we do, by way of the great port of Rangoon.

Rangoon.

Rangoon is Burmese enough, but it has its European quarter, its up-to-date rice-mills and saw-mills and factories, and a hundred and one other things which remind us that Rangoon is a " city of the world," like other great sea-gates of the Far East. In a single street, for instance, we could see a Christian church, a Jewish synagogue, a Hindu temple, and a Chinese joss-house, as well as the inevitable Bud-dhist pagoda. Along the water-front we meet people of all the trading nations under the sun, from farthest East to farthest West ; and in Rangoon itself we are likely to come across representatives of all Burma's peoples, except, perhaps, the wildest and most remote of the tribes, who never leave the depths of the great forests and jungles of the Far North.

For although Burma is only about four times the size of England and Wales, with no more than 14 millions of people, there are 128 different languages spoken in the country—and this is not counting those of the foreigners living in the land. (Remember that *we* are foreigners, too, when we go to Burma !)

Burma's Peoples.

The *Burmese*, whose cheery, happy-go-lucky ways and whose habit of

Topical Press.

IN A BURMESE MARKET AT RANGOON

Though Burma is only about four times the size of England and Wales, 128 different languages are spoken in the country and we might meet representatives of all Burma's peoples in the market place. Buddhist law and religion stand for a great deal in the lives of the Burmese, although superstition and belief in familiar spirits called *nats* are prevalent in many parts.

speaking with tremend-
ous politeness about
quite ordinary things
has caused travellers to
nickname them " The
Irish of the East," make
up at least three-
quarters of the popula-
tion. They are dwellers
in the valleys and plains
along the rivers,
villagers and growers of
rice and fruits, living
easily in that fertile land
where the hot sun and
the heavy summer rains
between May and Octo-
ber ensure good crops
without much labour.

The hill people have
a much harder life, for
they must clear forest
or jungle away if they
want to grow crops, and
fight it all the time to
prevent it overgrowing
their little fields again.
Elephants may come
when there are no bam-
boo shoots for them in
the jungle, and trample
down more than they
eat. And there is al-
ways the danger of the
tiger, the leopard and other wild
beasts.

The *Shans* are the best known of the
hill-folk. There was a time when there
were Shan kings in Burma ; but nowadays the Shans are the labourers of the
hill country, and the raftsmen who
bring down to Rangoon the mighty
rafts of teak from the forests up-
country during the time of the rains.
Many are tattooed from waist to knee.
They wear few clothes when working,
but all have wide hats of cane or straw
to protect their heads from the hot sun.

Among the mountains of the middle
and north live the *Chins* and the
Kachins. The Kachins, or Jingpaws,
as they call themselves, live in villages

Will F. Taylor.
LOADING THE RICE BOATS
Rangoon is one of the great sea-gates of the Far East, and we
are here shown coolies or native workmen loading the rice
boats which have just been moored along the water-front. Rice
provides more foodstuff for the support of human beings the
world over than any other crop grown.

on the hillsides, and are not Buddhists,
but worship the spirits of Nature.

The *Karens* are quite different from
all other Burmese people. They are
as solemn and dour, timid and silent as
the Burmese are jolly, outspoken and
high-spirited. In past times Karens
were constantly raided and persecuted
by the Burmese, who looked on them
as inferiors because of their belief in
evil spirits which must be kept happy
and well fed by strange offerings in
lonely places. The Karen lives in a
poor land, where farming is hard, and
where he must use his *dah* (heavy
knife) to clear away the cane and
bamboo growths, and to make the
simple farming tools he uses.

o 2

Along the North-eastern Frontier live the wild *Was* in a region about which little is known. The Wa resents the intrusion of strangers, and waylays them when he finds opportunity. In some parts the Wa is a head-hunter, and sets up skulls on poles at the entrance to his village, so that the ghosts of the former owners of the skulls may keep others out !

The Andamans.

Far away in the sea south-east of Burma are the Andaman Islands, where live the Andamanese, who are negritos and so short that they are really pygmies. They wear no clothes, use primitive weapons, and build flimsy shelters instead of houses. They are divided into several tribes, and rarely mix with white men. There is a European settlement, however, at Port Blair, near which is a convict station to which evildoers from India are often sent.

Burma, we see, has peoples in every stage of civilisation, from primitive savage head-hunters and folks who are still in the Stone Age, to highly-educated Burmese, some of whom have attended British universities and are doing much to introduce European systems of education among their countrymen.

As we steam up the Rangoon River, past the tall-pointed pagoda on a hill to starboard, we pass ships of all the seafaring nations of the world, it seems. When we come to the Rangoon water-front we can see the gilded spire of the splendid Shwe Dagon pagoda, the wonder of Burma, and a sacred place to all Buddhists, for within its shrine are eight hairs from the head of Gautama Buddha himself.

Teak Yards at Rangoon.

Rangoon was only a village sixty or seventy years ago : now it is a great modern city-port, with its wharves fronting the Strand for several miles along the river. Teak yards, rice-mills and oil refineries tell us plainly whence the wealth to which Rangoon owes its growth and prosperity comes ; for teak, rice and petroleum, with tin and rubies, are the chief products of this part of the Indian Empire. Down-stream come the great teak rafts, the laden rice-boats, and the little steamers with all kinds of produce to the port.

Teak yards are among the sights of Rangoon, for there we can see the wise elephants hauling the great logs across the black squelchy mud to pile them up in neat heaps in the yard. The male elephant is strong and picks up a great log between trunk and tusks and carries it to its place ; the female drags or pushes, but rarely lifts. The elephants feed on the tall grasses cut from the riverside upstream. We are a little sorry in some ways to see in up-to-date teak yards modern hauling and lifting machinery that in time will do away with the help of elephants altogether.

The Shwe Dagon.

The teak is cut in the hot, wet forests, and got out in the rainy season. European supervisors have a most unpleasant time of it up there in the wet weather, what with the water and the rain, the mud and the leeches, the fevers and the hordes of stinging and biting insects. Only the elephant with his strength and intelligence can move the huge logs out of the forest to the nearest water course. Teak trees grow among large numbers of other and less valuable trees, and never in a forest by themselves. Before they are cut they are ring-barked, so that they dry where they stand. Teak is heavy, hard, close-grained wood that stands all weather, resists the ravages of insect pests, and defies the boring of marine worms. Hence its wide use in tropical lands.

Let us look at the Shwe Dagon, which sits on its hill like a great bell, on the other side of the Royal Lakes. Two thousand years ago there was only a

AN ELEPHANT-SHAPED FUNERAL CAR

Will F. Taylor.

This curious car, surmounted by the effigy of an elephant, is the vehicle used at the funeral rites
of a Buddhist archbishop. The casket containing the remains is carried on this car and our
photograph was taken near the old city of Mandalay, far up the Irrawaddy. Here one may see
no fewer than 450 white pagodas grouped in a square around a large gilded one in the centre.
Here also is the palace of Thebaw, the last of Burma's kings (1876–1885).

simple village shrine on this hill ; it was not until the sixteenth century that the great and glorious pagoda was erected. Its dome is heavily gilded with the gold leaf brought by pious Buddhists as an " act of merit." It is topped, like most other temples, with a metal umbrella-like *hti*. Around the base of the pagoda are many other shrines, outside which is a kind of paved courtyard shut in by halls and canopies, screens and arches, altars and shrines, and adorned with many images of Buddha.

The Burmese seem much shorter than the people of India—some, especially the women, almost doll-like in their coloured silks. Both men and women wear the *lungyi*—a sort of skirt skilfully folded about the waist without the use of buttons or pins ; and the *eingyi*, a short jacket, generally white. Men wear bright silk scarves in turban fashion ; women wear them thrown over the shoulders. Both men and women wear their black hair long —men gathering it into a top-knot, women coiling it on the crown of the head and ornamenting it with a flower placed jauntily over one ear.

A Burmese Village.

A Burmese village is a collection of little brown houses perched on stilts to avoid the damp, and crawling things. The space below is used for numbers of purposes : as a store, as a fowl-house, or perhaps as a rubbish heap. Even to-day many villages are still protected by a stout fence or

A SACRED BUILDING IN BURMA

Topical Press.

This picture gives you an excellent idea of what a Burmese temple is like. It is the Shweh-mawdaw, a sacred building of Pegu, and is said to contain two hairs of the Buddha. Most Burmese temples, like this one, are topped with a metal, umbrella-like *hti*. From the *hti* hang the temple bells which when swayed by the breeze, give forth a musical, tinkling sound.

BURMA'S "LORD OF HEAVEN"

Will F. Taylor.

In all the bell-shaped pagodas of Burma one may see images of Buddha, before which the natives pray. Here is one such image, of giant proportions, the natives reverently placing offerings of hair, candles and flags in front of it. Compare the size of the human beings below with that of the stone figure. Buddhism is the religion of Burma and Ceylon, and there are forms of it in China and Japan, as well as in Tibet. Each form possesses its own bible.

palisade, and are entered by a gateway which is carefully shut by the watch-man every night. Around are the paddy fields in which ugly water-buffaloes work all day in the ploughing time—and dangerous animals they are to white folk, although they answer to the lightest word of the village boys.

Mandalay and Bhamo.

A village home has little furniture : a mat and a bamboo pillow for each person, a few food vessels of earthen-ware or lacquer work, one or two tables 6 inches high, round which the people squat for their meals and their tea, some water-pots—and, of course, the family betel-box, for everyone chews betel just as he smokes cheroots. In the top partitions of the betel-box is the lime paste and the spices ; in the second are tobacco leaves and areca (or betel) nuts, and in the bottom are the fresh green betel leaves. Betel-chewing stains the mouth crimson.

Far up the Irrawaddy is the old city of Mandalay, where we go to see the 450 white pagodas grouped in a square around the large gilded one in the centre ; the palaces of the old kings and queens of Upper Burma ; the Arakan Temple with its giant brass figure of the Buddha ; and the moated Dufferin Fort within its great square red walls, pierced on each side of the square by three gates—named after Lord Dufferin, who was the Viceroy of India when in the middle of the nineteenth century armed forces had to set Upper Burma in order and put down the tyrant King Theebaw.

Farther still up-stream is *Bhamo*, at the head of the Irrawaddy navigation, only twenty miles from China, in whose streets we can see Kachins from the hills, as well as Chinese from across the border.

A WAYSIDE RAILWAY PLATFORM IN BURMA   *Topical Press.*

Though Burma has but indifferent roads and most of her traffic is water-borne, she is fairly well equipped with railways. Rangoon and Mandalay are connected by a fine line, which extends altogether for upwards of 700 miles and leads to the far north of the country. Here is a typical scene at one of the country stations on the route. In the rainy season the railway lines are frequently damaged by heavy floods.

The Story
of the
World and
its Peoples

The Empire
on which
the Sun
Never Sets

Canadian National Railways.

THE AMERICAN BISON

The Bison belongs to the same great family as the ox, but has enormously high shoulders, a heavy mane and also a beard.   When the continent of America was in the early stages of its settlement, bisons roamed over the prairies in huge numbers, some of the herds being estimated to contain from 1 million to 4 millions of the animals.   Now these creatures are protected and the ones we see above are at Wainwright Park, Alberta, Canada. Bisons are often called buffaloes, but this is a mistake.   The only true buffaloes are found in India and Africa.

THE DOMINION OF CANADA

THE Dominion of Canada, with Newfoundland, which is not part of the Dominion but has its own government, includes more than half of the North American continent.

As yet, Canada has only about ten millions of people, but there is room for many millions more, and opportunities of making a good living for all who are not afraid of work. Canada has not only large areas of fertile lands awaiting the plough, and even wider spaces capable of supporting vast flocks and herds ; she has also great mineral wealth, which up to the present has been only partly exploited, and the probability is that her undiscovered mineral resources far exceed those whose location and extent are more or less known to the prospector and the surveyor. In addition to her wide lands awaiting occupation, and her huge mineral wealth, Canada has great forests stretching almost from ocean to ocean, and rich fisheries ; and although a great deal of timber and fish are turned into wealth by the Canadians every year, the untouched forests are vaster by far than those which have been cut by the lumberjacks, and the fish that are caught are only a small part of the myriads which swarm in the seas, lakes and rivers.

Our great grandfathers used to think of Canada as a very cold land in which life was hard and full of adventure— chiefly, I think, because a famous poet called Canada "Our Lady of the

Snows." There are even now some people who think that the greater part of the Dominion is a cold and barren land in which life is difficult and Nature cruel. Nothing could be farther from the truth.

The Canadian Winter.

It is a fact, of course, that most of Canada is much colder in winter than any part of the Motherland ; that the St. Lawrence and the Great Lakes are sealed by ice for five months in the year ; and that even in large and populous cities like Montreal and Toronto the thermometer in winter sinks to levels which startle us in our warm little Homeland, where even ten or twelve degrees of frost set us shivering unless we wrap up or snuggle down by the fire. But go to Canada and spend a winter there ; see how boys and girls enjoy the snow and ice ; find out for yourself how much cosier Canadian houses are than ours, and how little you yourself feel the cold,

even when there are thirty, forty, or fifty degrees of frost, because the cold is a *dry* cold and not a damp chill like we often get in Britain !

The great gateway of Canada for those of us who visit the Dominion from the Homeland is the St. Lawrence, which with its five great lakes provides a waterway for at least 2,000 miles into the very heart of the North American continent. For seven months in the year, large ocean liners can steam up the St. Lawrence to the great Canadian city-ports of Quebec and Montreal, beyond which a series of rapids bars the way ; although smaller ships, by using the canals which have been made to avoid the rapids, can pass up the river to the Great Lakes and on to the grain-shipping ports at the very head of Lake Superior.

At the Gateway of Canada.

As a matter of actual fact, there are only about 120 miles of rapids between Prescott and Montreal that

ENGINES OLD AND NEW   *Canadian National Railways.*

Railways are essential in the development of any great trans-continental country, for the ranchers and settlers must have ready means for sending their products to market and obtaining supplies from the cities. Canada to-day has about 40,000 miles of railway, and we see above one of her finest and latest locomotives named "Confederation." Alongside this monster of the iron road is one of the early engines known as "Trevithick." The largest Dominion system is that of the Canadian Pacific Railway Company.

H. J. *Shepstone.*

A CANADIAN DOG-TEAM

Though Canada now has its air liners, its wireless and every up-to-date means of communication, mails in some parts are still carried by dog sledge during the winter. The dog-team, however, in addition to its comparative speed and great reliability for utility purposes, is much employed in sporting events, and races between teams over wide tracts of snow-covered country afford the utmost interest. The team above is owned by Chateau Frontenac.

prevent ocean liners from reaching Toronto, and at the present time there is under active consideration a plan for making a great new deep water canal to improve this bad stretch of river, and to harness the rapids to power stations to earn the money to pay for it. If and when this scheme is completed, Toronto and not Montreal will be the head of ocean navigation, and Toronto will quite probably rapidly outstrip Montreal in size and importance.

Two great nations, however—the Canadians and the people of the United States—are concerned in this plan, for the international boundary at that spot passes down the middle of the St. Lawrence, and Canada and the United States must come to a suitable agreement before the work of improving the channel can be begun.

The winter sea-gates of Canada are the "warm water" ports of Halifax in Nova Scotia and Saint John in New Brunswick; and of Portland, Boston and New York in the United States.

DWELLERS IN THE NORTH

FUR TRAPPING IN LABRADOR

In the wintry scene above the man is setting his trap to catch a mink. These animals live near rivers, where the ground is most likely to be an unbroken stretch of white waste. The trapper therefore builds over his trap a little house of tree boughs to keep out the snow. Minks are members of the weasel family and the fur of the Canadian variety possesses considerable value.

THE DOMINION OF CANADA extends in a tattered fringe of archipelago far towards the Pole. Its northern mainland is at the edge of the Arctic, and a wide strip of it lies well within the Arctic Circle. Here the long winters are severe, and the short summers often quite warm and pleasant, but on the barren islands of the Polar Sea climate conditions are much more difficult.

There are no trees, but a great deal of this tundra country is covered with coarse grasses, and in many places is brilliant with flowering plants during the brief summer. Berry-bearing bushes, too, are common, and at the end of summer give a pleasant change to the diet of the people who live in this scantily-populated land.

By the Air Mail.

The northern islands are the home of the Eskimo, and the mainland tundra of both Eskimo and Indians, most of whom get their living by hunting and fishing. On the mainland these people are more or less in touch with civilisation at the many trading posts, some of which are now in communication with the rest of Canada, not only by wireless, but also by the air mail, which can bring news and letters from the outside world every week, instead of once in two or three months, as was formerly often the case when the mails had to be carried by dog-sledge in winter, or by canoe or coasting vessel in summer.

Many Eskimo of the Canadian north have their own schooners, some of which are quite fine craft fitted with auxiliary motors, and capable of almost anything required of them in these difficult waters. Others have motor boats, or boats bought from ships which call at various trading posts in the summer when the sea is free enough from ice. Some have quite comfortable shacks of drift wood and turf in which they live during the winter; in summer they prefer to use their tents and kayaks, which are just the things for the roving life they lead during the better weather.

Those of us who do not realise how much the world has changed during the past ten or twenty years would be astonished to find Eskimo at a northern trading post listening to wireless programmes from the great American transmission centres, or sitting in their summer tents or in their winter huts enjoying the music of their gramophone, and perhaps even eating canned meat that has come from the more civilised lands of the south.

The Real Eskimo.

But it is true. The Eskimo whom we believed when we were very young to live always in his igloo, in an eternally frozen land, never did exist. Even far north among the great islands of the Polar Sea, where the Eskimo live to-day, very much as their ancestors did 1,000 years ago, there is a short summer as well as the long and bitter winter; and during the summer these Eskimo take to the land with their hunting kit and their tupic or skin tent, as well as to the sea in their light and wonderfully-made kayaks, and gather what food they can from both. As winter comes down from the north, the Eskimo retire to their winter huts or *anis*, built of stones and turves, and often slightly underground, and perhaps built partly of drift-wood found on the summer beaches. Here they live snugly while the blizzards rage and howl outside, until the sea ice is strong enough to bear them on their winter hunting trips.

Each little Eskimo winter village is strung out over a considerable distance to give the people of each home a fairly wide area over which to hunt. Igloos or houses of hard blocks of frozen snow form the hunting and fishing headquarters of each family.

On the mainland, Eskimo hunters and Indian trappers collect furs and skins to exchange at the trading posts for things they need. But the big fur-trading is carried on in the great conifer forests, which lie to the south of the tundra lands. This forest belt stretches practically from ocean to ocean across Canada, and in parts is 600 or 700 miles in width. Its southern edges are fast being eaten into by the busy axes of the lumber-jacks, especially in Quebec, Ontario and Manitoba; but in the virgin depths of the forest and along its northern edges where it merges

Will F. Taylor.

A TYPICAL LABRADOR TRAPPER

You have probably read many thrilling stories of Canadian trappers. Here is one of these men, just as you might meet him in the depth of winter in Labrador. He is wearing snow shoes and sealskin boots; sealskin mitts; and hooded and fringed "dickie." You will see that his traps are on his back and that he carries an axe for blazing his trail, in addition to rifle and cartridge belt.

almost imperceptibly into the tundra, the trappers—Indians, half-breeds, and Canadians—set their traps, collect the furry pelts of the creatures they catch, and take them to barter at the Hudson Bay posts for food, clothing, and other things.

Trappers and Fur Traders.

The trapping season is in winter when the fur-bearing animals are wearing their finest coats, and when the snow not only aids the trappers to conceal their traps, but enables them to get about more easily by sledge and snow-shoes.

As winter comes on the trapper collects from the store of the fur trader the flour and bacon, the coffee and tobacco, the blankets and clothing, traps and snares, guns and ammunition, and whatever else he is likely to need during his lonely sojourn in the winter wilds. He may not be able to pay for all these goods, but the trader knows that the average trapper can be trusted to settle his debts in furs after the trapping season is over.

He sets out with his dog-sledge over lonely trails and arrives at last at his wooden shack, built of strong logs, with every crevice stopped and stuffed to keep out the bitter cold. This shack is his winter headquarters. He sets his traps and snares about three-quarters of a mile apart in a wide circle of perhaps thirty or forty miles, which he calls his "trap line." He has to be very cunning to deceive the wary, knowing creatures of the wild, whose sharp eyes and keener scent enable them quickly to detect the work of a "human." At times he may be absent from his cabin for several days— perhaps a fortnight—inspecting his traps, collecting his catch and resetting his traps for another.

The Trading Post.

The skins or pelts of the creatures he catches—of the marten and beaver, fox and otter, wolf and ermine, musk-rat and other animals—he pegs out and dries, piling them in bundles ready for transport by canoe when the spring unlocks the frozen streams and lakes and enables him to make an easy journey back to the trading-post. Here, as a rule, no money passes ; for money is useless in such country as this. The trapper is credited with the value of his pelts, and against his credit he

THE HOLLINGER GOLD MINE   *H. J. Shepstone.*

There s gold in the west of Canada and this wonderful country is now the second largest gold producer in the British Empire.   In the above illustration we see the famous Hollinger Mine, the richest of those on the Porcupine Goldfield.   In 1897 finds of gold in the Klondike region of the Yukon drew men helter-skelter from all parts of the world, but the " Canadian Shield," east of the Rockies, is the great gold-bearing region now.

Will F. Taylor.

IN THE KLONDIKE COUNTRY

Here we see gold miners at work in the Klondike country. Their methods are primitive compared with those where expensive and elaborate machinery is available and their appliances consist of a simple sluice for washing the gravel as a means of extracting the " pay-dirt." In streams and rivers the world over, including those of our own islands, some traces of gold may be found.

draws what goods he needs for his summer use ; and later, when he once again sets out for his trapping ground, his stores for the long and lonely winter.

A Gold Rush.

What has drawn, not only Canadians, but men from all parts of the globe to the far north-west of Canada, is gold. In 1897 rich finds of gold were discovered in the Klondike region of the Yukon basin ; a gold rush immediately set in, and in spite of the difficulties of reaching the Klondike in winter, swarms of gold-seekers attempted the perilous passage of the snowy passes from the North Pacific coast ; and, when spring came, made their way in hastily-built scows down the roaring Yukon to the gold-field. Thousands perished long before they came in sight of their goal. Thousands reached the diggings only to find that gold was not to be picked up anywhere, and that it was only the lucky ones who made sudden and enormous fortunes. Mining camps grew up ; some developed into towns, *e.g.*, Dawson City, while others became derelict as soon as the quest for gold proved unavailing.

Very large quantities of gold were got by the primitive and haphazard methods of early diggers. When these methods began to fail, gold-mining and gold-digging on a scientific plan, employing expensive machinery, for a time proved successful. But in recent years the yield of gold from the Klondike has greatly decreased ; and as a result people began to leave Yukon territory instead of swarming there from all parts of America and Europe as they had done in the gold rush of '98. Indeed to-day the population is much less than it has been for the last thirty years.

Canada as Gold-producer.

Although Canada is now the second largest gold producer in the British Empire, by far the richest yield to-day is from the Canadian Shield, and the rich-est gold mine is the famous Hollinger Mine on the Porcupine Goldfield there.

It may be that the future wealth of these northern lands will lie in the rich grasses on which animals like the caribou and the reindeer can be raised in large numbers. The caribou are already there in considerable herds that migrate north or south according to the season in search of pasture ; some reindeer have already been introduced and are flourishing there, for the Canadian tundra is no nearer the Pole than Lapland, where the chief wealth of the people is in their reindeer herds.

Sport and General.

ESKIMO AND THEIR IGLOO

At some of the northern trading posts one might find Eskimo listening to wireless programmes from the great American transmission centres. Yet these simple, hardy folks still live in igloos, such as the one shown above. Every little Eskimo winter village is strung out over a consider-able distance to give the people of each home a fairly wide area which they can regard as their own hunting ground.

LUMBER JACKS AND THE FORESTS

LUMBERMEN AT THEIR WORK

H. J. Shepstone.

The forests of Canada stretch in an unbroken line almost from the Atlantic to the Pacific and afford work for an enormous number of men. The swift-flowing rivers are much used to float the lumber from forest to factory, and the men depicted above are sorting out logs for the making of pulp for paper. To understand the work of these lumbermen of the St. Maurice River, Quebec, you must realise that they are standing precariously upon floating logs.

CANADA has many millions of dollars' worth of valuable timber as yet untouched, although the eastern forests have been greatly cut into by the lumbermen, who have also made considerable inroads into the southern parts of the forests in Quebec, Ontario and Manitoba.

Forest Rangers.

As we have already seen, these great forests stretch in a wide and almost unbroken line from Atlantic to Pacific. The trees are mostly conifers like larch and spruce, whose soft woods are particularly valuable to the paper-maker and the manufacturer of artificial silk ; and tamarack and pine, with hemlock and birch and other trees. The great printing presses of the world, however, consume paper at such a rate that Canada is taking every possible step to conserve her forests, prevent waste, and arrange for new trees to be planted to take the place of those cut down.

Large areas have been set apart as National Forests to be strictly preserved and cut only when there is need. No lumber company can cut timber where, when and how it pleases. It is under more or less strict supervision everywhere, so that young trees are not cut or damaged, and cutting is done in the most economical way.

Forest rangers are appointed to prevent waste and damage, to fight pests that damage trees, and, above all, to guard as far as possible against the worst peril there is—the danger of forest fires. Look-outs and other posts have been established whence the rangers can detect outbreaks of fire, and by means of the telephone and wireless can summon help and fire-fighting appliances to extinguish the blaze before it can spread over large areas. Hydroplanes, too, are used for fire detection and forest protection, for they can settle on the surfaces of the many lakes in summer. Like the planes used for carrying the Canadian air-mails, they are equipped with runners and skids in

ON THEIR WAY TO THE SAW MILLS   *Ewing Galloway, N.Y.*

Larch and spruce are known as soft woods and are particularly valuable to the paper-maker, the great printing presses of the world consuming an enormous amount of Canadian lumber. In this picture you are shown a riverful of logs, raw material for the saw mills or pulp plants, floating down the Thessalon River in Ontario.   It cheapens the product considerably when transport along a stream can be arranged.

winter so that they can land on the snow-covered ice of the lakes and streams.

The following is part of a warning notice that appears in many of the Canadian railway time-tables :—

" Nine out of ten forest fires are let loose by human hands.   An abandoned camp-fire, a glowing cigarette, a pipe-heel, or other innocent-looking cause ! Only a tiny point of flame which an hour hence becomes the fuse to a gigantic disaster."

It is in British Columbia that the Canadian conifers attain the greatest size, for there the country is moister, and winters on the whole much milder than in the central and eastern portions of the great Conifer Belt.   Here grow the magnificent Douglas firs, whose feathery tips rise to a height sometimes of 300 feet ; the splended Sitka spruces, and the fine-grained red cedars whose timber is in great demand for building.

Lumber-jacks.

Lumbering is carried on chiefly in winter over the greater part of Canada, for the heavy snowfall makes it easier to move the weighty logs by sledges or by slides to the nearest stream, there to await the break-up of the ice and the spring floods that will carry them down by the million to the saw-mills and the pulp-mills on the main rivers and the lakes.

TURNING TREES INTO NEWSPAPERS

Mondiale.

The mountain of logs here depicted was photographed at Iroquois Falls, Quebec. Powerful cranes lifted the timber from the water and here the stuff is stacked waiting to pass through various intricate stages before being made into pulp.

Mondiale.

The bark is not required in the process of paper-making and so the logs have to pass through wood barkers—the bark itself being used to feed the fires that drive the machinery. Here you see the barking appliances (B), and the logs have also to be sprayed (C) as they pass on to the pulping process. At point A you see the timber progressing swiftly along a moving platform towards the barkers, whilst at " D " is the endless belt which takes it forward to the next stage.

P 2

This provides work for many men who otherwise would be idle because their ordinary jobs have been stopped by frost and snow and bitter weather. They move up-country from towns and villages and farms to the lumber camps, where they live strenuous lives, but earn good money. After the spring "runs" of logs on the rivers are over, many of the lumber-jacks go back to their warm weather work in town and village, farm and factory.

In many parts of British Columbia, however, the lumbermen do not wait for winter before they begin their cutting, because the snows are not heavy enough to make it worth while. They fell the huge trees during the good weather, cut them into giant logs, and, by means of wire cables and donkey engines, lug them out of the forest and place them on lumber trains which convey them to the river, or very often to an arm of the sea—for the Pacific shores of Canada are in many parts indented by long deep inlets much like the fjords of Norway.

Mondiale.

AN OVERHEAD ROPEWAY FOR PULP

This picture shows how bales of pulp are picked up by a " grab " from the water in which they have been soaking and conveyed along an overhead ropeway to the rolling mills. The paper upon which this book was printed may once have been part of a tree in Canada. Much Canadian pulp in a raw state is imported into this country to be manufactured into paper.

THE PRAIRIES AND WHEAT

A WHEATFIELD OF THE PRAIRIES *Canadian National Railways.*

This photograph, taken at Melfort in Saskatchewan, gives you an excellent idea of what a vast prairie wheatfield is really like. " Prairie " means a meadow, or natural grass-land, and the soil is particularly suitable for ploughing and will grow grain for several years before it needs to be further fertilised. The prairies are by no means level, but sweep across the horizon in giant undulations. Before the white man came, Indians and the bison roamed the prairies.

THE CANADIAN PRAIRIES lie south of the forest belt, and between the Rocky Mountain foot-hills and the Lake of the Woods east of Winnipeg. The name means " meadows " or natural grass-land. The prairies are by no means level ; they rise gently in three broad steps or very wide terraces from Winnipeg westward to the Rocky Mountain foot-hills ; and the top of the east of those three gigantic " steps " is gently undulating country, with few trees and open horizons.

Products of the Prairies.

The " prairie provinces " are Manitoba, Saskatchewan and Alberta, although it should be remembered that all three stretch far north from the prairie lands into the great belt of conifer forests. Manitoba, indeed, stretches from the international boundary of the forty-ninth parallel to the shores of Hudson Bay, where she has built her new port of Churchill.

The soil of the prairies is extra-ordinarily fertile, and in many places will grow grain several years before the farmer finds it necessary to restore its vitality by scientific manuring.

Although grain—especially wheat—is the chief prairie product, there are regions where the rainfall is hardly enough for grain, but where large numbers of cattle, sheep and horses can be reared, as they are on the eastern foot-hills of the Rockies. Grain farmers, too, do not lock up all their capital and spend all their energy in grain-growing ; they grow other crops as well, and rear farm animals too. It is true that when a man first takes up his land, and breaks it up for farming, he generally grows wheat first, because wheat is pretty certain of making him a return of ready money. But after that, he begins to lay out his farm so that he can grow other crops too, and rear animals.

The prairies, however, are the real " golden lands " of the West, and rich hard wheat sown in spring and reaped the following autumn is the main crop.

ON THE GREAT CANADIAN PRAIRIES—

Canadian National Railways.

The four beautiful horses here illustrated are drawing a reaping machine over one of the enormous prairie fields of golden grain.   The picture was taken at Swan River Valley in Manitoba.   Manitoba, Saskatchewan and Alberta are the three prairie provinces, forming Canada's wheat-belt.

Canadian National Railways.

This scene is not so romantic or picturesque as the one above, for the latest mechanical appliances have taken the place of fine horses.   This photograph comes from North Battleford in Saskatchewan and we are shown a machine, drawn by a petrol-driven tractor, that not only cuts the wheat but threshes it at the same time.   The farmer's saloon motor-car in the background is a contrast to the fiery mustangs formerly ridden.

ONE OF THE WORLD'S WHEATFIELDS

Canadian National Railways.

This picture is a good companion to the one on the left, for here our friends the horses are still holding their own. The team of workers is collecting stooks of corn from a field in Saskatchewan. The appliance on the right, like some huge dust-pan, gathers up the sheaves that form the stooks. They are then raised aloft by the mechanical conveyor and dropped into the huge four-wheeled waggon, to be transported direct to——

Canadian National Railways.

The threshing machines. This illustration comes from Portage La Prairie in Manitoba. The motor-driven power plant is on the left, connected by an endless band with the thresher. Here you see sheaves being fed into the machine and the heaps of straw beyond. What looks to be steam emerging from a powerful exhaust is the chaff, husk and dust cleared from the grain.

But we must think of them also as great stock-breeding lands where grain would not be so profitable, and we must bear in mind that although a farmer's mainstay may be wheat on the richer and moister lands, he also goes in for a good deal of mixed farming.

The Bison.

Before the coming of the white men, the Indians roamed the prairies, hunting the bison (or "buffalo"), and following the great bison herds as they migrated in their millions yearly across these vast natural grazing grounds. When white men came, and the Indians found a ready market with them for hides and "buffalo robes," both whites and Indians (now armed with guns capable of far swifter execution than their bows and arrows) carried on a campaign of ruthless slaughter, bringing down the bison in uncountable thousands, stripping them of their hides, and leaving their carcases to the coyotes and the buzzards. The greed that prompted this wholesale extermination of the bison herds soon brought its retribution, and it is not too much to say that in a comparatively few years the bison was in danger of becoming as extinct as the prehistoric monsters whose remains we find in the rocks.

The magnitude of the slaughter may be realised when we read records which tell how, in the middle of the nineteenth century, travellers saw the plains covered with grazing bison from horizon to horizon. Yet the day soon arrived when only a few hundreds were left. Luckily, some of these were captured and at last preserved in the great National Parks of Canada and

Canadian National Railways.

IN THE SHIPPING CORRALS

Bison are carefully preserved in the great national parks of Canada and the United States of America, where they live unmolested, perfectly happy in their freedom. The herds in Wainwright Park, Alberta, are famous corrals and here we see some one and two-year old bisons rounded up in shipping corrals. These animals are to be sent by Canadian National Railways to form a new herd at Wood Buffalo Park in the Fort Smith district of the great North-West.

WILL HE MAKE BETTER BEEF ? *Canadian National Railways.*

Though the bison, being so strong and hardy, can roam the prairies all the year round in perfect safety, the domestic cattle to which we in the Motherland are accustomed are not so well adapted to life in the great open tracts. To overcome this difficulty an animal known as the "Cattalo" has been bred. His father is a bull bison and his mother a domestic cow. He is very strong and not likely to be overtaken by disease, and may be the means of bringing still better beef from Canada to the meat markets of the world.

the United States, where they could live and multiply unmolested. The buffalo herds of Wainwright Park in Alberta are famous ; like some others, they have so increased in numbers in recent years that hunters are employed from time to time to thin them out.

Where the bison herds formerly roamed in yearly migration over the prairies are now broad lands of golden grain. More and more land is being taken up by the wheat farmers, who now grow wheat, especially in Alberta, much farther north than was formerly thought possible. On these northern wheat-lands, the great length of day amply compensates for the shorter summer, and the long hours of con-

tinuous sunlight ripen the grain more quickly. In Alberta, too, and Saskatchewan, the warm Chinook winds come down from the west, licking up the winter snow as if by magic, and giving the farmers the chance of early spring sowing.

How Wheat goes to Market.

It is one thing to grow wheat and quite a different thing to market it. Were it not for the amazing network of railways serving the prairie lands and the wonderful organisation that permits growers to despatch, store and export their crops, the business of wheat-growing on this gigantic scale would be an unprofitable one.

Co-operation among the farmers has led to the creation of what are known as wheat "pools"—the collection and storage of the grain at one or two great central points which are most convenient for storage and for transport to tide-water. The threshed grain is stored in giant buildings called elevators, some of which can hold as much as six millions of bushels.

Smaller elevators are set up at central points on the railroads all over the grain-lands; and it is to these that farmers bring their harvests by wagon and lorry. From these the grain is sent to monster elevators, at Winnipeg, for example, whence a comparatively short haul by railroad delivers it to other great elevators at Port Arthur and Fort William at the head of Lake Superior, whence the wheat can be loaded into specially constructed lake-steamers for transport as required, to the ocean ports of Montreal and New York.

Grain Export.

More and more grain nowadays is being sent westward to the Pacific ports, instead of eastward. The Alberta wheat " pool " has constructed giant elevators at Prince Rupert, one of the Pacific terminals of the Canadian National Railways; there are others, too, at Vancouver, which is the Pacific terminal of both the Canadian Pacific and the Canadian National. From these ports grain is shipped to Britain and Western Europe by way of the Panama Canal—a long sea voyage of six weeks or so, it is true, but cheaper in the long run, because of the shorter railroad haul to the sea, and because of the fewer changes from land transport to water transport by the western route.

Grain going east from the Winnipeg " pool " must change from rail to lake steamer at Lake Superior, and very often from lake steamer to rail again at Georgian Bay on Lake Huron, and from rail to ocean steamer at Montreal. All these changes add to the cost of transport and greatly increase the price at which the wheat can be sold. The sum paid to the farmer for his wheat is usually less than half the price charged for it when it is exported from Montreal to Liverpool.

The Wheat Pool.

The wheat " pool " has other advantages than those we have already mentioned. First of all, the wheat can be held back in the big elevators until the price is good enough for it to be released; and secondly, the " pool " arranges for the farmer to receive his money in three parts if he chooses—one on receipt of the grain, one when he sows his spring crop, and the third to help pay for harvesting it. This means that farmers need not borrow money to keep themselves going, nor be practically a year behind with their profits.

The transport of grain on the Great Lakes is carried on in specially-built " lake freighters " with engine-rooms at their sterns and navigating bridges and living quarters at their bows—all the rest being cargo space. The need for many of these freighters is easily seen when we read in some recent Canadian official records that 380,000,000 bushels of grain had to be shipped from Fort William and Port Arthur during the season. This partly explains why Ontario and Quebec, both inland provinces of the Dominion, have nearly 13,000,000 tons of shipping on their registers. The largest of these grain carriers is 633 feet long, with a gross tonnage of 10,480.

Queen City of the Prairies.

The great centre of all this business is *Winnipeg*, the " Queen City " of the prairies, which has grown from a small prairie town of wooden shacks to a splendid city with fine buildings and all the requirements of civilisation in a remarkably short time—and is still

THE WAY WHEAT GOES TO MARKET

Canadian National Railways.

The prairie lands of Canada are served by an immense network of railways, by means of which the wheat harvest is collected from the farms and carried first to local centres and then to large main stores, from which it can be marketed to the best advantage. Most of these stores are within touch of shipping, and the elevators at Montreal are illustrated above.

Canadian National Railways.

Here is the Canadian National elevator at Port Arthur. The threshed grain is stored in this elevator, which is at the head of Lake Superior, and is then easily transferred to specially-constructed lake steamers for transport as required to the ocean ports of Montreal or New York.

growing fast. It is often called the "Keystone of Canada," because all traffic across Canada east and west must pass through this central point. A glance at the map of Canada reveals the reason.

First of all, it is almost midway between the Atlantic and Pacific Oceans; second, it is in the "bottle-neck" between Lake Winnipeg and the international border, at the confluence of the Red River and the Assiniboine River, forty miles south of the lake and sixty miles from the boundary between Canada and the United States. And to this "bottle-neck," commanded by Winnipeg, traffic must converge; the C.P.R., the C.N.R., the Midland Railway of Manitoba and the Northern Pacific of the U.S.A. all meet there. The Winnipeg railway sidings are astonishingly large, to accom-modate the huge movements of grain, cattle and other products from the west, and of manufactured foods from the east. Winnipeg has flour-mills, meat-pack-ing, clothing, food products and sheet metal industries; and with its suburbs a population exceeding 304,000.

Other Prairie Cities.

Other prairie cities are much smaller, but are fast growing, as more and more lands are brought under yield. *Cal-gary*, the centre of the stock-raising and agricultural region of Southern Alberta, has, with its suburbs, a popula-tion of 87,640. Important oil wells are near, and the town has 150 different industries. Both C.P.R. and C.N.R. serve the area. Another large town is *Edmonton*, the capital of Alberta, near good coal, on the N. Saskatchewan, and the gateway to the famous Peace

Mondiale

INDIANS OF THE PLAINS

This is a photograph of a most interesting and life-like model to be seen in the American Museum of National History. It shows Indians of the Plains with the curious method of transporting their goods by tying the bundles to a pair of rods trailed behind a horse or dog. These appliances are known by the name " Travois."

THE NOBLE RED INDIAN

Canadian National Railways.

The natives of the great American continent, who roamed the prairies before the coming of the white man, were named "Indians" by Christopher Columbus, who actually believed at the time that his voyage across the Atlantic had led him to India by a westerly route. In the above impressive picture we see Red Indian warriors in full dress. The race is a noble one, now living peacefully in reservations, though clinging to the picturesque costumes of those who have long since gone to the "happy hunting grounds." In Canada alone there are still over 100,000 Redskins.

Natural gas (50,000,000 cubic feet daily) is brought in pipes to the city from the oil regions. Both C.P.R. and C.N.R. serve Edmonton ; the city has the first municipal aerodrome constructed in Canada, and its industries include engineering, meat-packing, flour-milling, coal-mining, timber-working and butter and cheese-making. It is a great fur-trading centre for the north-west.

Farming in Eastern Canada is rather different from farming on the prairies. Wheat-

Canadian National Railways.

A SCENE IN THE ROCKIES

The scenery of the Canadian Rockies is positively majestic, as is confirmed by this view of Mount Robson, the highest peak, upwards of 13,000 feet. At its base is Berg Lake, so called because of the many icebergs dotted on its surface.

River country to the north, now being rapidly settled and developed. Oil wells have been bored at Wainwright, 100 miles from the city, and at Turner Valley.

The E.P. ranch, owned by H.R.H. the Prince of Wales, is in the neighbourhood, and has oil wells near it ; it probably has oil beneath it too.

Will F. Taylor.

SWITZERLAND IN CANADA

This Swiss-like vista is a landscape introducing the trio of peaks known as "The Three Sisters." The photograph was taken from Bow River Valley, Canmore, in the Province of Alberta. Contrast this with our prairie views.

A PEAK OF THE WILDS

H. J. Shepstone.

We think of Canada as a " Land of Forests, Lakes and Rivers," and its sons are proud of its limitless aspects and resources. To preserve some of its wildest beauty spots and form homes for bison, moose, elks, grizzly bears and other animals she wishes to preserve, Canada has established vast national parks, the finest of which are among the Rocky Mountains. Jasper National Park is the largest of these reservations. It is the greatest wild game sanctuary in the world and the above picture was taken in the Bastion Park section in Tonquin Valley.

growing and mixed farming are the chief businesses in the prairie provinces ; but in the east dairy-farming, stock-breeding and fruit-growing are the most important branches of the farming industry.

Canada's Great Cities.

Conditions in the east are different from those of the western prairies. The climate is different, and the soil is different too. The needs of the east for farm produce are greater than those of the west, for in the valley of the St. Lawrence and the Lake Peninsula of Ontario is the densest population in the Dominion ; all Canada's great cities, except two, are there, and

Mondiale.

AN OIL WELL IN ALBERTA

The resources of Canada seem almost limitless, but we must remember that this vast country stretches from the Atlantic to the Pacific and from the Arctic down to the Great Lakes.   Even oil is found and some recent discoveries in this direction lead us to hope that great development is probable.   The towering derrick seen above belongs to the Wainwell No. 1 in Wainwright, Alberta.   It produces 300 barrels of oil a day.

CANADA'S "GREAT DIVIDE"

H. J. Shepstone.

Does not this fine photograph make you wish to travel overseas? It depicts a beautiful scene of forest, stream and mountain in Canada, and marks the dividing line or boundary betwixt British Columbia and Alberta. The actual spot is the Banff National Park. There are National Parks in both Eastern and Western Canada, with fine hotels and bungalow camps. Here holiday-seekers make their headquarters for hunting, fishing and canoe trips, and climbing.

Canada's biggest manufacturing industries have their homes there. It is more profitable from the point of view of the ready market in this populous region of the Dominion for farmers to go in for dairy-farming, poultry-rearing, raising stock for meat, and fruit-growing; and it is fortunate that the moister climate favours these businesses to a far greater extent than the drier climate of the prairies.

Across the St. Lawrence.

A glance at the map will show the marked difference between the east and west of the Dominion. Nearest to the Mother Country comes Newfoundland. Then, in Canada proper, we see the huge Province of Quebec, bounded on the north-east by Labrador. This vast tract has the sea on three sides, for Quebec's western extremity is bounded by Hudson Bay. South of Quebec, across the St. Lawrence, are New Brunswick and Nova Scotia; whilst the section containing Ottawa comes between the frontier of the United States of America and the Great Lakes.

The prairie wheatbelt is therefore mainly in the centre of the continent. Here it has a purely inland climate, unaffected by the sea summer or winter. To the south of Alberta, Saskatchewan and Manitoba is the boundary of the U.S.A., with the Missouri River not far away.

THE BUSIEST PARTS OF CANADA

MONTREAL, CANADA'S LARGEST CITY

Though we know of the majestic Rocky Mountains, the snowy Yukon, the prairie provinces and similar great open spaces, we must not forget that Canada possesses some very fine and most important cities. The largest of these, illustrated above, is Montreal, with a population of nearly a million people. It is also a vital seaport and draws electrical power from the Lachine Rapids. In the city are the Cathedral of St. James, the McGill University and some 2,000 factories. The port is closed by ice from November till March.

THREE-FIFTHS of Canada's population live in Ontario and Quebec, and the greater number of these dwell in the lowland of the St. Lawrence, where all Canada's cities of over 100,000 people are situated, except two, and where we find the only cities with populations of more than half a million—Montreal and Toronto.

Canada's Largest City.

Montreal is the largest city in Canada, with a population (including its suburbs) of nearly a million people. It is at the head of ocean navigation on the St. Lawrence, and is therefore a great seaport, with routes converging in it from the Lakes and the Canadian west, and from New York and the busiest regions of the north-eastern United States. It has abundant hydro-electric power from the Lachine Rapids close by, and can therefore carry on a large variety of manufactures independently of coal. Nearly 2,000 factories of various kinds have been erected in the city or in its immediate neighbourhood.

It is amazing to think that this vast business metropolis of the Dominion has grown up from the tiny settlement founded on the island of Mont Real in 1642 by the Sieur de Maisonneuve. You can see his statue to-day in the old Place d'Armes in the heart of the city. The French element still predominates ; newspapers in French are as common as those in English, and four out of every five inhabitants can speak French.

Montreal's great cathedral of St. James is a reproduction on a smaller scale of St. Peter's, Rome. Near Mount Royal Park, on the lower and eastern slope, is the famous McGill University.

The French University of Laval is in the French quarter of the city.

Canada's two great railway systems have monster stations there; the bigger is the C.P.R. terminal of Windsor Street Station. Montreal has thirty miles of water-front, with dock and wharfage accommodation for vessels up to 25,000 tons; a huge network of rail connections; and giant grain elevators (some capable of storing nearly 3,000,000 bushels), which can handle a million bushels of wheat a day.

The great disadvantage from which the port suffers is that it is closed by ice from November till March.

Toronto.

Toronto (600,000), the capital of Ontario, bids fair to outstrip Montreal; if and when the St. Lawrence is rendered navigable to ocean liners between Montreal and Lake Ontario, as has been proposed, Toronto is bound in time to usurp Montreal's position as Canada's leading port, and to grow proportionately in population and importance.

In its business quarter, Toronto's skyscraper buildings remind one somewhat of New York; and, seen from a high viewpoint, its principal thoroughfare, Yonge Street, looks like a road ribbon at the bottom of a deep canyon of masonry. Its fine harbour on the lake is protected by a low sandy island, where people amuse themselves much as New Yorkers do on Coney Island. Power from

Canadian National Railways.

THE PLACE D'ARMES IN MONTREAL

This view of the fine city of Montreal shows us Notre Dame and the Place d'Armes. The vast business metropolis of Canada grew from a tiny settlement founded on the island of Mont Real nearly 300 years ago by the Sieur de Maisonneuve. His statue may be seen in the above photograph, and the Place d'Armes is the heart of the modern city. Four out of every five inhabitants of Montreal speak the French language.

WHERE CANADA'S PARLIAMENT MEETS

Canadian National Railways.

Ottawa is the capital of Canada and stands on the river of the same name, which is of Indian origin. In our picture is shown the Parliament Buildings, which occupy a lofty bluff overlooking the river. The tower is called the "Tower of Peace" and is a memorial to the 60,000 Canadian soldiers who gave their lives in the Great War.

Mondiale.

This bird's-eye view of Hamilton shows you another of Canada's fine cities. It stands on Lake Ontario and is about 40 miles from Toronto. Hamilton is sometimes referred to as "the Birmingham of Canada," for it has great steel and ironworks and many other industries.

WINTER AND SUMMER SPORTS

Mondiale.

Canada in winter is much colder than the Motherland, but if you were to visit the Dominion when the temperature was below zero you would scarcely feel the cold because it is a dry cold and not the damp chill that we usually experience. The frost and snow, too, provide unequalled winter sports, and this picture shows the Park Slide at Mount Royal, Montreal, over which four lines of toboggans rush at top speed.

Canadian National Railways.

Though Canada has colder winters than ours, her summers as a rule are much warmer and drier. There is, indeed, a vast gulf between summer and winter temperatures. As a contrast to the toboggan slide, here is a view of Sunnyside, Toronto, at the height of summer.

Canadian National Railways.

AN INDIAN MAID

This lithe and happy Indian girl, so warmly clad
against the winter blast, was snapped at Metis,
in Quebec. She seems to have an inherent love
of animals by the way she is fondling her pet
beaver.

Niagara has made Toronto one of
Canada's leading manufacturing centres.

A favourite excursion from Toronto
is, of course, to the famous *Falls* themselves.

Niagara Falls.

They occur where the whole of the
Niagara River plunges headlong over
a great ledge of limestone into the pool
below, to gather speed rapidly as it
enters the Niagara gorge, through which
it foams and leaps and boils in raging
whirlpools. By the time the flood has
reached Queenston it has calmed down,
and makes exit to Lake Ontario with
a quiet that strangely belies its mad
energy a few miles up-stream.

Ages ago, geologists tell us, the Falls
were seven miles or so down-stream,
but since that time they have gradually
cut their way back—a process that is
still going on. What will happen when
they have receded to Lake Erie no man
can tell ; it is not likely to concern the
present generation, at any rate !

The Falls are divided by Goat Island
into the Canadian or Horseshoe Fall
(158 feet high, 3,100 feet wide), and the
American Fall (167 feet high, 1,080 feet
wide). You can go to the foot of the
Falls in a tiny steamer and view the
great rushing torrent at close quarters ;
you can even pass behind the American
Fall, clad in oilskins ; and led by a
guide through the onslaught of wind
and spray, amid the noise of thundering
waters, you may dare to open your
frightened eyes to see the fall rushing
in sheets of light and darkness in a great
curve that seems within reach of your
outstretched hand.

The rapids in the Niagara Gorge are
even more terrifying than the Falls
themselves. The Falls are liquid moving translucent Majesty ; the whirlpools in the gorge are howling demoniac
Force that threatens.

No wonder Niagara is a sort of Mecca
for all the tourists of the globe. Hundreds of thousands visit it every year ;
for despite the great power-houses

ON THE ST. LAWRENCE RIVER

The St. Lawrence River is the great gateway to Canada and the view above is one of the Port of Quebec. In the foreground you see coal barges being loaded. On the opposite side of the basin are the great shoots by means of which grain is transferred to the holds of steamships from the elevator. The name Quebec is of Indian derivation.

This is the Saquenay Power Plant at St. Joseph D'Alma, Quebec. This plant supplies mines and mills, villages and towns, factories and canneries with electrical power, light and heat, so saving coal. The system is brought into being by damming the course of a swift-flowing river.

Canadian National Railways.

In the Far West of Canada the railway tracks have to be carried on high trestle bridges, over stupendous gorges, down the deep canyons of zig-zag rivers and along perilous ledges skirting the mountain precipices. In this illustration we see the " Confederation, Ltd.," at Cisco, British Columbia. This crack train is built entirely of steel and is even equipped with wireless.

Mondiale.

In this picture we have an aerial view of the city of Vancouver, with its water front. Vancouver is the largest town in British Columbia and (including the suburbs) has a population of a quarter of a million. Its main interest is shipping, and liners leave this port for Australia, China and Japan.

BIG PROVINCE IN THE FAR WEST

Prince Rupert, where the above photograph was obtained, is about 500 miles north of Vancouver, and is an important town and seaport. It is a great centre of the fishing industry and some of the boats are illustrated. Salmon, halibut, cod and herrings are all caught in this neighbourhood.

This is the cooling room in a huge cannery in British Columbia. The salmon are carried on a conveyer into the cannery and pitched into a moving machine that cuts off fins and heads, scrapes off the scales, splits open and cleans the bodies and sprays the fish with water. They are then sliced into chunks the right size for the cans. The cans are filled by machinery, the tops soldered on and then they go to a steam oven for the cooking. Afterwards they are cooled, as seen above.

Mondiale.

THE "NARROWS" AT ST. JOHN'S, NEWFOUNDLAND

St. John's is the capital of Newfoundland, which was discovered by John Cabot in 1497, and has
regular steamer services to Liverpool and New York.   This illustration shows us the "Narrows"
and the seaward side of the Battery at the harbour entrance.

built to steal some of the energy of the
rushing river, there has been no visible
diminution in its resistless flood, and no
detraction from the marvellous beauty
of the Falls—unless you cannot shut
your eyes to the hotels, the trams, and
the establishments and activities of
those who cater for tourists who must
have amusements, and souvenirs, and
picture postcards and other things to
make them really happy !

Ottawa.

Ottawa is the beautiful capital of the
Dominion on the Ottawa River, opposite the busy lumber and pulp-mills of
Hull, which, like its regal sister across
the river, derives power, light and heat
from the Chaudière Falls. Its fine
Parliament Buildings and Government
Offices stand on a high bluff overlooking
the river.   Its wide and shady streets,
and its lovely houses with fine lawns
and beautiful gardens, make Ottawa a
city of wonderful homes.

There are other cities, too, in this
busy region of the lower Lakes and the
St. Lawrence.   There is *Hamilton*, west
of Toronto, with its great steel and
iron works, its chewing gum and confectionery businesses, and the famous
works that send out vacuum cleaners
to eat up the dust of a million homes
in Europe and America.   There is *Trois
Rivières* (Three Rivers) on the St.
Lawrence about half-way between
Quebec and Montreal that draws its
power from the great Shawinigan Falls
on the St. Maurice River and runs one
of the biggest paper and pulp plants in

AT THE FALLS OF NIAGARA

Mondiale.

Niagara is a Mecca for all the tourists of the globe, and hundreds of thousands of people visit it every year. The Falls are divided into Canadian and American sections by an island, and the river separates Canada from the United States. Above we see the river and the Falls.

Canadian National Railways.

Ontario is one of the famous fruit-growing districts of Eastern Canada, and the busy girl workers illustrated above are gathering in the cherry harvest at Grimsby, in that Province. Eastern Canada is noted not only for its fruit, but also for its dairy-farming, and has cheese factories besides other agricultural interests.

the Dominion, as well as cotton factories and shoe factories.

Canada To-day.

All this mighty energy in process of development, all this activity that is spending itself in the building up of flourishing manufactures, remind us that the Canada of to-day is a very different Canada from that of even twenty or thirty years ago. She no longer imports most of her manufactured goods from Britain and other lands; she has become a manufacturer herself, and is beginning to penetrate into the markets of the world in competition with those very countries to which she formerly looked for manufactured goods.

Testimony to Canada's extraordinary progress appears in a report of the Royal Bank of Canada issued in 1927: "Canada is now the leader in the production of newsprint, asbestos, nickel, cobalt and salmon; and produces the world's largest exportable wheat surplus. She stands second in the number of telephones in use, and in the production of automobiles and lumber; third in gold and silver production; seventh in steel production; and tenth in that of coal."

Mondiale.

IN THE JASPER NATIONAL PARK

This magnificent view is one that you might obtain in the Jasper National Park in Alberta, Canada. With such a perfect background, composed by Mother Nature herself, it is not surprising to know that it has been used for the making of a talking film. A company of performers numbering thirty travelled by packhorse through the valleys of this mountain playground to take this picture.

The Story
of the
World and
its Peoples

The Empire
on which
The Sun
Never Sets

KRAALS OF THE KAFFIRS

Will F. Taylor.

The word " kraal " is of Dutch origin and may indicate a complete village or encampment of the Kaffirs, who are natives of South Africa. On the other hand, it may mean a single hut, similar to those shown above. These huts are most ingeniously made of mud, which bakes hard in the fierce sun-rays, and are strongly thatched with reeds and grasses over an umbrella-like framework of wood.

BRITISH SOUTH AFRICA

EIGHTEEN days' voyage in one of the splendid motor ships of the Union Castle Line takes us to Cape Town, the sea-gate of the Union of South Africa, calling on the way at Las Palmas, the chief seaport of the Canary Isles, famous for their bananas and their supplies of early vegetables for British and Continental markets ; or perhaps at Funchal, in Madeira.

It was Sir Francis Drake who said of the Cape of Good Hope : " This Cape is truly a most stately thing, and the fairest Cape we saw in the whole circumference of the earth." Earlier voyagers called it the " Cape of Storms "—one, indeed, said it was *Cabo tormentoso*, the " Cape of Torments," because of the heavy weather he encountered in trying to round it. His kingly master, however, brushed the name away with the remark : " Rather let it be called *Cabo da bona speranza* "—" Cape of Good Hope " ; and Cape of Good Hope it has remained unto this day.

Cape Town.

Cape Town stands on its beautiful bay some distance to the north of the famous Cape, off which sailormen still believe old Vanderdecken, " the flying Dutchman," cruises in his ghostly vessel in unending efforts to weather it. Over the city towers Table Mountain, which, at certain times of the year, has its flat top shrouded in mists that overhang it, and form what is popularly known as the " Tablecloth."

To one side of Table Mountain is the Devil's Peak, and to the other is the Lion's Head, so called for a reason that is perfectly plain as soon as you see it !

Directly we land we know that we are in Africa, the continent of the black man, for many of the workers on the water-front and in the streets are negroes who do most of the labour in South Africa, both in town and country. The fine old Dutch houses that still remain in and around the city remind us of sturdy Johan van Riebeeck, who founded the Dutch colony there in 1652. The splendid buildings and wide streets tell of the work of the British who succeeded the Dutch. Adderley Street is the finest thoroughfare in Cape Town, with its restaurants and shops, electric cars and public buildings; but even there on the pavement opposite the Post Office we see coloured folk selling bunches of the wonderful Cape flowers on Saturday mornings.

From Cape Town runs the great railway northwards for many hundreds of miles to the Victoria Falls of the Zambezi, and on into the coppermining country of the Belgian Congo, forming the southern part of the " Cape-to-Cairo " railway that was the cherished dream of Cecil Rhodes, the most famous of South African Empire builders.

What is South Africa ?

What is meant by South Africa ? In its widest sense it means all-Africa south of the Zambezi, all-British save for the strip of Portuguese Mozambique on the east and the big rectangle of Portuguese Angola on the northwest. The Union of South Africa forms the greater part of it ; it includes the Cape Province, Natal, the Orange Free State, and the Transvaal ; South-west Africa is governed by it under a mandate from the League of Nations, and Basutoland, Swaziland and Bechuanaland are protectorates. But to the north of all these lie Southern Rhodesia, and (north of the Zambezi)

South African Railways.

CAPE TOWN AND TABLE MOUNTAIN

Cape Town is the sea gate to the Union of South Africa and is the capital of Cape Province. Here we have a panoramic view of the city from the sea, with Adderley Pier in the foreground. Behind the busy and most important town Table Mountain towers, its top often enshrouded in the mists that are called the " Tablecloth." Table Mountain is upwards of 3,000 feet in height.

Will F. Taylor.

CAPE TOWN'S SHOPPING CENTRE

Adderley Street is the chief shopping centre of Cape Town, and the photograph above was taken on a busy Saturday morning. This fine city has its cathedral, university, Government House and Houses of Parliament, and is the scene of the first white settlement in South Africa. It has splendid docks and its position at the foot of the vast continent gives it a delightful climate, with bright blue skies for months at a stretch.

Northern Rhodesia and Nyasaland Protectorate—all of which must be reckoned as belonging to British South Africa, making a vast territory as big as British India, and about half the size of Australia or one-third the size of Canada.

The Native Africans.

This great land has five times as many native Africans as white people. These natives are members of the great Bantu race of negroes. Large numbers of them live in their kraals or

Will F. Taylor.

SOME NATIVE WOMEN AT HOME

The Kaffir woman in the foreground of this picture is preparing on her flat stone some corn for cookery purposes.   In South Africa we can find five times as many native people as there are whites.   Most of the Kaffirs live in kraals or villages, growing maize and other foodstuffs crops and tending their cattle.   In Africa maize goes by the name of " mealies."

villages, growing maize and other crops, or keeping cattle.   In the old days they fought, tribe against tribe ; raids were common, and life was held cheaply by the great black kings who swept as conquerors over wide areas. To-day, far from civilisation, these natives live in peace and lead healthy, free lives in the open air.   But in the

towns the Africans too often drift into bad habits, and live in what we should call slum conditions, learning only the evils and neglecting the good things of European civilisation.

How the Natives Live.

The natives do not roam about the country as they did before the rule of

AN HOTEL FOR THE TRAVELLER

Will F. Taylor.

You would consider it very strange to have to live in this curiously-shaped kraal, but it is thoroughly well-suited to the climate of the country by whose people it was erected. It is a grass-covered hut provided by a chief in Basutoland as a rest-house for any wandering tribesmen who happen to be visiting the village.

South African Railways.

Externally, the thatched kraals are so different from other types of dwelling as to be most fascinating to our Western eyes. The interiors, however, are even more intriguing, and we are here shown the inside of one of the Zulu type of huts. Notice the orderly assembly of utensils.

the white men; many live in prosperous, independent countries under British protection—like Basutoland and Swaziland. Others in South Africa are gathered into "native reserves," much as the Indian tribes of Canada and the United States have been settled on the "Indian reserves." Here they own their own little farms and live happy and contented. Other Africans live among white folks, but keep to their own quarters. They are in great demand as labourers on the farms, and in the gold and diamond mines; they are employed as domestic servants in town and country. But always in the towns they live in parts set aside for them, where they have their own churches, schools and colleges. If they travel by train they must ride in the carriages that are specially reserved for them. Many are well educated and speak English quite well: large numbers, indeed, speak no other language nowadays. Perhaps the finest of them all are the Zulus, some of whom you are sure to see when we visit Natal.

In Natal, too, you will be surprised to find large numbers of East Indians, and will wonder what these Asiatic people are doing in South Africa. They come there to work on the sugar and tea plantations, bringing their families and their own civilisation with them —even their own merchants and their own entertainers!

The Build of South Africa.

What is the country itself like? The map tells us that most of South Africa is a series of great tablelands, whose average height above sea level is from 3,000 feet to 4,000 feet. This fact is very important, for it means that South Africa is not so hot as it would be if it were lower, and is one of the reasons

Topical Press.

THE SNAKE PARK AT PORT ELIZABETH

The important harbour of Port Elizabeth is on Algoa Bay, rather more than 650 miles from Cape Town. Round about is the country where the ostrich breeding industry has been developed, and the town possesses a special feather market. It has also a snake park in which are exhibited fine specimens of the snakes to be found in South Africa, and we see in the above photograph one of the attendants with his charges.

South African Railways.

BUILT IN THE DUTCH STYLE

This illustration depicts the Homestead of Groot Constantia, the Government Wine Farm that was first established by Dutch settlers in the long-ago.   In many of the mountain valleys of South Africa, notably the district lying behind Table Mountain, are extensive vineyards, from the produce of which excellent wine is manufactured.   There are also orange groves, whilst apricots, peaches, pears and other fruits are grown, very largely for export to the Motherland.

why South Africa has the sunniest climate in all the world. Wherever you enter it from the sea, South Africa rises steeply and suddenly a little way from the coast. If you leave the sea at the shore of the Cape Province, you climb up a giant " step " to the plateau of the Little Karroo ; cross this plateau and climb another " step," and you are on a still higher table-land called the Great Karroo ; go farther north still and up another " step " and you reach the High Veld — the rich grass-land country of the Orange Free State and the Transvaal.

The Great Rivers.

The South African plateaus are crossed by three great rivers : the *Zambezi*, which divides Northern from Southern Rhodesia ; the *Limpopo*, whose monster bend forms the northern boundary of the Transvaal ; and the *Orange*, whose tributary, the *Vaal*, divides the Orange Free State from the Transvaal. All three of them have falls and rapids where they cut through the table-land edges ; on the Zambezi are the famous Victoria Falls, discovered by Livingstone in 1855 ; and on the Orange are the high Oughgrabies Falls. The Orange flows west down to the sea through dry and desert country and has no port at its mouth ; but the Zambezi and Limpopo flow east and down to hot, wet shorelands on the edge of the Indian Ocean.

South African Railways.

A map of South African railways is an astonishing thing If we take the great main Cape-Cairo route as a dividing line, we see to the east of it a network of railways serving busy towns, prosperous farms and rich mining areas ; but to the west of it there are very few towns and hardly any railways at all. The reason is a simple one. The eastern part of South Africa

BOTH GOLD AND PRECIOUS STONES

If you were being taken as a visitor over the diamond mines at Kimberley, you would come to a workplace such as the one illustrated above. Here you would see highly-skilled men sorting over the gravel in their search for diamonds. Years ago prospectors dug in the sand with rough spades and found a fortune in diamonds ; now heavy and expensive machinery is in use.

Johannesburg sprang like magic out of a wilderness directly gold was discovered, and has been growing ever since. In the scene above you note the underground workings of the Crown Mines. In many of these mines, shafts up to 7,000 feet in depth lead down to the gold-bearing reef.

IN A VALLEY OF DIAMONDS

South African Railways.

Not far from Pretoria, in the Transvaal, is the Premier Diamond Mine and our picture affords a splendid view of the marvellous workings. It seems wonderful that man should burrow after precious stones so much as completely to change the surface of the earth over a wide tract. The famous mine above is the one which yielded the Great Cullinan diamond, one of the largest ever discovered. It actually weighed 1¾ lbs. and was presented to King Edward VII. by the Government of the Transvaal.

is not only sunny, but it has plenty of rain brought by the onshore wet winds from the Indian Ocean; while the western part becomes drier and drier the farther west you go, until you come to real hot desert—the Kalahari, "land of the Great Thirst," where only a few Hottentots and bushmen can find a living. The western half is no home for human beings; the eastern half is rich in all things that make human life happy and prosperous.

Vines and Fruits.

The region at the back of Cape Town is a land of vineyards and fruit farms, yielding wine, grapes, raisins, oranges and other fruits that adorn our shop windows when such fruits are not in season in the northern hemisphere. For South Africa is on the other side of the world and has seasons opposite to ours. This fruit-growing business is much like those of the Mediterranean lands and of California; for this part of the Cape Province has rain chiefly in winter, and the long, dry sunny summers that favour fruit-growing if only enough water can be supplied.

A great contrast to these South African fruit-lands are those of Natal, where the climate is hotter, and where rain is much more abundant and spread more evenly over the year. In Natal grow pineapples and bananas, as well as tea, coffee, sugar-cane and tobacco—just as they do in the hot wet coast-lands of Queensland.

The Veld.

Farther away from the sea are great stretches of natural grass-land, known generally as the Veld, and in many ways like the grass-lands of Australia or the Argentine. Millions of sheep are raised on these splendid pastures, and wool is one of South Africa's chief exports as a result. In the drier grasslands such as are found on the

Topical Press.

A SCENE IN THE "CITY OF GOLD"

Johannesburg is a veritable "city of gold," for near it is the richest goldfield on the globe—the Witwatersrand ("white waters ridge"); or, as it is generally called, the "Rand." Above we see Eloff Street, Johannesburg. Thirty years ago this city occupied nine square miles. To-day it has an area of about ninety square miles and nearly 1,000 miles of streets and roads.

JOHANNESBURG AS SEEN FROM THE AIR

Photo Press.

"Jo'burg," as it is often called, is built on a rectangular plan, with the streets running at right angles to one another, so forming "blocks," like those of modern American cities. The main thoroughfare above is Commissioner Street West, and you can see in the distance the enormous heaps of waste material produced from the gold-mines. It is almost 1,000 miles from Cape Town to Johannesburg, and this city of the Rand contains a quarter of a million people, more than half of them negroes.

Karroos, goats and ostriches are reared; but since ostrich feathers went out of fashion, fewer ostriches are kept. The richer and wetter grass-lands of the Transvaal and the south-east are fine cattle country, for cattle need much more water than sheep, which flourish best on the richer parts of the Great Karroo. In the cattle-lands dairy-farming is a very profitable business.

Riches of the Mines.

But rich as South Africa is, in fruits and grain, in sheep and cattle, we think of it first and foremost as the land of gold and diamonds; for its fortunes were largely built on these two valuable minerals, and gold and diamonds are still very important among its products to-day.

Johannesburg is the "city of gold," for near it is the richest goldfield on the globe—the Witwatersrand ("white waters ridge"), or as it is popularly called, "The Rand." The Rand stands on a high plateau nearly 6,000 feet above sea-level, and the rock in which the gold is found is now got from deep mines by expensive and up-to-date mining machinery, to be treated by scientific methods to make it yield its golden treasure.

Johannesburg of To-day.

Fewer than thirty years ago the total area covered by Johannesburg was but nine square miles; to-day its municipal boundaries enclose an area of about ninety square miles, with nearly a thousand miles of streets and roads.

FROM CAPE TOWN TO VICTORIA FALLS

Will F. Taylor.

THE TUGELA RIVER, IN NATAL

The Tugela River forms the boundary between Natal and Zululand, and is best remembered by the battles fought in its vicinity during the Boer War for the relief of the besieged town of Lady-smith. At its mouth the river is tempestuous, but here we see a placid upper reach with a motor car and passenger being ferried across, a process that takes about twenty minutes.

WE can get a very good idea of what South Africa is like by taking a journey along the great railway backbone of the South African system from Cape Town to Victoria Falls, and at the end of our long journey of 1,640 miles we shall have something to see that makes such a journey more than worth while.

From Cape Town we steam for many hours through a rich fruit-growing region, past towns with beautiful old Dutch houses, and with sparkling streams of water running down the sides of their shady avenues. We are over 100 miles from Cape Town before the train begins to make the steep ascent to the Karroo by many rising bends and tunnels. Up and up we go, but it is not until the morning of the second day of our journey that we are really on the Karroo, rolling across the dry lonely plains, past kopjes that stand out like high islands of steep red stone above the general level. At evening the drab plain becomes almost wonderful—it takes on new colours, the scent of thyme and bush-herbs fills the air. Kaffir fires flicker in the dusk, and noises of cattle come from the distant farm, snug amongst its clump of gums and willows.

The "Valley of Diamonds."

At *De Aar* junction we pass the cross-roads of South Africa, where a long line of railway branches off north-westwards to cross the Orange and link up with the railway system of South-West Africa ; and another runs south-east across the Karroo to the coastal plain and the seaports of East London, Port Alfred and Port Eliza-beth. We continue our journey north, and 470 miles from Cape Town we cross the Orange and at last arrive at *Kimberley*, in the "Valley of Dia-monds," 547 miles from our starting-

A "CASTLE" LINER HOMEWARD BOUND

The animated scene depicted above shows us one of the towering liners of the Union Castle Company lying in Table Bay being loaded with the glorious fruits of South Africa and other cargo. The fussy little tug-boat is coming forward to carry out her special task, and it seems that the enormous vessel is like a hound upon the leash, eager to be off on her homeward-bound trip to the Mother Country.

point, where fortunes were won in a day when the diggings were first opened up, and where a diamond like the famous " Star of Africa," worth £25,000, could be picked up on the banks of the Vaal. Since then many great stones have been found—one, the Porter-Rhodes diamond, discovered near the centre of the Kimberley mine, was valued at £60,000.

Vryburg and Mafeking.

But diamond-digging is not for us. We are to see a little of the mines, but not a great deal, as we continue our run towards *Vryburg*, the capital of Bechuanaland, where we could, if we wished, purchase outfits and hire native guides to take us hunting hartebeest, gemsbok and wildebeest on the dry plains to the west. *Mafeking*, 100 miles farther along the line, reminds us of its famous siege during the Boer War. Not far from the town is the native " Stad," where blacks of the Baralong tribe live under their chiefs ; it has a population to-day of 3,000 natives.

When we arrive at *Palapye* we are fewer than forty miles from Serowe, which is perhaps the biggest native town in the whole of South Africa, and the headquarters of the Ba-mangwato tribe, once ruled by the famous black king, Khama, who died not long ago at the great age of ninety-three.

Bulawayo.

About 1,360 miles from Cape Town we reach the city of *Bulawayo*, which was founded in 1893 on the very spot where the chief kraal of the Matabele had stood until the downfall of the Matabele King, Lobengula. To-day it is the capital of Southern Rhodesia ; the governor lives in Government

Will F. Taylor.

ON AN OSTRICH FARM

Of all the birds in existence in our time the ostrich is the largest.   To the top of its back and not counting its neck, the creature may be 5 feet in height.   In parts of South Africa are large farms devoted to the breeding of flocks of ostriches, whose value lies chiefly in the wonderful plume feathers—though the fact that they are less fashionable than formerly has reduced their worth. The feathers are cut about once in eight months and the bird feels no more pain than you do when trimming your finger nails.

AMONG THE FRUIT FARMS—

The climate of South Africa is well-adapted for the growing of luscious fruit of many kinds and modern ocean-liners are specially equipped with cooling machinery which allows the fruit to be brought safely through tropic seas.   Here we see a sun-browned gang gathering fruit at Orchard Sidings in the Cape Province.

Only a comparatively small proportion of the fruit is exported in a fresh condition, a great deal of it being first sun-dried and then packed for shipment.   In this illustration we are shown fruit in the course of being dried in trays beneath the strong African sun.

'NEATH AFRICA'S AZURE SKIES

Topical Press.

Fruit grows as well in South Africa as it does in California, for both are lands of unfailing sunshine. Here we see the produce of the orchards brought in carts and waggons, placed on a platform at the sidings and then loaded into ventilated railway trucks. The picture was snapped at De Doorns, in Cape Province, and, in the same neighbourhood, large crops of tobacco are raised.

Topical Press.

Many of those luscious, gaily-coloured pears which adorn the windows of our shops at a time of year when we have no such fruit that is home-grown, come from South Africa. Here we see happy natured " coloured " women handling these pears in a packing-shed at Orchard Sidings in Cape Province. The wooden corners of the boxes project upwards for the support of the box above.

243

House, which is connected with Bula-wayo itself by a great avenue nearly two miles long. Like most South African towns, Bulawayo is built on the rectangular plan that is usual in very modern cities in the southern hemisphere. A great bronze statue of Cecil Rhodes reminds all who come that way of the man who developed the vast territories called after him—"Rhodesia."

The Victoria Falls.

Visitors make a point of visiting the Matoppo Hills, to the south of Bulawayo, to see the last resting-place of Cecil Rhodes, at the top of a rounded granite hill, from whose summit the surrounding scenery is so wonderful that it is known as "The World's View."

From Bulawayo the main line strikes north-west, by way of the Wankie coal-fields to Victoria Falls Station, which is about a mile from the famous Falls, and not far from the Victoria Falls Hotel, which we can make our centre for the trips to the chief points of interest.

The Victoria Falls are even more astonishing than Niagara. The Zambezi River, here closely approaching a mile in width, plunges bodily into a narrow chasm 400 feet deep, to rush madly through a narrow zig-zag gorge that straightens out eventually; and after forty-five miles of pent-up energy in this long cleft, the Zambezi recovers its normal width and its stately progress to the sea.

The Smoke that Sounds.

David Livingstone discovered these famous Falls in November, 1855. In his account of this discovery he tells how he saw in the distance five tall columns of vapour, white below and dark above, as if vast areas of grass were on fire, and thus accounts for the native name given to the Falls by his followers—Mose-oa-Tunya, "the smoke that sounds." He describes his canoe journey to the island, which hangs perilously over the lips of the Falls (now called after him "Livingstone Island"). "Creeping with awe to the verge," he says, "I peered into a large rent which had been made from bank to bank of the broad Zambezi. . . . On looking down into the fissure on the right of the island, one sees nothing but a dense white cloud, which at the time we visited it, had two bright rainbows in it. From this cloud rushed up a great jet of vapour exactly like steam, which condensing, came back in a constant shower, which soon wetted us to the skin. This shower falls chiefly on the opposite side of the fissure, and a few yards from the lip there stands a straight hedge of evergreen trees, whose leaves are always wet."

The Rain Forest.

This "hedge" is the dense Rain Forest fringing the shore opposite the southern lips of the Falls, and divided by the chasm known as the Boiling Pot, through which the imprisoned Zambezi makes its escape from the Palm Grove opposite the south-eastern rim of the Falls. The railway from Cape Town skirts the edge of the Rain Forest, crossing the gorge at a point about 200 yards below the Boiling Pot in one magnificent arched span of 500 feet, at a height of 400 feet above low-water level. Trains cross this bridge at only about five miles an hour, and when the river is high, in the month of April, the spray from the Falls washes the carriage windows. You can cross this bridge on foot, if you pay the usual toll of 1s. "return." You may even descend by iron ladders fixed in the side of the gorge to the left of the bridge, into the gorge itself and view at close quarters the terrifying rush of waters.

The Rain Forest is a tangle of great trees linked by festoons of creeping vines, amid which fairy rainbows continually dance in the spray. Sometimes you may see a troop of baboons busy among the greenery, and if you hunt among the tree roots and the stones

THE NIAGARA FALLS OF AFRICA

H. J. Shepstone.

The Victoria Falls are even more astonishing than those of Niagara. They are to be found in Southern Rhodesia and were first discovered by David Livingstone, whose black followers called them Mose-oa-Tunya, which means "the smoke that sounds." We see above the Devil's Cataract of the Falls and the flying spray enables us fully to understand the native name. The Falls are formed by the Zambezi River, at this point closely approaching a mile in width.

you will find hundreds of *crabs* of all sorts, sizes and colours—land crabs, of course.

The most beautiful of the cataracts into which the Falls are divided are the Rainbow Falls, which can be best viewed from Danger Point; but the most awe-inspiring are the Main Falls, by the side of Livingstone Island.

Victoria Falls and Niagara.

A comparison between the Victoria Falls and Niagara is very startling—the Victoria Falls are about 400 feet high, while Niagara at its highest is only about 167; and Victoria Falls discharge 100 million gallons of water a minute, while Niagara discharges about 84 millions. For a long time there has been talk of harnessing the Victoria Falls to power-stations, and of sending electrical power by transmission lines to the great gold-fields of the south, just as the Canadians and Americans have harnessed Niagara. But up to the present the Victoria Falls remain free.

From Livingstone we could, if we chose, continue the journey by rail to Broken Hill, a rich lead and zinc-mining district, and a good starting-place for a hunting trip; but one has to remember that animals cannot be used for transport there because it is partly in the "fly" belt, where the deadly tsetse fly brings slow death to horses, oxen and other animals. From Broken Hill we could go by way of Elizabeth-ville, in the province of Katanga (Belgian Congo) and Kambove, both in a rich copper-mining region, to Bukama on the Upper Congo, and on to a river port on the Kasai River, whence in the best time of the year we could travel by air, if we liked, by Belgian hydro-plane service to Kinshasa, the capital of Belgian Congo, on the mighty Congo itself.

Rhodesia.

But we think better of it, for there are very interesting things for us to see in Southern Rhodesia, which we missed on our trip through it to the Falls. So we take train back to Bulawayo,

South African Railways.

A STATUE OF CECIL RHODES

This fine bronze statue of Cecil Rhodes stands in Main Street, Bulawayo, and reminds us that not only Rhodesia, but British South Africa as a whole, owes much of its development to this great Empire Builder. Bulawayo is the business capital of Southern Rhodesia, and the stones upon which this statue rests were brought specially from the Matoppo Hills, where Rhodes was buried.

A. J. Shipley.

A CITY OF THE ANTS

Even in England one may find quite large ant-hills, but these homes of the intelligent creatures are completely dwarfed by the ones to be found in Africa. Here, for example, we see natives of Rhodesia breaking up and removing a giant hill that has been reared above an ant-city.

changing into another for Gwelo and Fort Victoria, twelve miles from which are the remarkable ruins of Great Zimbabwe, about which there has been more argument than about the Pyramids.

Nobody really knows who built this city stronghold, although all sorts of stories have been told to explain it. Its origin is hidden in the mists of the past, but it is evidently the work of a forgotten people who knew that gold was to be got in large quantities in the neighbourhood, for abundant traces of their workings have been discovered. For a long time it was thought that this was the city whence the Queen of Sheba procured gold to present to King Solomon when she paid him the State visit recorded in the Old Testament,

but this has been proved to be only a romantic tale.

Zimbabwe.

Zimbabwe ruins lie in three great groups, which all at one time probably formed parts of a well-populated city, of which the so-called citadel formed the central point. The Zimbabwe people had wonderful systems of irrigation for their fields, carrying water for hundreds of miles along the hillsides. The stones of which the temples, forts, walls and palaces are built are set in place without mortar. One of the strangest buildings is a mysterious conical tower in front of the court of the temple. Yet the people who inhabit the region to-day are the simple Makalanga tribesmen— blacks whose best efforts at architecture are their little huts of wattle-and-daub.

Bushman Paintings.

Great Zimbabwe, once a king's capital, a great trading centre, with its fortress and temple, its gold-mines, craftsmen, builders and skilful farmers, is now nothing more than heaps of ruins for learned men to squabble over while the Makalanga squat at their hut doors and wonder in their simple minds what all the fuss is about.

If we explore the Matoppo Hills carefully, we shall find things far older than Zimbabwe that are the works of men. On the rocks are strange paintings in colour done by the prehistoric bushmen—hunter-artists who lived there long ages ago. More than one such rock painting shows the Victoria Falls as five streams of white water falling over red cliffs, with a cloud of white vapour rising high above all.

Did the race of men who built Zimbabwe come from far-away Arabia ? No one can say, but the Arabs have always been wonderful traveller-traders.

Southern Rhodesia Publicity Bureau.

AN AFRICAN MYSTERY—

(1) In Southern Rhodesia are to be found the remarkable ruins of Great Zimbabwe, about which there has been more argument than about the Pyramids. Here are the conical tower, platform and sacred enclosure of the Temple.

Southern Rhodesia Publicity Bureau.

WHICH PUZZLES EVERYONE

(2) And in this photograph we see the outer parallel passage of the Temple. The Zimbabwe ruins indicate that at some remote period there existed hereabouts a well-populated city. These unknown people built stone structures without mortar.

NATAL AND THE ZULUS

THE VALLEY OF A THOUSAND HILLS

South African Railways.

Natal is, generally speaking, a country of high hills. It rises in monster steps or terraces from the sea ; and, in between these mountain ranges, are deep and interesting valleys. Here, for example, is the Valley of a Thousand Hills. Though the climate at lofty points is excellent, the sheltered valleys are tropical. The views in the highlands of Natal are among the wonders of the world.

IT was Vasco da Gama who gave Natal its name. When, in 1497, he " doubled " the Cape and began feeling his way carefully along the shores of South Africa, he came on Christmas Day to a dim coast-line which he called in honour of the day the " Land of Natal."

To-day Natal is one of the most prosperous members of the Union of South Africa. She is different from all the rest. The long slope from the high ridges of the mighty Drakensberg down to the Indian Ocean looks towards the sea and the warm trade-winds which bring abundant rains to all the province. Natal is warmer and wetter than the rest of the Union ; the land rises from the coast in three wide terraces or belts, each of which offers its own

special advantages to farmers and planters.

The Terraces.

Nearest the sea is the subtropical belt, moist and warm, where planters grow sugar-cane and tea, maize and tobacco, subtropical fruits like bananas and pineapples, mangoes and oranges, as well as cotton, arrowroot, spices and ground nuts. The workers on the plantations, especially those growing tea and sugar, are not African negroes, but Asiatics who have come from India, bringing with them their families, their priests, their shops and their amusements. You can see them at work in the green cane, the bright dresses of the women giving gay spots of colour here and there ; you can hear the beat of their drums at night, and the thin pipe of the Hindu flute ; you may come upon a small Mohammedan mosque or perhaps a white plaster Jain temple in the heart of the sugar-cane country ; and you meet in your walk home in the cool of the evening sturdy Jats, tall Sikhs, slender Hindus, and quiet Tamils—all of different religions but all from India and working in Natal sugar-cane plantations.

The Higher Belts.

Beyond the coastal belt there is another and higher terrace where maize, wheat, millet, Kaffir corn and other grains are grown, and where cattle, sheep and horses are reared. It is chiefly in this " midland " belt that the wattle grows, whose bark is of great value in tanning, and is used not only to make South African leather, but also in the tanneries of other countries.

Up in the Drakensberg.

Above this belt rises the third—the " upland " belt, which is cooler than the others because it is much higher above sea-level. This is a land of cattle and sheep, of wheat and barley, of potatoes and garden vegetables.

Behind all three belts rise the slopes of the Drakensberg Mountains, a giant rampart 600 miles long, separating Basutoland from Natal. The highest peaks are Giant's Castle (12,000 feet) and Mont aux Sources (10,600 feet). You can go up to these grim

Topical Press.

THE RICKSHAW " BOY "

A favourite form of transport in Natal is the rickshaw, which may be said to take the place of taxi-cabs. These vehicles are drawn by tall, powerful Zulus picturesquely garbed and wearing strange headgear. Many of these rickshaw " boys " are upwards of 6 feet in height, and can pull their loaded carriages at a rapid pace mile after mile without tiring. Owing to the nature of their work, however, these men are said to be short-lived.

IN THE DRAKENSBERG MOUNTAINS

The beautiful and awe-inspiring Drakensberg Mountains form a giant rampart 600 miles in length, and divide Basutoland from Natal.   In few parts of the world can one see wild nature to greater advantage and the climate at the heights is distinctly cold.

Nearly 100 years ago Sir Benjamin D'Urban occupied the present capital of Natal for the British and after him the city of Durban took its name.   It is a splendid and thoroughly up-to-date town and above we see one of the chief squares, with the Post Office, City Hall, and Gardens.   It is nearly 7,000 miles from England to Durban by sea.

S 2

heights from the coast at Durban, taking the train to Bergville, where you leave the railway for a mountain hotel near the deep gorge of the Tugela River.

Very early in the morning you start out with the guide, breakfast at "Breakfast Rock" before 8 a.m., and go up and up through woods of wild elder and tree-ferns to the magic colour of the base rocks of Mont aux Sources in the sunlight. It is cold up there, especially to those who have come from the lazy warm lands by the sea ; but the view is one of the world's wonders.

There is a famous pass in the Drakensberg at the head of the Goodoo Gorge, over which the dignified Basuto farmers stalk beside their shaggy ponies loaded with bags of grain or rough bales of wool from their farms in the valleys of Basutoland to sell in Natal. There are places, too, where you can see the rock paintings of the first people who lived among these mountains—the Bushmen, who dwelt in this part of Africa long before the advance southwards of bigger, stronger and more intelligent people from the north.

The natives who lived in Natal when first the Dutch and then the British began to make their homes in the country were the Zulus, who live to-day mainly in their own country of Zululand, ruled by their chiefs under the supervision of the British.

A Race of Warriors.

The Zulus are a splendid race of Africans, tall and well-built, living in their neat huts of beehive shape in their kraals or villages, sometimes on the hilltops, sometimes on the slopes just above the bottom of a valley. Their homes are marvellously constructed of pliant twigs and poles bent over and plaited with smaller ones, and then covered with long grass thatch. The furniture is of the simplest—a few mats, vessels for cooking and storing food, a kaross (skin) or two, and that

is all. Around the kraal are the mealie patches in which maize is cultivated ; a cattle enclosure is close by, for the Zulus rear many cattle.

When the white men first made treaties with the Zulus, the terrible Chaka was lord of the land ; he was slain by his brother Dingaan, another powerful Zulu king whose *impis* (regiments) "ate up" all the smaller peoples who dared to resist him. Cetewayo, a later king, fought the Zulu War with the British, but was defeated after a brave struggle, and Zululand was taken over at last in 1897 by Britain.

In the towns, especially in Durban, you will see Zulus most wonderfully decorated with ostrich feathers or horns on their heads and ornaments and bangles on their arms, drawing the rickshaws that are commonly used by people just as we use taxicabs in London.

The Zulu of To-day.

It is only in remote Zululand that you will see Zulus as they were when Chaka, "the great elephant whose tread shakes the earth," ruled with a rod of iron ; and that only on special occasions—tall warriors with skin karosses about them, white tails of gnus at their knee, with hide shield and assegais. To-day the Zulus are peaceful farmers growing mealies, Kaffir corn from which their favourite drink, *tshwala*, is made, pumpkins, beans and sweet potatoes. Cattle, sheep and goats are looked after by the boys. Gardening near the kraal is done chiefly by the women and girls. Men set up the framework of the huts, but women always do the grass-thatching. The real power in the Zulu kraal is the witch doctor, although he is prohibited by law, for the Zulus are very superstitious, and believe in a multitude of "spirits," most of which are entirely unpleasant, but all of which are easily persuaded by the witch doctor and his powerful "charms"! Some of these

CONSULTING THE WITCH DOCTOR

Photochrom.

This photo was taken near Pietermaritzburg and shows a Zulu warrior in his full fighting equipment.

Will F. Taylor.

Here is another type of African native. He is a member of the Ba-ila tribe, to be found in Northern Rhodesia.

South African Railways.

The witch doctor, seen performing his mysterious rites in the above illustration, is a real power in any Zulu kraal. Zulus are a very superstitious people and believe most firmly in the powerful " charms " of their witch doctors. These weird magicians are able to cope with almost all the multitude of spirits that exist in the minds of these simple natives.

P.C. KAFFIR ON DUTY

The sturdy fellow seen above, heavily armed, but with feet innocent of boots or shoes, is a Kaffir constable such as you might meet at Durban, in Natal. As a policeman he is both trustworthy and dependable.

spirit of Chaka, "that great one" who wanders at night with his ghostly *indunas* and *impis* over the old battlefields when it is not well for men to be abroad, not even a strong young man who has but newly won his *isicoco* (head ring).

There are many more than a quarter of a million people living in Zululand and the country is well watered and fertile. The famous battles of Rorke's Drift and Isandhlwana were fought against the Zulus in 1879 and also that of Ulundi.

spirits, they say, live in the forest, some in the bush, some even in the water.

At Rorke's Drift.

Some can bring the rain, if only the witch doctor can be bribed to ask them ; some kill cattle in strange ways, unless the witch doctor prevents it, which costs money ! But there is one spirit, say the Zulus, that no witch doctor can persuade, and that is the

IN A NATIVE BEAUTY PARLOUR

The vanity of Kaffir women is expended mostly upon the arrangement of their hair and the display of beads and ornaments. Here we see the "beauty parlour" of one of the kraals, with hair-dressing in progress.

The Story
of the
World and
its Peoples

The Empire
on which
The Sun
Never Sets

A PATIENT NATIVE FISHERMAN

Francis Birtles.

" Black Fellows," as some of the aboriginals or native Australians are called, are by no means all short, those in the north being fine, upstanding men, 6 feet in height, or more. Here is one of these men, patiently fishing, and seeming most intent upon the task in hand. Some States of Australia give official protection to the aboriginal population and provide mission stations for the benefit of these people—who were the first owners of the " Island Continent."

THE ISLAND CONTINENT

MEN dreamt of a great southern continent for 2,000 years before they had enough definite knowledge of it to set down in scattered bits upon the maps of the world of the fifteenth and sixteenth centuries.

Arabs and Malays knew of it, and doubtless gave news of it to traders from the west, but the first definite record of it appears to have been set down on an old map of 1489, now in the British Museum. It is just an odd shoulder of land appearing mysteriously out of the map-space and vanishing again, proving that the Portuguese makers of the map must have had fairly accurate knowledge of

part of it, at any rate. On a later map of 1536 there is no doubt about it ; for part of the northern coast, with capes and bays much as they are to-day, appears there, and is called Java la Grande.

Early Explorers.

The Spaniards came that way in 1605 ; one sailed through the Straits that to this day bear his name— Torres Straits—between Australia and New Guinea. The Dutch, too, were there in the same year, and gave the great southland much more careful attention, for they already possessed rich islands in the East Indies, where a Dutch governor, Pieter Carpenter, ruled for the prosperous Dutch East Indian Company. It was in his honour that the Dutch explorers of the northern shores of Australia named the Gulf of Carpentaria. You find several other Dutch names along its shores. By 1616 they had worked their way along the arid western shores to the better country that is now the south-western corner of Western Australia. But more important still were the voyages of Abel Janz Tasman, a Dutch navigator, who charted most of the south coast, named the great new continent " New Holland," and found what he called Van Diemen's Land in honour of his patron, Antony van Diemen, Governor of the Dutch Indies. In later years this land was renamed Tasmania in memory of its discoverer.

The Dutch made attempts to colonise Northern Australia, but failed. All that remains of their efforts are the Dutch names on the map, and the descendants of the water buffalo, which the Dutch introduced from Java and which now roam in large herds and are shot by hunters for their hides. The fact is that Spaniards and Dutch saw the most uninviting coast-lands of the island continent—either mangrove swamp backed by tropical forests in the north, or dry and thirsty country in the west—except for Tasmania, which was far away.

Captain Cook.

It was left for an Englishman to discover, explore and chart the East Coast of Australia, and to see the best

IN THE GRAMPIANS OF VICTORIA

Victoria is the State in the south-eastern portion of the Australian continent. In the western portion of this State are the Grampian Mountains, rugged and lofty, with the peak of Mount William rising to 4,500 feet. The extraordinary rock formation shown in this photograph is to be seen in the Grampians and this particular portion is known as " The Silent Street."

AUSTRALIAN NATIVES WITH THEIR BOOMERANGS   *Will F. Taylor.*

Here is another group of aboriginal tribesmen of Australia. They are descended from hunters and warriors and their boomerangs are illustrated. These weapons are usually about 2 feet 6 inches in length, and those which are used in hunting are so shaped that they return to the thrower if they should miss their mark. It is believed that there are nearly 100,000 aboriginals in Australia, but the people lead such vagrant gipsy lives that they cannot easily be counted.

part of it. This man was Captain James Cook, the greatest navigator-explorer the world has ever seen, who sailed the whole length of Eastern Australia in 1770, and saw beautiful and fertile country, where Europeans could make new homes for themselves. The names of capes and bays, reefs and rivers along this coast record imperishably the story of Cook's eventful voyage. The lands behind these shores are to-day the most densely populated parts of the Island Continent, where people of British race have founded a new nation and a great Commonwealth beyond the seas, which in days to come will probably outstrip the little Motherland in wealth and population.

Australia is twenty-five times the size of the British Isles, and nearly as big as the whole of Europe. At present it has fewer people than Greater London, but there is room for millions more.

A Land of Many Climates.

So great a land has many climates. Nearly half of Australia is tropical, and the rest lies in warm, temperate regions. The northern parts, where there are hot, wet forests and mangrove swamp, are as near the Equator as Ceylon and Southern India ; the southern parts lie in the same latitudes as the Cape Province of South Africa and have much the same kind of climate. On the Queensland coast the climate is wet and hot enough for planters to grow sugar-cane, bananas, cotton and rubber, and to cultivate coco-nut palms in great groves facing the sea ; for this is the region where the South-east Trades sing their eternal song and bring moisture from the wide Pacific. In many of the southern parts the climate is not unlike that of the Mediterranean with its long, hot dry summers and its mild, wet winters—ideal country for the cultivation of oranges, grapes, olives, coco-nuts and other fruits, or for growing grain. It is fortunate that in these regions artesian wells can be sunk to fetch up water from great depths; water from these wells or from large reservoirs among the hills can be led to fields and orchards in myriads of channels during the dry weather.

Grassland and Forest.

Other parts of Australia are great natural grass-lands, especially in the interior of New South Wales and Queensland, where sheep are reared in enormous numbers and where cattle can be fed on the moister lands.

Australia has forests, too, of splendid timber and rich deposits of coal and metal ore; so that Australians who speak in praise of their homeland, as all real Australians do, make no vain boast when they say they have the finest climate in the world and one of the richest countries on the globe in which to live.

The Australians.

But although Australia is a land of splendid opportunities for those who love a free life in the open air, we shall make a great mistake if we suppose that most Australians live active lives on the sheep stations and cattle stations, the farms and the orchards, and the plantations. The plain truth is that at present by far the greater number of Australians live in the large towns—they are townsmen and city folk, and get their living much as people of that kind do throughout the civilised world, except perhaps that the splendid Australian climate tempts them to live a freer and more enjoyable life in

A WEST AUSTRALIAN GOLD MINE

In the dry country, some 300 or 400 miles from Perth in Western Australia, is Kalgoorlie, one of the great gold mining centres. Here we have a view of the Golden Mile Mine. Australia supplies the world with one-sixth of its output of gold and Western Australia is the greatest gold-producing State of the Commonwealth.

"WHERE ALL ARE SLAVES TO GOLD"

G.P.A.

This picture gives you a clear idea of the old-time gold prospector, with his humble tools and " pan " for washing through the gravel in search of the precious metal. It was one man who discovered in a flash the concealed natural wealth of Western Australia.

Contrast the upper scene with the lower one. In the latter is shown a gold dredge at work in the Araluen Valley, New South Wales. All the important mines are equipped with elaborate and costly machinery for getting and crushing the gold-bearing reef and for extracting the gold.

the open air. Sydney and Melbourne alone contain nearly one-third of the total population of the Australian Commonwealth.

A famous Australian writer says : "Probably not two out of every 200 Australians have ever seen a wild kangaroo, although there are thousands of them in the distant 'bush.' Many Australians have never set eyes on a flock of sheep or a herd of cattle larger than one which might be seen within twenty miles of London ; yet on some of the large sheep stations out-back, over 100,000 sheep are shorn annually, and herds of 50,000 cattle are not uncommon."

The kind of people Australia needs are those who will make use of the rich farming and stock-breeding lands, which can easily support a hundred millions of people.

The Australian Interior.

There are parts of Australia which can never support many people ; some of them, indeed, will never provide homes for settlers, for they are desert lands, dry and waterless, where not even goats and camels could find a living ; but even among these desert patches there are areas of good pasture with here and there prosperous little townships.

People once believed that the whole of the Australian interior was a great desert—perhaps because of the unfortunate experiences of the early explorers who made their way into the interior at times of great drought. It

ONE OF THE COVES OF SYDNEY HARBOUR

Sydney, with its suburbs, has a population of over a million, and stands on what is perhaps the finest harbour in the world. Large liners can enter the very heart of the city and berth at Circular Quay. The beautiful environs of Sydney, where the business men make their homes, are on lovely coves, such as the one seen above, and on arms of the Harbour. The city is connected with many of the suburbs by ferry-boat.

is a fact, however, that many parts which their discoverers condemned as arid barren lands quite unfit for human habitation are now among the richest and most fertile regions of the Australian continent. Irrigation has brought about this wonderful transformation, by leading water in canals and channels from thousands of deep artesian bores, or from great reservoirs created by building dams across river valleys among the hills where there is generally plenty of rain. One of the most famous of these dams is the great Burrinjuck Dam on the Upper Murrumbidgee in New South Wales.

Conquering Drought.

Irrigation, too, has done much to rob drought of its terrors — the terrible drought that in past years dried up all the springs and made rivers mere chains of muddy waterholes; that withered all green and growing things, and brought the torture of death by thirst to the squatter's sheep, the stockmen's cattle, and even the wild creatures of the bush; the drought that brought misery and ruin to men and to all other living creatures.

Drought is still a thing to be reckoned with, especially in the wheat districts and in the great pastoral lands where lack of rain at the proper season may do untold damage. But modern rail and motor transport can bring food and water to starving flocks and herds, or can carry the animals to other parts where there is still pasture to be found.

Sport and General.

THE NEW SYDNEY HARBOUR BRIDGE

Our illustration shows the new Sydney Harbour Bridge in course of construction. It spans the Harbour between Dawes Point on the southern and Milson's Point on the northern side. The bridge has been the work of a famous firm from Middlesbrough, in Yorkshire, and its main span is 1,650 feet in length and 172 feet above the level of high tide. Across the bridge are four electric railway tracks, a wide road and two footways. More than £5,000,000 have been spent upon the bridge.

AN AUSTRALIAN SHEEP STATION

FATHERS OF THE FLOCKS

Topical Press.

Here we are shown some types of splendid Merino rams, which become fathers of the wool sheep in Australia. About one-fifth of the whole world's supply of wool comes from the Commonwealth and a really large sheep station may cover an area up to 1,000 or 2,000 square miles and muster perhaps 100,000 sheep. In each " paddock " there may be 5,000 of the animals.

IF you want to know what sheep-farming in Australia is *really* like, the only way is to become a " jackeroo," and actually work on one of the big stations. But that is not possible for many of us, although sturdy lads, fond of outdoor life and not afraid of plenty of hard work, might do much worse than go out to Australia as jackeroos or apprentices to a sheep station in order to learn the business in the proper way by starting at the bottom.

The " Run."

Among the things a jackeroo quickly learns is that the big estates on which sheep or cattle are reared in large numbers are always called " stations," and not farms ; the owner (or the manager, if the station belongs to a company, as some do) is always the " boss "; and the men who work for him are "stockmen," and never shepherds or cowmen, although you are quite in order if you speak of them as " hands." The land over which the sheep roam is the " run," which may cover an area

of anything up to 1,000 or 2,000 square *miles* if the station is a big one, and can muster perhaps 100,000 sheep. It is true that nowadays the tendency is for very large stations to be cut up into several small ones, but even then they are far larger than anything of the kind one sees in Britain. A large station will probably be divided into what we should call " fields," but which the jackeroo soon learns to call " paddocks," by long fences, each paddock big enough for about 5,000 sheep. It is the boundary rider's job to keep an eye on these fences and report instantly to the head station (by telephone if possible) any break in them before the sheep have become aware of it.

Shepherds on Horseback.

It is a good thing for a jackeroo if he is a good rider—if not, he soon will be— or he will give up his job ! For on stations like this, a man on foot could never cover the necessary ground in time to be of any use. He must have a mount, and a good one ; and that is one of the reasons why every large sheep station will have some hundreds of horses; and there may also be some thousands of cattle which feed on the moister ground, and provide fresh beef for the many hands, as well as meat and hides for marketing, especially if the station is in Queensland, which is Australia's largest cattle-rearing State.

The station will probably be forty or fifty miles from its next-door neighbour, and very much farther from the railway. Although these distances are smaller now than they used to be, thanks to the almost universal use of motor cars and lorries over the " bush " roads during the greater part of the year, they do mean that a station must be as self-supporting as it can be, and that it must keep fairly large stores of things which it cannot produce or make for itself.

Life at the " Station."

We must remember that a really big station has more people working on it than live in many small English towns, and the needs of its population are pretty considerable. It has large store-rooms full of all sorts of things likely to be wanted, and all arranged so that they can be got at by the store-keepers at a moment's notice. There are foodstuffs —flour by the ton, tinned fruits and bottled fruits, everything, in fact, except meat and such products as can be got on the station. There are clothes, harness, wire for fences, tools, machines, repair outfits, spare parts—in fact,

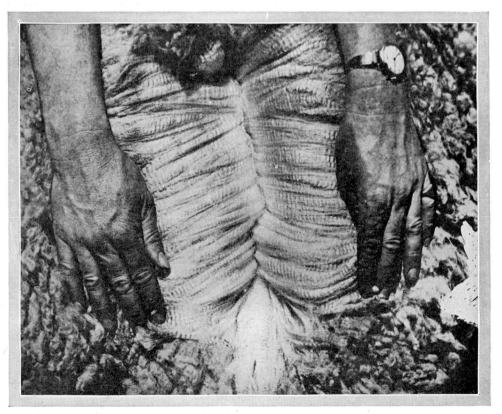

SHOWING THE " CRIMP " IN THE WOOL

Well crimped or frilled wool is crisp, elastic and most satisfactory from the point of view of spinning. Good Merino fleece counts high, and the Australian sheep farmer goes in for the best stock he can obtain. Apart from its great woollen industry, the Commonwealth produces enormous quantities of meat and grain, dairy produce and fruit.

READY FOR THE SHEARING SHED

When the time for shearing approaches the first step is to muster the sheep, as seen in the photograph above. This work is done by the jackeroos, who ride over the " run " on their hardy horses, gathering together the roaming sheep. On a large station there will be jackeroos or riders in considerable numbers, and these men live in " barracks " on the station.

Topical Press.

After the mustering the sheep are gathered into gated pens made of strong hurdles. They pass in a long string from one pen to another, always drawing nearer to the shearing shed. Eventually, first through a narrow lane, they make their way into the building, are grabbed by one of the shearers and made to yield up their woolly coats in an amazingly short space of time.

AMIDST A WEALTH OF WOOL

Topical Press.

Here is an interior view of the shearing shed and it will be seen that the work is done entirely with labour-saving and intricate machinery. In days gone by " swagsmen " moved from station to station in season doing the sheep-shearing by hand, but modern methods have brought about a revolution so that the work now is done with greater speed and far more efficiency.

Topical Press.

To the ordinary person wool is just wool. To a man of experience, however, there are many different qualities and the fleeces have to be carefully sorted and graded. Here is a picture of a showroom in which wool is displayed for the inspection of expert buyers. The number of fibres in the wool denote its value and Australian Merino has the highest " count."

everything down to patent medicines for animals as well as human beings. Many stations have their own libraries, and good ones, too. Nearly all have their own telephone system, which keeps the head station in touch with boundary riders' huts perhaps fifty miles away, as well as with neighbouring stations and the nearest post-office and railway station.

The jackeroo soon discovers that there are many other people working on the station besides the stockmen. There are blacksmiths and carpenters,

saddlers and harness-makers, butchers and bakers, horse-breakers, engineers and builders, clerks and store-keepers. And when shearing time comes the station is invaded by perhaps a couple of hundred extra hands who earn big wages at sheep shearing, moving from station to station as work offers.

Rarely are all these people at the head station at any one time, however ; they are off away in the bush in many base camps which are moved from place to place according to the work that has to be done—mustering the sheep for " dipping " to protect them against parasites, for instance. The fence gang is away somewhere repairing a boundary fence or building a new one. There is always work to be done at many places at the same time on this " run " of between 1,000 and 2,000 square miles.

The Home Buildings.

In what sort of place will the jackeroo and his companions live when they come back from riding ? Up-to-date stations have quite excellent home buildings. They are usually built of timber cut and put together on the station itself. The head station near the centre of the run consists of the owner's house, the " barracks " or building where the jackeroos and unmarried men of the station have their bedrooms, and a big dining-room ; the stores and office ; and the kitchen and servants' quarters. There are, besides all these, many other smaller houses and buildings away from the head station itself.

Water is generally sup-

USING THE WOOL PRESS

When all the sheep have been mustered and sheared the wool must be carefully packed for transport in such a way that it occupies the least possible space—for the steamer charges are calculated not by weight, but by space occupied in the hold. This work is done by means of the wool press, seen above, which packs the produce into the smallest possible compass for baling.

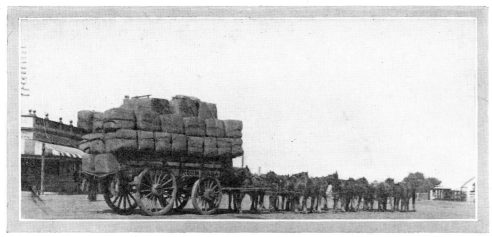

THE WOOL TEAM STARTS ON ITS JOURNEY

Tightly baled and ready for the journey to the nearest railway station or else to the seaport, the wool is now loaded on to a ponderous waggon drawn by perhaps ten or a dozen horses. This waggon and its string of horses is called the " wool team," but the tendency is now more and more to use motor lorries or heavy vehicles propelled by steam.

plied by an artesian bore, going down perhaps 500 feet or even 1,000 feet to bring up pure water from the depths of the earth. A large station will have more than one bore, especially in dry country where sheep would suffer greatly without such an unfailing source of supply. If the water is hot when it comes to the surface—and it sometimes is, especially if the bore is a deep one—it is directed into big cooling tanks, perched on high platforms above the station roofs, from which supplies are led to all points where water is required.

Sports and Pastimes.

A modern station will also have its own electric plant and generating station, not only for lighting, but for driving some of the machinery. Nowadays a great deal of sheep-shearing is done by means of electric shears fixed to a power-shaft by flexible metal tubing, so that shearers can use them at any angle. One man can satisfactorily shear a hundred sheep in an eight-hour day.

It might seem that life on a station whose nearest neighbour is fifty miles off, and post-office and railway farther still, is a dull affair. But in these days of motor cars and wireless such is by no means the case. Unless the bush road is bad because the weather is wet, it is but a short run to the next station, where a party or a match is being held ; and it is not much farther to the railway when there is a brief spell for the jackeroo and his friends to visit the town.

The Way to Success.

In any event, the station itself will probably have tennis courts and other facilities for games ; and there is generally good shooting to be had in the bush or somewhere in the neighbourhood of the station.

On the whole, being a jackeroo is a fine experience for healthy fellows fond of an active life out of doors, and is generally the beginning of a training that finds its reward at least in manly independence, if not in the ownership of a fine station of one's own. The first is what every jackeroo can achieve ; the second, of course, depends also on the amount of money he can command when he wants to start on his own account.

Jackeroos of Australia, ranchers of Canada and veld-riders of Africa can at least all claim to lead a man's life.

THE CITIES OF AUSTRALIA

THE PARLIAMENT HOUSE, CANBERRA

Canberra is the capital of Australia. It stands on its own Federal Capital Territory and has beautiful scenery, including several peaks over 5,000 feet. The process of actual building is being carefully planned and Australia hopes in Canberra to create the most beautiful capital city in the world. Above is the Parliament House, opened by H.R.H. the Duke of York.

PEOPLE who think of Australia only in terms of " settlers," and kangaroos, and " black-fellows " would be astonished to find in the Commonwealth some of the finest cities in the world, where you can buy anything and everything, and where you can live as luxuriously as you could live in London or New York—if only you had the money !

It is hard to realise, but true nevertheless, that nearly a third of all Australia's people live in Sydney and Melbourne, both of which have populations that exceed a million.

Sydney stands on what is perhaps the finest harbour in the world, and large liners can come right up to the very heart of the city and berth at Circular Quay. Its streets are lined with many splendid buildings, some of which, as might be expected, are distinctly American in type.

There are huge " department stores " of the kind common in America, but less common in Britain, where goods of every kind can be bought ; some have over thirty " floors," and employ 4,000 or 5,000 assistants.

Sydney's beautiful suburbs where business men make their homes are on the many arms of its harbour ; one of the most important is Mosman Bay, with its pretty houses embowered in trees overlooking the blue waters. Ferry-boats ply constantly between the suburbs and the city.

Bathing Beaches.

Sydney's bathing beaches are immensely popular, for all Australians, thanks to the delightful climate, are great sportsmen and lovers of the open air, and bathing is the greatest of all summer attractions. Bondi, Manly Beach, Freshwater, Collaroy, Avalon, Palm Beach and other spots are the week-end haunts of thousands. At one bathing beach as many as 10,000 may be in the water at one time !

At Bondi and Manly the joy of bathing is sometimes interrupted by the clang of an alarm bell, and those who do not know what it means are astonished to see the whole 10,000 bathers rush to shore as quickly as possible. The bell is sounded from one of the towers by the watchman on

MARTIN PLACE, SYDNEY, N.S.W.

The streets of Sydney are lined with many splendid buildings, and some of the department stores have over thirty floors, and employ 4,000 or 5,000 assistants. Sydney is the capital of New South Wales. Its harbour extends inland from the sea for upwards of a dozen miles. Sydney has its University. One-third of all Australia's people live in Sydney and Melbourne.

Here is a view of Rushcutters' Bay, Sydney, as seen from the air. The city and its suburbs are grouped round the world-famous Harbour. Not only is the harbour used by the ships of all maritime nations and by men o' war, but it also affords bathing beaches and opportunities for yachting, fishing and other aquatic pastimes. At look-out stations men sound bells to warn the bathers against sharks when necessary.

Adelaide is the capital of South Australia, and we see in the picture above King William Street. The city is beautifully planned at the foot of the Mount Lofty range of hills. It was named after Queen Adelaide and is divided into two parts by the Torrens River. It has a University and also a most important wireless station.

COMMONWEALTH OF AUSTRALIA

Melbourne stands upon the River Yarra, where it enters Hobson Bay, and our illustration shows St. Kilda Road. Melbourne is the capital of Victoria and was the site of the Commonwealth Houses of Parliament before the building of Canberra. It possesses a University and was named after the first Lord Melbourne. The wide straight streets run at right angles to one another.

Here is a view of the Victoria Bridge at Brisbane, the capital of Queensland. The city is built on both sides of the Brisbane River, the sections being connected by the bridge seen above. The University of Queensland is situated at a bend in the river, but this city differs from the other state capitals because it is in a subtropical latitude and its trees and flowers savour more of the hot countries of the world.

WINNING THEIR SPURS

Among the natives of Australia a " corroboree " means usually a dance, but the same term is applied in the Northern Territory to a tribal ceremony known as " Making Young Men." Boys on the threshold of manhood are called upon to face this ordeal, which lasts some time and is made up of several phases. In this picture the Ordeal of the Bull Ants is in progress, the master of the ceremony scattering the fierce insects over the candidates, whose faces are covered.

Photos : Francis Birtles.

Here is a master of the ceremonies with his plumes of Brolga feathers and sword of office. He is sharing the Ordeal by Sun Heat and also keeping watch on the candidates. You will observe that he has a neck rest to support his head so that he can see what is happening.

Francis Birtles.

OUT OF THE STONE AGE

This Australian aboriginal is a warrior of one of the tribes in the Northern Territory. He carries a stone spear and tomahawk and his rank is shown by the number of rings of plaited bamboo on his arm.

Francis Birtles.

WITH HIS " THROWING STICK "

The " Throwing Stick " of this aboriginal is constructed with a lever, which comes into action when the spear is thrown. This lever adds very greatly to the distance to which the spear can be hurled.

the look-out for sharks ! Mighty sea-tigers they are, too, and very cunning. As soon as the danger is passed, the signal is given, and the 10,000 scamper joyously down the sand and into the water again.

Sydney's Giant Bridge.

Sydney's great interest at the moment is her mighty new steel bridge that has been constructed by a famous Middlesbrough firm across the harbour. Its main span is 1,650 feet long ; with its approaches, the bridge is 3,770 feet from terminal pier to terminal pier. It is to carry four electrical railway tracks, a road and two footways across the harbour at a height of 172 feet above high tide level. Although a British company secured this £5,000,000 contract, the steel was all fabricated in Australia, and the granite and cement were local products.

Melbourne on the Yarra, where it enters Hobson Bay, is another splendid State capital, with wide straight streets at right angles to one another, fine shops and public buildings, and beautiful parks on the outskirts of the city. The best-known street is Collins Street, a wide, tree-lined thoroughfare with many handsome buildings. Melbourne has the advantage over Sydney at present of having excellent electric railways.

Adelaide, the capital of South Australia, is most beautifully planned at the foot of the Mount Lofty Range, with its ring of lovely parks and open spaces enclosing its business heart, and its pretty suburbs.

Perth, the Western Australian capital,

SOME INDUSTRIES OF AUSTRALIA (1)

By permission of the Agent General for Queensland.

In the industries of Australia, especially those to do with agriculture, the most up-to-date and scientific methods are brought into use. Here, for example, we see the interior of a butter-making factory in South Queensland, with churns and other appliances operated by the latest machinery. Dairy produce is a most important item in the activities of the Commonwealth.

By permission of the Agent General for Queensland.

This picture gives us a peep at the inside of a cheese factory, situated on the Darling Downs, one of the great farming regions of Queensland. The large appliance in the centre is the pasteuriser, which ensures the complete preservation of the cheese in a fresh and wholesome condition.

By permission of the Agent General for Queensland.

This is a scene such as you might come upon whilst travelling in an agricultural district of Queensland. It shows the drying of arrowroot. The roots of this herb are reduced to a pulp in water. The pulp is then dried, as illustrated above, and so forms a kind of starch which is largely used as a food for delicate and invalid people.

By permission of the Agent General for Queensland.

Here is another farm-like scene from Queensland. It depicts an enormous number of hams and sides of bacon in the curing-room at a bacon factory. Queensland is the largest of the three states on the east of Australia. In addition to its dairy produce, it raises maize, sugar cane, pineapples, bananas and tobacco.

is on the Swan River, twelve miles from its outport of Fremantle.

Brisbane, capital of Queensland, is different from all other State capitals, because it is in subtropical latitudes and is rather warmer; its subtropical trees and flowers, too, give a different aspect to the city. It is twenty miles up the river, on both banks, which are connected by the Victoria Bridge.

The Commonwealth Capital.

Hobart, Tasmania's capital, and the smallest of all, is on the deep estuary of the Derwent, with Mount Wellington behind it. Like Sydney, Hobart can receive large vessels into its very heart. It is a favourite summer resort for Australians because of its cooler climate

None of these fine Australian cities is the capital of Australia. That honour is reserved for *Canberra*, which stands in its own " Federal Capital Territory," whose beautiful scenery includes several peaks over 5,000 feet; and, unlike any other capital in the world, it is in actual process of building according to a carefully-planned scheme. Nothing will be put there that is not in keeping with the plan, for in Canberra, Australia hopes to create the most beautiful capital city in the world. Its streets will radiate from a magnificent Capitol, and from other subnodal points already planned in its austere geometrical layout. The Parliament House was opened by H.R.H. the Duke of York in 1927.

By Trans-Australian Railway.

Australia's capitals are linked by railways which make a fine show on the

By permission of the Agent General for Queensland.

IRRIGATION FOR THE THIRSTY CROPS
In hot countries the absence of moisture in the parched ground is one of the chief difficulties of farmers and cultivators. This trouble is now being more and more overcome by the use of modern scientific appliances and we see here the system adopted in the sub-tropical parts of Queensland for conveying water by artificial means to a field of young tobacco plants.

"MANY A FAIR PEARL—"

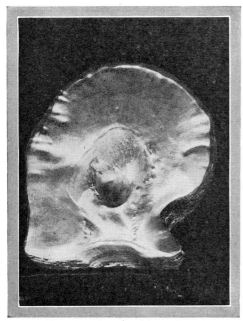

Pearls are found in the shells of oysters and sometimes appear as "blisters" on the inside of the shell, between it and the fish. Such a blister is shown above.

The man here depicted is swiftly opening the shells of oysters in his search for pearls. This photograph was taken in the north-west of Western Australia.

Photographs by permission of the Agent General for Western Australia.

Here is a collection of pearls, the harvest of Australian waters. The chief centres of the pearling industry are in the seas of the tropics. Both Queensland and Western Australia have their pearl beds and there are other " grounds " off Ceylon, South America, China, and elsewhere.

map, but which suffer from the great disadvantage of being constructed on three different gauges, which prevent long " through " journeys from east to west, or *vice versâ*. Australia's crowning achievement was the construction of the Trans-Australian Railway connecting Kalgoorlie in Western Australia with Port Augusta in South Australia, by way of the Nullarbor Plain, so-called because of its wide areas covered here and there with salt bush and bluebush, but absolutely treeless.

The train journey from Fremantle to Brisbane, however, involves the following changes because of the varying gauges :—

	Miles.	Gauge.
Fremantle to Kalgoorlie	387	3 ft. 6 in.
Kalgoorlie to Port Augusta	1051	4 ft. 8½ in.
Port Augusta to Terowie	120	3 ft. 6 in.
Terowie to Albury	814	5 ft. 3 in.
Albury to Wallangarra	893	4 ft. 8½ in.
Wallangarra to Brisbane	223	3 ft. 6 in.
Total	3488	

Another transcontinental line is in process of completion from north to south, following the route of the Overland Telegraph, built in 1872. The section from Port Augusta to Oodnadatta has been long in operation, and has now been extended to Alice Springs, a thriving township in the very heart of Australia ; the northern section from Palmerston on Port Darwin has reached Emungalon, and will soon be completed to Daly Waters.

Aeroplane and Motor Transport.

Aeroplanes are very widely used in the Commonwealth, and several regular air routes are in operation. The great distances and the fine weather make the aeroplane ideal for linking up city with city, and outlying townships with the heart of things. The use of *motor* transport has spread amazingly ; no cattle or sheep station of any size is without its fleet of cars, which are chiefly imported from the United States and Canada.

We see therefore that Australia is a vast Island Continent with a main industry that centres round wool. Second in importance comes farming in its broadest sense, and the statement may be repeated that this great Commonwealth is most willing to welcome young people who will work hard to wrest a living from the land itself.

Francis Birtles.

AN AUSTRALIAN ANT-HILL

A species of ant known as the Termite is found in Australia and forms strange hillocks, such as the one illustrated above. A colony of termites is said to consist of workers ; soldiers, who keep guard ; and a single queen and king who live together in the middle of the nest, waited upon by the workers.

The Story
of the
World and
its Peoples

The Empire
on which
The Sun
Never Sets

By permission of the High Commissioner for New Zealand.

THE WAR DANCE OF THE MAORIS

Present-day Maoris are descendants of the original natives of New Zealand, who were fierce
and warlike when Captain Cook first circumnavigated the Islands. There are now upwards of
60,000 Maoris, some of whom are shown above in kilt-like costume giving an exhibition " haka."
or war dance.

NEW ZEALAND

THE Dominion of New Zealand is often called " the Britain of the South," not only because it is the home of a million and a half people of British race, but also because, like the British Isles, New Zealand consists of an island group on the edge of a great ocean, and largely in the west-wind belt.

Early Explorers.

But New Zealand is not *exactly* at the opposite point of the globe to Britain, as we can easily discover if we look at the latitudes within which it lies. North Island is in similar latitudes to those of middle and Southern Spain, and South (or Middle) Island is in latitudes corresponding to those of Northern Spain and Southern France.

This is important, because it largely explains why the climate of New Zealand is, on the whole, warmer and sunnier than ours.

Again, Britain is on the eastern side of the great ocean ; but New Zealand is on the western side of the Pacific, and is 1,200 miles or so from the nearest continent, instead of being only about 21, as it is the case with Britain and Europe. So we must reject the idea that New Zealand has the same position in the southern hemisphere as Britain has in the northern. But the New Zealanders are indeed " intensely and patriotically British," regarding the Motherland with honour and affection.

Tasman, who had charted much of the southern shores of Australia, discovered and mapped a small part of the great northern peninsula of North Island about the middle of the seventeenth century. One hundred and twenty years later Captain Cook sighted the eastern shores of New Zealand, and conjectured that it must be part of the great southern continent which the geographers of his day believed to exist. He sailed north round the cape which Tasman had named after the daughter of Anthony van Diemen, Governor of the Dutch East Indies, and then voyaged south along the western coast of North Island until he found a wide passage leading east again. This was Cook Strait. Evidently the land he had seen was a large island, and not part of a great southern continent, for he had sailed round it. Cook then circumnavigated South Island (1770) and passed on to explore the eastern shores of Australia. But he had learned enough about New Zealand to astonish people at home with his descriptions of the native people, the plants and the creatures of the new islands far away on the other side of the world.

Cook and the Maoris.

He found the islands inhabited by the fierce and warlike Maoris, who lived in " pahs " or villages surrounded by high, strong palisades. " They are a strong, rawboned, well-made, active people rather above the common size," he writes in his journal ; " they are of a dark brown colour with strong white teeth. Both men and women paint their faces and bodies with red ochre mixed with fish oil. They wear ornaments of stone, bone and spills at their ears, and about their necks, and the men generally wear long white feathers stuck upright in their hair."

To-day about 63,000 of the Maori still live in New Zealand, principally in North Island. They have their own land, their own schools, and their own representatives in the Dominion Parliament. Many are wealthy, progressive and influential citizens of the British Empire.

Splendid Mountain Scenery.

New Zealand is a very beautiful country, and not a little of its fine scenery is due to the fact that the islands are mountainous. South Island has the great mountain backbone of the Southern Alps, whose highest peak, Mount Cook, rises to an altitude of over 12,000 feet. The Maori name for it is Aorangi, the " Cloud Piercer." This mountain backbone, which lies nearer the west coast than the east, is difficult to cross, and it is only in comparatively recent years that a railway has been constructed to link up the prosperous cities of the east coast with those of the west. There was a road which went by way of Arthur's Pass, and whose general direction is followed by the railway which goes through the Otira Gorge in a series of cuttings and tunnels, linking up Christchurch on the east with Hokitika, Greymouth and Westport on the west.

The Southern Alps are well named, for their towering snow-peaks, deep valleys, huge glaciers, and dark forests are very like those of the Swiss Alps ; and every year those who love the mountains or seek the risk and thrill of hazardous climbing, go there for holidays, just as people flock to Switzerland. The finest glacier is the great Tasman glacier, which challenges comparison with any other in the world.

New Zealand's Fjords.

In the south-west the mountains come steeply to the sea much as they do in Norway ; and, as in Norway, the coast has undergone submergence there in past ages, allowing the sea to invade the long deep-cut valleys and turn them into tortuous and narrow inlets like the Norwegian fjords—steep-walled, profound and still. The best-known of these New Zealand fjords is Milford Sound. Some of them have the tongue-like ends of great glaciers within 600

MAORI MANNERS AND CUSTOMS

By permission of the High Commissioner for New Zealand.

When two Maori women meet, they greet each other by rubbing noses. This salutation is shown above. The Maoris came originally from Polynesian Islands and were long years ago addicted to cannibalism. Now they are Christians and happy, contented people, with their own land, their own schools and their own representatives in the Dominion Parliament.

By permission of the High Commissioner for New Zealand.

This illustration depicts the romantic " poi " dance, as given by aboriginal women. It conveys to the watchers an idea of the voyage from Polynesia to New Zealand. Starting with the launch of a long canoe, it goes on to show in actions the buffeting in storm, a quick righting again and the eventual landing on the beach of the new country. All this is most artistically conveyed.

LIKE A WITCH'S CAULDRON

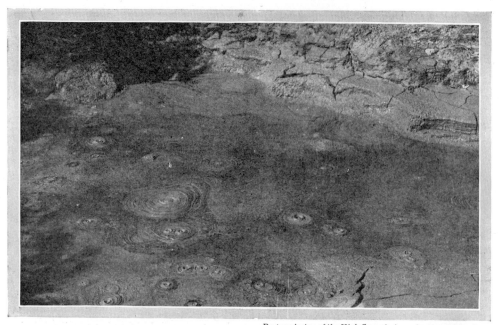

In the North Island of New Zealand, near the old Maori village of Whakarewarewa, one may see a lake of mud that is literally boiling. This is the " thermal " region of the Dominion, which is visited by thousands of people every year. They come to watch the mud pools seethe and bubble and swirl like the dark contents of a witch's cauldron.

Will F. Taylor.

Rotorua is the principal centre for visiting the thermal region, and here we see the Malfroy Geyser in the grounds of the Sanatorium at that place. From this geyser great jets of boiling water spout into the air, driven by giant forces that lie beneath the ground. As you approach Rotorua you detect the smell of sulphur in the air.

A GEYSER IN OPERATION

By permission of the High Commissioner for New Zealand.

This photograph gives you a " close-up " idea of what a geyser is like when in action. The one illustrated is the famous Pohutu Geyser at Rotorua. Sometimes these geysers burst forth, spouting a column of scalding water anything up to 1,500 feet into the air, the water being accompanied by black mud and stones. Yet, in the very midst of this region, the Maoris have built their villages, and erected shed-like houses with quaintly carved gable ends.

feet of the sea, and yet with graceful tree-ferns spreading their curling fronds within sight of the glacier ice—a sight to be seen nowhere else in the world.

Natural Grass-lands.

The Southern Alps lie across the track of the prevalent westerly winds, so that the western side of South Island has very much more rain than the long slopes and the coastal plains on the eastern side. Forests clothe the wetter western slopes, but the drier eastern plains are natural grass-lands, ideal for sheep-rearing. These are the famous Canterbury Plains, whose name is associated all the world over with the finest New Zealand lamb and mutton. Much dairy-farming is carried on there, too, especially in the moister parts ; but the real dairy country of South Island is the rich pasture land of the northern regions of South Island, in the neighbourhood of Nelson, facing North Island across Cook Strait.

North Island.

North Island is very different in structure from South Island. The mountain backbone in North Island is nearer the *east* coast ; it is broken into several ranges which nowhere exceed 7,000 feet. To the west of it lies one of the most remarkable volcanic regions in the world. It is a great volcanic plateau, pitted with geysers, mud volcanoes, and hot springs, with Lake Taupo in its midst, from which issues the Waikato River to run many miles north to the sea. Lake Taupo covers an area of 250 square miles, and is fed by thirty rivers.

Above the plateau three great volcanoes raise their triple cones ; Ngaurohoe, mightiest of all, is still active, but his brothers, Ruapehu and Tongariro, are quiescent or extinct—who can say ?

Hot Springs and Geysers.

This " thermal " region of North Island is visited by thousands of people every year; fine hotels have been built for their accommodation, and Maori guides make good money during the tourist season. Rotorua is the principal centre. There you can see great jets of boiling water spouting into the air, driven by giant forces that lie beneath the ground, and can watch the mud pools seethe and bubble and swirl like the dark contents of a witch's cauldron. The sulphur springs of Rotorua fill the marble baths of a wonderful sanatorium built there to give new life and vigour to those who come from afar to seek health.

You can smell sulphur in the air as you approach Rotorua, but this is not nearly as astonishing as the sights you see. From green valleys and hills rise mysterious puffs of steam, and by the very roadside are mud-holes that seethe and bubble like boiling porridge, and hot lakes of yellow, or blue, or green or pink.

In the valley of Tikitere, ten miles from Rotorua, " the earth is hot beneath your feet, the country gapes with steaming cracks, and if a cane is thrust a few inches into the soil a jet of steam or a spout of boiling water reminds you that, just beneath, the very bowels of the earth are seething towards the surface."

Geyser Valley.

Go to Wairakei and see the marvels of the Geyser Valley, where geysers with strange names, like the Champagne Cauldron, the Dragon's Mouth, the Prince of Wales' Feathers and the Donkey Engine, throb and boil and spout aloft in giant columns of boiling water, only to gurgle and hiss back again into their craters. You can set your watch by some of them, they are so regular. The Paddle Wheel performs with unfailing regularity every ten minutes ; the Twins every four minutes and a half. Te Reke Reke takes rather longer to make up his mind ; he spouts once every $4\frac{1}{2}$ hours.

Tarawera is a mountain of grim memories ; its appalling eruption in

NGAUROHOE BELCHING MOLTEN ROCK

By permission of the High Commissioner for New Zealand.

Ngaurohoe, one of New Zealand's three great volcanoes, is here seen in a full burst of activity, belching forth its smoke and molten rock. The two brothers of this terrifying peak are no longer active and it is possible that they have become extinct—though no one can say.

By permission of the High Commissioner for New Zealand.

The cave here shown is to be seen at Waitomo, between Rotorua and the western coast. The visitor is taken by his guide through an insignificant opening in the mountain side and then passes from cavern to cavern, each with wonderful stalactites hanging from the roofs and strange limestone formations. The cave depicted is picturesquely called "The Bride's Jewels."

1886 altered the whole countryside and spread ruin and death for many miles around. Millions of acres of fertile land and scores of happy villages were destroyed, and the famous Pink and White terraces of Rotomahana which all the world came to see were utterly wiped out.

Maori Villages.

In 1900 the giant geyser of Waimangu, the greatest in the world, burst forth near this spot, spouting its 1,500-feet column of scalding water, black mud and stones from a quiet pool which no one had dreamed capable of such astonishing activity.

It is difficult to imagine human settlement in country like this, yet the Maoris have built some of their villages in the very midst of it. Not far from Rotorua is the old Maori village of Whakarewarewa, with houses perched like match-boxes often at the very edge of boiling springs and fumaroles (steam holes). The Maoris regard these terrifying things as advantages, and make use of them as " fireless cookers " and " free hot baths." Over a fumarole they place a small box with its bottom of laths, and in it they put food wrapped in green leaves to be cooked. Washing day presents no problems ; it is done out of doors in the grim wash-tubs which Nature has provided, and there is never a queue for the bath, no matter how big the family

In this thermal region the Maoris not only act as guides, but, attired in the native dress, often perform some of their ancient dances and sing the old, old songs that have come down to the present from the far-distant past when the Maori came in their long canoes from over the sea to the " Long White Cloud," which to-day we know as New Zealand.

Maori Dances.

This ancient Maori tradition is told in action and in song in the *poi* dances performed by the women. The launch of the long canoe, its swaying rhythm, its buffeting in storm, its overthrow and quick righting again, and its landing on the beach are shown in rhythmic pantomime. The paddle-stroke is heard in the regular flick of the two *poi* balls tied with flaxen cord and wielded by the dancers, and the swish of the water is suggested by

Will F. Taylor.
A DINNER COOKED BY NATURE
So hot is the earth in parts that Maori women can actually cook their dinners in an oven provided by Nature. Fireless cookers and free hot baths are simple when one dwells near fumaroles (steam holes) and even laundry day presents no problems.

By permission of the High Commissioner for New Zealand.

THE MITRE PEAK AT MILFORD SOUND

New Zealand presents a wide diversity of scenery and in the south-west the mountains come steeply to the sea, so forming long, deep-cut valleys and narrow inlets that make one think of Norwegian fjords. This happens particularly at Milford Sound, seen above, with Mitre Peak and Sindbad Gully. Here are great glaciers within 600 feet of the sea.

the rustling skirts of stiff flaxen fibres.

More vigorous still is the *haka* or war dance performed by the men, each clad in a kind of kilt of stripped flax, and brandishing his *tewhatewha* or long-handled fighting axe.

But Maori boys and girls who have of course been to school, and have become as interested in " going to the pictures " and dancing as any other young modern folk, are not very intrigued by the old tales and songs and dances, which may quite possibly soon die out.

Waitomo Caves.

People who visit the thermal regions of North Island usually find time to inspect the famous caves of Waitomo, between Rotorua and the western coast. Through an insignificant opening in the mountain side, the visitor passes through cavern after cavern with wonderful stalactites pendent from their roofs, and with strange limestone formations that resemble fantastic turrets, or cathedral aisles, or perhaps fine shawls marvellously carven in old ivory.

Presently he is led steeply down to the brink of a subterranean river whose waters gleam blackly in the gloom. There he steps into a boat and pushes off into the darkness—a little apprehensive and perhaps afraid, until his eyes become accustomed to the place and he sees above him a myriad of tiny stars of blue and green and opalescent sheen twinkling from the roof, flickering, fading and twinkling again as if alive.

And they certainly *are* alive, for the guide tells how multitudes of curious glow-worms have made their home in the roof of this strange cavern, turning it into an Aladdin's Cave of jewelled splendour. No one who has ever seen it can forget the mysterious beauty of the Glow-worm Cave of Waitomo.

We have our Cheddar Caves at home, but the caverns at Waitomo are perhaps the most beautiful in the world.

NEW ZEALANDERS AT WORK

ON A FARM IN NEW ZEALAND

New Zealand is a most important farming country, with first-class grass-lands and a soil that responds admirably to skilful tillage. In the picture above we see a huge field which has been ploughed with the aid of the motor tractor. It is now being "disced," which means that the furrows made by the plough are in course of being levelled and pulverised with disc harrows. This brings the brown earth into good tilth for seed-sowing.

NEW ZEALANDERS make the most of their fertile country and its genial climate both in their work and their play. They get their living mainly by using the opportunities offered them by the great stretches of natural grass-lands in both islands, where very large numbers both of sheep and cattle are reared, and by farming in the rich soil.

Dairy Produce.

We can gather some idea of their most important industries if we look at a list of exports from New Zealand — £18,000,000 worth of wool; £11,000,000 worth of frozen meat; £10,500,000 worth of butter; £5,750,000 worth of cheese; £4,000,000 worth of skins and hides; £1,000,000 worth of tallow; and £500,000 worth of preserved milk. Besides these exports, all others from New Zealand are of little importance. All of them, notice, are the products of the pastures; add their value together and remember that all these millions of pounds' worth of pastoral products

have been exported from a land whose population is only a million and a half.

New Zealand butter and Canterbury lamb are always in demand, because their high quality is maintained by a careful system of Government inspection. Large freezing plants have been established at many centres, especially at and near the meat-exporting ports of Christchurch, Dunedin and Invercargill in South Island, and Wellington and Napier in North Island. Co-operative creameries and dairy-factories have done much to make dairy-farming successful, and so has the Department of Agriculture, which is always ready to lend its scientific aid in solving farmers' problems and so increasing the quantity and raising the quality of production.

Some mining is carried on in New Zealand. All the coal the Dominion needs can be got in the country, especially from the large coal-field on the western shores of South Island, where Westport is the chief outlet. There is good coal, too, in the Waikato

MILKING BY MACHINERY

New Zealand is a great dairying country, exporting every year butter, cheese and preserved milk worth many millions of pounds. Here we are given a peep into a milking-shed, where the precious fluid passes straight from the cow to the cooling plant without being touched by human hands. In the Dominion upwards of 600,000 cows are always milked by this modern machinery.

Photos by permission of the High Commissioner for New Zealand.

These two Maori men have been digging for kauri gum, a kind of resin found in association with the kauri pine. This is a large New Zealand tree and the men here shown seem to have won a fitting reward for their labours. The gum in this form does not come from growing trees, but is found on the sites of ancient forests. It is used in the **manufacture of linoleum.**

TWO FINE NEW ZEALAND CITIES

The city of Wellington is in North Island and is the capital of New Zealand. We see here a view of the waterfront, and it will be noticed that ocean-going ships come right up to the city. The Houses of Parliament and Government House are at Wellington.

Photos by permission of the High Commissioner for New Zealand.

So beautiful is the setting of the city of Auckland that it has been called " The Naples of the South." It is situated in the North Island and was formerly capital of the Dominion. The harbour can accommodate the largest vessels and the view of Queen Street, shown above, features a magnificent and up-to-date thoroughfare well worthy of so fine a city.

IN THE SOUTHERN ALPS

New Zealand is a magnificent country, with scenery that is widely varied, and it may come as a surprise to you to know that its islands are mountainous. The South Island has for its backbone the Southern Alps. The highest peak, Mount Cook, illustrated above, rises to an altitude of over 12,000 feet. Maoris call the mountain Aorangi, which means " The Cloud Piercer."

New Zealand's Southern Alps are well-named, for their towering snow-peaks, deep valleys, huge glaciers and dark forests are very like those of the Swiss Alps. The finest glacier is the great Tasman Glacier, illustrated by this print. Those who enjoy mountaineering visit these parts, just as people at home flock to Switzerland in the season.

district of North Island. But, thanks to her mountain streams, New Zealand has abundant " white coal " in her water-power, some of which is already harnessed to provide homes and factories and cities with electric light, heat and power. One of the largest power-stations is at Arapune on the Waikato River, forty miles west of Rotorua in the geyser country.

There are gold-mines, too, in both islands, but these are not nearly as important as those of Australia.

Good Sportsmen.

The New Zealander, like the Australian, is a good sportsman as well as a hard worker. Their tennis champions, rowing champions, and Rugby teams have made names for themselves throughout the world of athletic sports. Like the British at home, these British people of the Antipodes know how to " play the game " in sport and every walk of life. Golf and cricket are everywhere popular. At Christmas-time, in the height of summer, the bathing beaches are thronged with swimmers and the bays are white with the sails of yachts. The lovely scenery and the wonderful climate tempts many to go riding, tramping and camping in the bush, or climbing among the mountains. The New Zealanders are great lovers of outdoor life, chiefly because their climate is never too unpleasant to prevent work and play in the open air.

New Zealand Cities.

All the big towns in the Dominion are either on the coast or near it. The largest city is *Auckland*, the former capital, which with its suburbs has a total population of over 202,000. Next comes *Wellington*, the capital, with 127,000 people in city and suburbs, closely followed by *Christchurch*, with 122,000. If we do not count dwellers in the suburban areas, Wellington has about 10,000 more people living in it than Auckland.

Wellington, on the splendid natural harbour of Port Nicholson, which could accommodate the whole of the British Navy if necessary, has a central situation in the Dominion which fits it admirably for its position as capital, and chief distributing centre of New Zealand. It exports butter, cheese, fruit, hemp, frozen meat and wool, and the bulk of its trade is with Britain, Australia and Canada.

Auckland, on Waitemato Harbour, at the head of Hauraki Gulf, is the great port of call for vessels using the Panama route to New Zealand. At the entrance to the harbour is the island of Rangitoto with its triple-coned volcano, now extinct. The water is deep enough to allow large ships to berth within a few yards of the main thoroughfare of the city. Auckland was founded in 1840 ; in 1841 its population was 1,500 ; to-day, only about ninety years after its foundation by Governor Hobson, it is a large city of over 200,000 inhabitants. For its beauty, Auckland has been called " The Naples of the South."

The Canterbury Plains.

Christchurch is the city of the Canterbury Plains. Its harbour is Port Lyttelton. From it the railway to Greymouth crosses the Southern Alps by the famous Otira tunnel, which is said to be the longest in the British Empire.

Dunedin got its name from its Scottish founders, who gave it the ancient name of Edinburgh. Its outport is Port Chalmers, near the mouth of Otago Harbour.

New Zealand comes under the control of a Governor-General, who is supported by two councils, after the manner of Houses of Parliament. We can say that the most important industry in the Dominion is that of sheep-raising, and it was mainly through New Zealand enterprise that steamships were first equipped with refrigerating plant.

The Story of
the World
and its Peoples

Some Jewels
of the
Empire's Crown

H.M. Eastern African Dependencies.

EAST-AFRICAN WITCH DOCTORS

It is surprising in what a large number of native races we find " witch doctors," men who claim to exercise charms for ensuring success in life or love, for curing disease and for many other mysterious purposes. Above we see these weird practitioners as they may be found in Uganda, a British Protectorate in East Africa. What precise tricks they are working it is not for us to know.

BRITISH EAST AFRICA

IN East Africa are broad lands which form part of the British Empire. They are (1) Kenya Colony and Uganda (which is a British Protectorate ruled by its native negro king) ; (2) Tanganyika Territory, formerly a German colony, but now placed under the care of Britain by the League of Nations ; and (3), off the East African shore, the Islands of Zanzibar and Pemba, ruled by a native sultan under British protection.

Most of these lands belong to the high plateau country of East Africa, which is crossed in the west by higher mountain ranges and studded with enormous lakes, and is famous all the world over as the " Land of Big Game " —the hunter's paradise. These lands drop steeply down on either side to the narrow, hot, wet coast-plain that fringes the Indian Ocean.

Great Lakes and Volcanic Peaks.

Two mighty volcanic peaks rise from the eastern half of this plateau— Kilimanjaro (19,328 feet), in Tanganyika territory, and Kenya (17,000 feet). The western half, too, is dotted with large volcanoes, some of which are active. The largest lake is Victoria, whose level is 3,700 feet above the sea, and whose deeply-indented shores belong partly to Kenya Colony, partly to Uganda and partly to Tanganyika Territory. The other great lakes, Nyasa, Tanganyika and Albert, are long and narrow, for they are flooded parts of a

WOMEN WHO GO TO THE WELLS

Will F. Taylor.

These strong, well-built women are water-carriers at Mombasa. They deftly balance the heavy water-pots (or any other load) upon their heads. Mombasa is one of the chief ports in Kenya, situated on the Indian Ocean. From this place the Uganda Railway runs to Nairobi, the capital of Kenya, and on to Lake Victoria.

SNOW-CLAD KILIMANJARO

Will F. Taylor.

Our picture conveys to you more than any printed words could do what the country is like in British East Africa. The party of natives is on trek across the grass-lands, and the colossal hump in the background is the contour of Mount Kilimanjaro. This mountain is formed of two extinct volcanoes and rises to a height very little short of 20,000 feet. Its summit is snow-clad.

deep valley formed by the sinking of part of the earth's crust to form a deep trench ; a similar trench, with lakes in it here and there, cuts across the table-land east of Lake Victoria ; both form parts of what is called the " Great African Rift Valley."

The chief ports of this part of the British Empire are Mombasa in Kenya and Dar-es-Salaam in Tanganyika. From each of them a great railway climbs up from the narrow coastal plain to the plateau and crosses it to the great lakes. The Uganda Railway runs from Mombasa on the Indian Ocean to Nairobi, the capital of Kenya, and on to Kisumu on Lake Victoria ; the Tanganyika line starts at Dar-es-Salaam, and goes by way of Tabora to Ujiji and Kigoma on Lake Tanganyika.

Nairobi.

Nairobi stands over 5,000 feet above sea-level and about 330 miles from Mombasa. A hundred miles away to the north is the snowy cone of Mount Kenya. Everybody who comes to Kenya, whether for big game-hunting, or for coffee-planting, or to see the country, comes to Nairobi, for it is the capital and the heart of things in the colony. Although it is clearly still in its growing stage, there are many fine buildings along its wide straight streets, among others that are evidently temporary ones. The large number of cars here remind us that the motor car is one of the chief ways of getting about in this region. One great motor road takes you to the Sudan ; another goes south to Nyasaland, but both are difficult in the rainy season.

In the neighbourhood are many coffee plantations owned by European planters who employ natives of the Kikuyu tribe to work on the land. Great numbers of sheep and goats are reared and land formerly the home of thousands of game has been fenced off for cattle runs.

Past Nairobi, the railway climbs up through hilly country dotted here and there with the kraals of the Masai people, who are perhaps the best of all the tribes of East Africa, and who live

Thomas Butler.

IN A LAND OF BIG GAME

The view here shown is typical of Kenya, in British East Africa, and the place depicted is Golbanti. This part of our Empire is famous all the world over as the " Land of Big Game," and a hunter's paradise. Antelope, zebras, rhinoceros, wild buffalo and even lions are seen. The animals are most numerous in the Great Game Reserve of this wonderful country.

Topical Press.

LOADING A COTTON STEAMER

The port illustrated is Jinja, in Uganda, and the work that is going forward so busily is the
loading of raw cotton into a Lake Victoria steamer. This product will then be taken by water
to the head of the railway line and so find itself on an ocean-going liner bound for the Motherland.
There are regular services of lake steamers linking up the native ports and towns.

on the Masai Reserve—territory specially set apart for their use by the
Government. At last we arrive at
Kisumu on Lake Victoria, where we
find regular services of lake steamers
linking up the native ports and towns
around the lake shores. From Kisumu
we could, if we chose, take steamer to
Jinja, where a short line of railway
would take us on our way to the
upper Nile, which we could reach by
car in the dry weather quite comfortably.

Zanzibar.

Now let us take a peep at Zanzibar
and Pemba, " the islands of cloves "
—for most of the world's cloves are
grown there. We find Zanzibar a
town of tall white, flat-topped houses,
of mosques and towers, set amid
the deep green of waving palms,
and " the myrtle-like green of giant
clove trees." We go ashore and lose
ourselves in the maze of dark crooked
streets, which are crowded with
people of all sorts, of every nation
under the sun, reminding us in many
ways of the native bazaars in Indian
cities. At the clove market every
Monday, all the East congregates.
Men with snowy turbans folded round
fine embroidered caps ; bearded men
hung with gold chains, and eager, fine-
faced men in white robes—Arabs and
Persians, Greeks, Jews and Gentiles—
bid for the stacks of cloves which glut
the stores, bursting from the high-piled
sacks.

The language we need here is Swaheli,
which we found useful in speaking to
the natives in Kenya, but in Zanzibar
you find people of every seafaring race,
and along the water-front you can hear
the tongues of all the nations that
" go down to the sea in ships."

IN ZANZIBAR—ISLAND OF CLOVES

H.M. Eastern African Dependencies.

Zanzibar is a town of tall, white, flat-topped houses and of mosques and towers. It consists of a maze of dark streets and you see above one of the bazaars or shopping centres. The Island of Zanzibar is nearly 50 miles in length and some 15 miles across and its chief town and seaport takes the same name. The Island has some good motoring roads and a light railway.

H.M. Eastern African Dependencies.

Zanzibar is sometimes referred to as an "island of cloves," for here most of the world's supply of cloves is grown. In the illustration above we see green cloves being weighed by the native foreman or checker, and it would seem from this picture that the gatherers of the crop are paid for their labours by weight. Writers refer to "the myrtle-like green of giant clove trees."

FASHIONED BY ARAB CRAFTSMEN

H.M. Eastern African Dependencies.

This door and its frame is a worthy example of the skill and patience of Arab craftsmen, and the carving suggests a delightful sense of artistic proportion. Once upon a time Zanzibar was a state owned entirely by Arabs and an important centre of this powerful race of traders. Along the water-front of Zanzibar one may hear the tongues of all the nations that " go down to the sea in ships."

BRITISH WEST AFRICA

F. Deaville Walker.

A CASTLE ON THE GOLD COAST

The British West African lands are all within 15 degrees of the Equator and the climate is too hot
for Europeans to live there in comfort all the year round.   Here is a photograph of Christianborg
Castle, near Accra, on the Gold Coast.   The Castle is the residence of His Excellency the Governor.

VERY different from South Africa are those parts of the British Empire in West Africa between Cape Verde and the Bight of Biafra— Nigeria and the Gold Coast facing the great Gulf of Guinea, and Sierra Leone and British Gambia facing the Atlantic, where it is narrowest between Africa and South America.

In many parts of South Africa, Europeans have made their homes ; but in West Africa, Europeans rule, direct businesses, run plantations and carry on trade, to leave the country as soon as their work is done. They do not make homes and bring up their families there, for it is not at all a white man's country. You can see that clearly if you look at any book that tells you the population of Nigeria, for instance ; 19 millions of people live there, but of these, fewer than four thousand are Europeans. The British West African lands, in fact, are all within fifteen degrees of the Equator, and the climate is too hot for Europeans to live there in comfort all the year round.

Rivers and Ports.

The great river of West Africa is the Niger, some of whose tributaries are many times longer than the English Thames. Like other large African rivers, its lower courses are spoilt by falls and swift rapids, but it has several hundreds of miles of open navigation, and is still one of the chief ways of taking goods from place to place. Many other rivers come down to the Gulf of Guinea, and along them the palm oil, the ground nuts, rubber and other West African products are brought to the ports. Few of these ports, however, are really good, for the Atlantic beats all along this coast in heavy surf, so that in many cases steamers must anchor a mile or two out, and send goods ashore or take them aboard by the surf boats manned by the sturdy black Kru men, who are the best sailors in Africa. A great new deep water harbour has, however, been recently opened at the port of Takoradi on the Gold Coast, a little to the west of the old port of Sekondi. Another really fine deep water harbour is the French port of Dakar, under the shelter of Cape Verde.

Cocoa and the Gold Coast.

The Gold Coast got its name from the gold found in its streams, but it is much more important to-day as the land which supplies most of the cacao used in the world's cocoa and chocolate factories. The cocoa grown by negro farmers and by planters who own large estates reaches sea by road or by river, by motor lorries and native carriers, and even in great barrels rolled for miles along the roadway by perspiring negroes. The new harbour of Takoradi is much more convenient for shipping the cacao than the

old port of Accra, where surf boats and lighters must be used. Even passengers who wish to land must be swung from the deck of the liner in "mammy chairs," lowered into the surf boat that rises and falls on the big rolling swells, and taken ashore through the boiling surf by native boatmen.

Kumasi, about 170 miles from the coast, is the chief town of Ashanti, which is a British protectorate governed from the Gold Coast, like the northern territories farther inland.

Many of the natives, especially those in the coastal belt, have learned European ways; European education is spreading, and there are some good schools and colleges; and, in many native villages, the people prefer to make the roofs of their huts with corrugated iron instead of the old palm thatch which their fathers used. English is spoken by large numbers of the natives, some of whom have

F. Deaville Walker.

THE NATIVE POLICEMAN

The man here depicted is a constable in the native police force of Nigeria. The cuts on his face are tribal marks and were made upon his cheek in childhood.

F. Deaville Walker.

DRUMS THAT TALK

In all parts of West Africa there is a definite language of the drums, which is understood by the natives. Only the chiefs are allowed to have talking drums.

A CITY BUILT OF MUD

The homely scene brought to our notice above conveys to western eyes laundry day on a stream in Sierra Leone. Though the native women appear to wear no superfluous clothes, they are at least particular that such washing as they have to do shall be a credit to their housewifely art.

The name of this mud city is Kano, and it is to be found in Northern Nigeria. The houses seen in this street are built of nothing but mud or clay thickly plastered on to a framework of sticks, many of them strongly laced together. The pinnacles on the right are characteristic of the quaint architecture of this part of the Empire.

visited England to be educated and trained for special work in their own land.

Tin Mines.

British West Africa is important to the Empire because it supplies the palm oil and palm kernels from which soap, candles and even margarine are made. It grows most of the world's cacao ; its forests are rich in mahogany and ebony, and the tin mines and cotton fields of Nigeria provide the Empire with increasing supplies of two much-needed things that are all too scarce in the British Empire.

Alex. Barns.

IN A NATIVE FISH-MARKET

On the Island of Sao Thome, in the Gulf of Guinea, you might see this woman of the native fish-market.   Among the finny wares for sale she might offer shark meat, turtle, sting-ray or a species of octopus, queer delicacies which figure on the bill of fare of the black people.

MALAYA: LAND OF RUBBER AND TIN

THE HARBOUR AT SINGAPORE

Will F. Taylor.

Singapore is known as the " Liverpool of the East." It stands on an island of the same name, and is connected with the mainland by a railway which runs the whole length of the Malay Peninsula. Singapore has been part of the British Empire upwards of 100 years.

THE Malay Peninsula stretches its long body southwards from Siam, the " Kingdom of the Yellow Robe." Its neck is Siamese, but the rest of the peninsula is partly ruled by the British, partly by the native sultans, and consists of (1) the Straits Settlements, governed by a British governor; (2) the Federated Malay States, which are under British protection; and (3) the Unfederated Malay States, which are ruled by native sultans or princes who have British advisers at their courts.

The whole peninsula is practically one vast tropical forest, which rolls in great waves across the country covering the mountain ranges in an ocean of green. It is true that here and there men have built villages, towns and even cities, and in some places they have stripped away patches of forest to get at the rich tin deposits, or grow their plantations of rubber and spices; but these clearings are only the tiniest of spots in that great ocean of forest which stretches from sea to sea on either side.

The railways and the roads are bordered by dense forest; mines, towns, plantations and villages are hemmed in by it as by a wall. The native villages, usually by the side of a river, consist of a row of neat brown houses on stilts, and overshadowed by fruit trees. Behind them are the wet paddy fields; in front is the river. But beyond the cultivated land and the village, " the dark heavy line of the forest uprears itself around and above it like the walls of a prison."

The People of Malaya.

Who are the people of this forest land of Malaya ? The chief are the Malays —lithe and well-built brown people with shining black hair, who live in the villages by the water-side, and grow rice and fruit. Those who live near the sea are expert sailors and fishermen; those inland are clever hunters as well as farmers. The Malays are mostly Mohammedans; they are very polite and very particular, very cheerful but very quick tempered, brave fighters and firm friends. You will find Malays all over the south-eastern shorelands of Asia from Ceylon to the East Indies. They are not, as a rule, too fond of hard work; the work in the rich tin-fields in Malaya is mainly done by Chinese coolies, and the labour on the rubber and coco-nut plantations is provided chiefly by Tamil people from India. The Malay hates to work for a master; he leaves that to what he calls inferior folk.

In the forest country, where civilisation has not yet reached, live the Sakai, who are great hunters and clever trackers of wild animals, using their blow-guns and poisoned darts with deadly accuracy. Some of the Sakai grow a little millet and rice and fruits on land cleared by burning; when this is exhausted they clear a new patch. Like the Veddahs of Ceylon and the Todas of Southern India, the Sakai are animists who believe their world to be filled with spirits—mostly evil, and therefore to be pleased by strange offerings in lonely places. When the white man wants to build a new railway or cut a new road through the living forest, he generally employs bands of these Sakai to clear away the dense tangle of vegetation as only these little brown people can.

Wilder and shyer even than the Sakai are the small, black, short and woolly-haired Negrito people of the remotest forests, who grow nothing, but live entirely by hunting, or by grubbing up roots, finding wild honey and fruits, and rooting out tortoises and burrowing animals from their secret haunts.

Will F. Taylor.

MALAY CHILDREN AT SINGAPORE

The Malays are lithe, well-built, brown people with shining black hair, and the above children are representative of the rising generation of this race. Many Malays live in water-side villages and grow rice and fruit. Others are expert sailors and fishermen, whilst numbers are clever hunters.

IN THE "LIVERPOOL OF THE EAST"

The above photograph is illustrative of a street scene in Singapore. You will notice the rick-shaw in the foreground. Malays and Chinese in the main form the inhabitants of Singapore, for the island of that name is situated just off the Malay Peninsula. It is about twenty-seven miles in length and half that distance in breadth.

The Sakai are small, black, short and woolly-haired people who dwell in the remotest forests of Malay. Their quaint homes with thatched roofs are shown in the picture above. These people do not cultivate land, but live by hunting, finding wild honey and roots and capturing tortoises.

Kuala Lumpur is the "rubber city" of Malaya; its fortunes are founded on the rubber plantations, just as those of Johannesburg are on gold, and those of Kimberley on diamonds.

Its port is Port Swettenham on the Straits, and rubber and tin exporting is the chief business there.

Kuala Lumpur is the capital of the Federated Malay States, as well as the chief city of Selangor; it has fine broad streets and many beautiful buildings. Roads and railways connect it with the many rubber plantations and with the tin-fields. Its population is at least 80,000.

J. Hornell.

A CHINESE JUNK UNDER SAIL

You will often have heard of Chinese junks and here is one of these vessels sailing just off Penang in the Malacca Straits. The ships have high sterns and are well known in the East for their seaworthiness. Junks are by no means exclusive to the Chinese, for our Japanese friends have countless numbers of these vessels in use.

THE BRITISH WEST INDIES

Sport and General.

TRANSPORTING PITCH IN TRINIDAD

Near the Port of La Brea in Trinidad is a famous lake of pitch or asphalt. The whole surface of the lake is in constant motion and here we see how the pitch is loaded into waggons from the lake and wheeled away over tram-lines. A hundred thousand tons of this pitch are taken every year from this source.

IT is strange how names "stick," even though they are quite wrong. When Christopher Columbus, one fine day in October, 1492, sighted the island of San Salvador (now called Watling Island, one of the Bahamas), he believed he had reached the Indies off south-eastern Asia, and the name West Indies soon came to be applied not only to the islands, but to the mainland of America. The islands were not the "Indies," nor were the natives whom Columbus found there "Indians," but both names still stick.

The West Indies fall into three great groups: (1) the Greater Antilles, consisting of the large islands of Cuba, Haiti, Jamaica and Porto Rico; (2) the Lesser Antilles, which include the long festoon of volcanic or coral islands stretching away from Porto Rico to the mainland of South America; and (3) the low coral islands of the Bahamas to the north of Cuba. Practically all of these were first discovered by Columbus on one or other of the four great voyages between 1492 and 1502.

Peoples of the Indies.

The Spaniards almost crushed out of existence most of the native peoples of these lovely islands, setting them to work in the mines of Hispaniola. Then they followed the example of the Portuguese and brought in large numbers of negro slaves from West Africa—a foul trade in which English seamen took a leading part. Not even the fact that England accepted the lead in after years in putting down slavery can wipe this blot from our national history.

Most of the people of the West Indies to-day are the negro descendants of freed slaves. They are a cheerful and happy coloured folk who are wonderful gardeners and excellent plantation workers. At one time large numbers of East Indians and many Chinese people went to work in the islands, and there are still a great

A WEST INDIES VILLAGE

Will F. Taylor.

When Christopher Columbus sailed westwards and discovered land across the Atlantic he believed he had reached India or the Indies. It was a mistake on the part of the great explorer and one that has never been corrected, for we still speak of Jamaica, Porto Rico and other large islands in this part of the world as the "West Indies." In the photograph above is shown a native village. Many of the people are negro descendants of slaves who were set free.

many of their descendants there to this day. You will find innumerable East Indians in Trinidad, Jamaica and St. Lucia, for example.

Volcanic Outbursts.

The British West Indies consist of the Bahamas, Jamaica, Barbados, Trinidad and Tobago, the Leeward Islands and the Windward Islands. The Bahamas and Barbados are low coral islands with no great depth of soil; nearly all the rest are volcanic, and are really the upstanding portions of great sunken mountain chains. The terrible forces that cause sudden and appalling changes in the earth's crust are still active there from time to time; Kingston, the capital of Jamaica, was overwhelmed by an earthquake in 1907, when 1,500 lives were lost and property destroyed to the value of nearly two million pounds. In 1902 the great volcano of the Soufrière on the island of St. Vincent burst into sudden violence, destroying farms and homes and killing 1,300 of

the inhabitants; and, at the same time, an even more frightful volcanic eruption of Mount Pelee took place on the neighbouring French island of Martinique, where the loss of life was still more appalling.

The large island of Trinidad, very near the South American mainland, has a remarkable " pitch lake," which makes one feel as one looks at it as if he were witnessing part of the earth's crust in process of manufacture.

Sugar and Rum.

The chief business of the West Indies is sugar-planting, and the production of sugar and rum. Banana-growing is very important, too, and so is the cultivation of oranges, spices, coffee, cotton, tobacco, and other tropical products. Most of the really important things grown in the West Indies are got from plants which are not native to the islands, but which have been imported from time to time. The Spaniards introduced the sugar-cane in the sixteenth century, and the

H. J. Shepstone.

DRYING THE ROOTS OF GINGER

Ginger is a herb which is grown very largely in Jamaica, and the article we use in commerce (for spice and for making ginger-bread, ginger-wine, and so on) is produced from the root of this plant. In our illustration ginger roots are being dried in the sun on a mat made from reeds.

PREPARING COCOA BEANS FOR MARKET

The preparation of cocoa in a raw state is a great business in Trinidad, and here we see the cocoa beans spread out to dry in the hot sun. The beans grow upon cocoa trees in pods, each pod yielding about forty beans. When gathered the pods must be opened and the beans inside freed from pulp before they are set to dry.

cacao tree, too. Coffee, cinnamon, nutmegs, bananas, oranges and ginger were all brought into the islands from other lands.

No one who has ever been to the West Indies forgets to tell his friends about the magnificent palms which flourish in many of the islands. The great Royal Palm grows to a height of 100 feet, and an avenue of royal palms is a sight to be ever afterwards remembered.

Jamaica.

Jamaica is the largest and the richest of all the British West Indies. It is about twice the size of Lancashire, and lies south of Cuba, almost on the direct route from Europe and the United States to the Panama Canal. Its divisions bear names that are familiar to Britishers—Middlesex, Surrey and Cornwall. The beautiful Blue Mountains rise inland to twice the height of Snowdon, and it is on their slopes,

between three and four thousand feet above the tropical sea, that splendid coffee is grown, known all the world over for its exquisite flavour.

Jamaica grows pimento (" allspice "), sugar and tobacco, bananas and oranges, grape fruit and limes, coco-nuts, and even tea. From its tropical forests are got ebony and dyewoods. Many factories are established on the island —tobacco and cigar factories, and others where banana " figs " and banana flour are made.

Kingston, its capital, has fine wide streets laid out on the chess-board plan. King Street is its main thoroughfare. Kingston Harbour is one of the finest natural harbours in the world.

Trinidad has rich volcanic soil in which enormous quantities of sugar-cane are grown. Cacao is at its best here. Coco-nuts and all kinds of tropical fruits flourish. The capital is Port of Spain on the flat plain at the foot of the Santa Anna Mountains. It is very

CAPITAL OF THE BERMUDAS

Mondiale.

This charming picture was taken in Paget Sound, and shows the town of Hamilton, capital of the Bermudas. Of these islands about a score are inhabited and they form a great health and pleasure resort for many Americans. The islands were discovered by a Spanish adventurer, Bermudez, in the sixteenth century and take their name from him.

Mondiale.

This lovely landscape in Jamaica is known as the " Blue Hole." The island is something like a long dish in shape, 144 miles from one end to the other and rather more than 40 miles in depth. It possesses scenery that is of marvellous beauty, with mountains, forests, valleys and plains. Around it is the blue Caribbean Sea. Jamaica is one of the Greater Antilles Islands.

A JEWEL OF THE WEST

Mondiale.

In this photograph we see Port Maria, in Jamaica, and the very picture seems to suggest a lovely climate. In this island bananas, sugar, coco-nuts, coffee and tobacco form the chief exports. Wonderful trees and ferns, waterfalls, tree-clad mountains, avenues of bamboos and an entrancing coast-line greet the visitor to Jamaica.

up-to-date with its electric light, electric cars and good telephone services.

Barbados.

Barbados is the outermost of the West Indies, and the nearest to Europe. It is about as big as the Isle of Wight. Bridgetown is its capital; its inner harbour is usually crowded with island schooners which have brought vegetables, and other things from the neighbouring islands. Along the water-front is the busy market where coloured folk bargain and chatter joyously in the sunshine.

Sugar laid the foundation of Barbados' fortunes. Huge sugar plantations cover large parts of the island, and among the dark green of the growing canes you can still see the old windmills that provide power for the former type of crushing-mills, although large and up-to-date crushing-plants are now the rule. Some cotton is grown, and on the cotton plantations at picking-time you witness much the same scenes as those which are common on the cotton-fields of the southern States of North America.

The island of *Tobago* is particularly interesting to boys and girls because it is the original of the island described by Defoe in "Robinson Crusoe," although Alexander Selkirk, the original of the hero, was not marooned in Tobago, but thousands of miles away in another ocean on the island of Juan Fernandez.

Mondiale.

A SNAPSHOT OF THE NATIVE MARKET

Once upon a time the sugar plantations of Jamaica were worked by slaves, but those days have gone long ago and now the toilers of the plantations are well housed and have even a medical service. In this picture we see the native market at Annatto Bay, where goods of many descriptions are displayed for sale.

THE COCO=NUT CARRIER

Mondiale.

Particularly along the northern coast, coco-nuts are grown with great success in Jamaica, and here we see a native whose duty it is to carry the crop from the trees to the store-house. The coco-nut tree is really a member of the great palm family and grows to a height of about 50 feet.

British Honduras.

This is perhaps the most convenient place for mentioning *British Honduras*, the only part of the British Empire in Central America. Mexico lies to the north of it, and the republic of Guatemala to the west and south. Its coast-lands are low, marshy, and fever-smitten; but inland the ground rises rapidly into mountains clad in dense tropical forest where mahogany, log-wood and cedar are cut for export—difficult and risky work carried out chiefly by negro woodcutters. The heavy logs are hauled to the nearest stream by bullock teams, and floated down to the sea when the heavy rains set in.

Belize is the capital on a river of the same name. On the lowlands there are plantations of cacao, bananas and oranges; the higher and more open country has good pasture for cattle.

A GOOD YIELD OF COCOA

H. J. Shepstone.

We must not confuse the tree from which cocoa beans are obtained with the coco-nut, for the two are totally distinct. Cocoa beans (or "nibs" as they are sometimes called) come from the pods of the comparatively small cacao tree, which is here illustrated. The native is in the act of cutting the pods and appears to have a splendid crop.

BRITISH GUIANA

H. J. Shepstone.

INDIANS IN THEIR DUG-OUT CANOE

The nearly naked Indians seen in this picture are propelling themselves upstream in a canoe laboriously made from a single tree-trunk, which they have burned and carved out to form a boat. The aboriginals of these parts are great builders of canoes, and many of them live in dwellings erected on piles well above the water level.

THE only British Empire territory on the mainland of South America is British Guiana, which is about the same size as Great Britain.

" God of Waters."

The Guianas—British, Dutch and French—are hot, wet lands within a few degrees of the Equator, and a great deal of their surface is covered with dense tropical forest. It is only in the lowlands near the coast that white planters, employing Asiatic as well as native labour, have made their plantations of sugar-cane, rice, cacao, coffee, spices and coco-nuts. The greater part of the country still belongs to the forest, which is very difficult to penetrate, except by way of the rivers, which with their tributaries form a great network of waterways ; but these are full of falls and cataracts that hinder free use of them as highways.

The most magnificent falls in Guiana —indeed, in the whole of South America—are the Kaieteur Falls on the upper Potaro River, which is one of the tributaries of British Guiana's great river, the Essequibo. They are nearly five times as high as Niagara, and the deep voice of the roaring waters can be heard miles away. The Indians call the falls " God of Waters."

Georgetown, the Capital.

Although the Essequibo is by far the greatest river, it is the Demerara that is most important, for at its mouth stands Georgetown, the capital of the Colony. In Georgetown you may see not only British and other European people, but also Chinese, East Indians and negroes, as well as some of the native people of Guiana who work for the white men. Chinese, East Indians and negroes have come to Guiana to work on the plantations, just as they went to Natal and to Kenya Colony for the same reason. Europeans, indeed, form only about

5 per cent. of the people, but the East Indians include nearly half of the total population of British Guiana.

Peoples of the Guianas.

The natives of Guiana are the "Buck" Indians, coppery-brown people with lank black hair, broad, flat faces with dark, narrow eyes, and very muscular. They live in their villages up-country, according to their tribes, unless they have come to work in the lowlands for the white men, or pilot boats on the rivers, or to act as carriers in the forest lands. Large areas have been set aside by the Government in which the native Indians may live in security; such lands are called Indian Reservations.

The Swamp Indians live a timid, squalid life in their riverside huts on the lowlands, but they are clever makers of dug-out canoes. The Arawaks are a much finer people; many speak English and dress in European clothes. They are good boatmen and expert foresters. Other tribes live in the forest depths, and are clever in the use of the blowpipe and in the making of poisoned arrows.

H. J. Shepstone.

PREPARING FOR A TAPIOCA PUDDING

The little Indian girl depicted in this photograph is busily engaged in grating the roots of a shrub which grows in British Guiana. The meal which she prepares is called cassava, but it is better known to us under the name of tapioca. By a baking process a bitter poison is removed from the roots, leaving the meal as a wholesome foodstuff.

The Story
of the
World and
its Peoples

Our Neighbours
and Friends
in
Other Lands

THE GATE OF NEW YORK HARBOUR

Mondiale.

The monster flying-boat in the centre of this picture is the famous Do. X., which is illustrated also in another volume, and the scene the entrance to New York Harbour. In the foreground is Bedloe's Island, upon which is reared the 111-foot Statue of Liberty, with its electric torch some 40 feet higher. The statue was given to the U.S.A. by the people of France when America celebrated her hundredth year of independence. Inside the figure is a staircase.

THE UNITED STATES OF AMERICA

THE Great Republic of the United States is not so large as Canada, but it has more than ten times as many people, for it lies in latitudes more favourable to the growth of a dense and busy population. The 120 millions of people living in the United States are mainly of European descent, but whereas the inhabitants of Canada are chiefly British or French, those of the United States have come from almost every nation in Europe to form a united new people under the Stars and Stripes. At least 10 per cent. of the population of the United States are coloured folk, the descendants of the slaves brought there to work in the plantations of the south-eastern States during the bad old days of slavery.

A rapid view of the United States as seen on the map shows us a great and fertile plain with the mighty Mississippi—"Father of Waters"—draining it with its giant fan of tributaries; on the eastern side of it the parallel ranges of the Appalachians and the Alleghany plateau with the great rich Appalachian valley between, and on the western side of the plains the Western Cordillera of high ranges, lofty plateaux and great valleys and basins, forming a tremendous complex of mountainous country 1,500 miles wide, and containing some of the most majestic highland scenery on the globe. The eastern high range is formed by the Rocky Mountains, which extend into Canada.

Lakes and Great Plains.

The northern part of the great plain of the United States is an extension of Southern Canada; there are the prairies golden with grain in summer and snow-swept in winter; there are the great cattle ranches of the drier prairies and the foothills; and around the southern and western sides of Lake Superior is part of the great "shield" of very hard old rocks containing the richest iron deposits in the world, where the ore is got out of huge open pits by monster grabs and electric shovels, taken in long lines of freight cars to the lake side, dumped into monster ore steamers and transported down the lakes to the big iron and steel works on the southern shores of Lakes Michigan and Erie.

But the southern part of the great plain is very different. It is much warmer, for one thing, and in the moister eastern and south-eastern parts maize and tobacco, cotton, sugar, rice and sub-tropical fruits are grown in enormous quantities. The south-western plains are very dry; parts, indeed, in Arizona and New Mexico are actual desert, although great irrigation works have done a great deal in recent years to turn barren desert arid lands into fertile grain-lands and fruit orchards.

The Busiest Region.

The busiest and most thickly-peopled part of the United States is in the north-east, where great cities manufacturing all kinds of goods and drawing to themselves the grain, cattle, ores and timber of the west give employment to many millions of people. South of them are the States where

Central News.

THE CROTON DAM

This great dam is one of the sources of New York's water supply. When this photograph was taken, it was estimated that the dam contained nearly 27,000,000,000 gallons of water. The spillway on the left of the photograph is quite dry, as the water was still some 2 feet below the highest possible level.

THE RED MEN OF AMERICA

H. J. Shepstone

The inhabitants of the North American continent were first called "Indians" by Christopher Columbus, who believed he had reached India by sailing westward. The noble Redskins, of course, have no connection with India, and form a race by themselves, with many tribes and varying customs and languages. The figure above, so truly typical of the race, is that of an Apache warrior.

E.N.A.

Red Indians made their homes in all parts of North America, and the representatives of the race depicted above were photographed in the Canyon de Chelly, in Arizona. The cliff in the background is 1,000 feet in height and the long, slender cleft looks as though it were made with the axe of a giant.

Mondiale

To-day the Redskin lives in large enclosures or reservations, both in Canada and in the United States of America. Here the descendants of the original natives live much the same lives as they did long years ago, and we see above a gathering of women attending a festival in Western Canada Note how the baby is carried slung between poles and drawn along by his mother's pony.

MRS. CREE INDIAN AND HER BABY

E.N.A.

The Crees formed a tribe of Indians who roamed mostly in Canada, being happiest in well-timbered tracts of country. In this picture we see a Cree mother with her baby, and it is characteristic of Redskin women to carry their little ones on their backs in this manner. An Indian baby is known as a papoose.

CLEVER HANDICRAFTS OF THE TRIBESPEOPLE

North-American natives are extremely clever at various forms of handicraft, and the girls seen above are engaged in basket making.   They belong to the Hopi tribe, and the photograph was taken in Arizona, U.S.A.

Photos: E.N.A.

In this picture we see Indians of the Navaho tribe.   They have set up their primitive loom and are busy weaving a rug, whilst their sheep graze not far away.   The scene is a canyon in Arizona, and the rugs which are so woven are wonderfully warm as well as being of the gayest colours.

H. J. Shepstone

The little maid seen above, at the entrance to her hut, is a member of the Apache tribe. This tribe existed mainly in Texas and Arizona, and the warriors were amazing horsemen.

G.P.A.

Here is another Redskin girl, plump and chubby, her frock decorated with cowrie shells. She has just received as a Christmas gift a monster buckskin tom-tom drum.

H. J. Shepstone

As a contrast to the picture immediately above, here is an old Apache squaw. She is cracking a nut with evident enjoyment, despite her years.

Will F. Taylor

Once a great chief of the Apaches, this old man, who is sitting for his photograph outside his tent, is the famous Geronimo. Note his head-dress.

SMOKING THE PIPE OF PEACE

Mondiale

There is something wonderfully picturesque in this scene, which shows us Indians at home, with their birch-bark canoes. Note how the tent or tepee is ornamented with crude drawings. The two men on the right are following the tribal custom of smoking the pipe of peace and friendship.

E.N.A.

In the gathering twilight we see above Navaho Indians camping in the Canyon de Chelly in Arizona, in the United States of America. The men and women are sitting round the camp fire and it seems that a welcome evening meal is in progress.

H. J. Shepstone

This quaint old woman, with her stockingless feet, belongs to the Campo Indian tribe, which once roamed the San Diego district of California. She is hard at work crushing acorns, pounding them with the big stone in her hands as they are placed in the hollow of the other stone. Indian women harvest acorns in the autumn and prepare them for food to be stored for rainy days.

MEDICINE MEN AND WOMEN

Though the Redskins now live in reservations they keep up many of their old customs and are still influenced by the mysterious rites of witch doctors. Above, we see a procession on the way to a sun lodge with blanketed medicine men and medicine women taking part in the proceedings.

Photos: E.N.A.

In this illustration we see Mohawk Indian warriors in full war paint, with their feathered head-dress and long bows. Early settlers in Canada encountered just such braves as these, and fights were of almost daily occurrence. To-day the Redskin is more worldly, and sells arrows, shields and such objects to the white visitors.

NEW YORK AND ITS SKYSCRAPERS

Topical Press.

Here are two of New York's skyscrapers. In the foreground is the Telephone Building, while to the right is Woolworth's.

Ewing Galloway, N.Y.

This curious photographic effect was obtained by making a picture, at close quarters, of a building in Wall Street.

Topical Press.

A photograph taken from the air, which gives a splendid impression of New York. The city is built partly upon Manhattan Island, which is 13½ miles long. Such a comparatively small piece of land forced the people of New York to economise in space by building skywards.

Keystone View Co.

Land is so scarce and buildings so crowded together in New York that the one way in which to provide the needed accommodation was to carry construction upwards. This has brought to the city a veritable forest of skyscrapers, representing some of the tallest structures ever reared by man. Our photograph was taken from the sixty-seventh floor of the Chrysler Building. If you were at that height you would look down upon the street below as is here illustrated.

UP AMONG THE CLOUDS

This wonderful snapshot was taken in the course of a survey of New York by aeroplane, and shows the tower of the great Woolworth Building completely surrounded by cloud. Nothing could bring home to us more realistically the height of these enormous skyscrapers, raised storey after storey, each one of them housing from 10,000 to 15,000 workers during business hours.

tobacco and cotton, rice and sugar have built up big business, and where other large cities flourish.   West of all is the great basin of the Mississippi, with the second largest port of the United States, New Orleans, near its mouth. West of the Mississippi Basin are the Mountain States, with their treasures of gold and silver, copper and lead and other minerals, and between these and the Pacific are the States of the Pacific seaboard, the best known of which is the lovely land of California, with its port of San Francisco on the Golden Gate.

The capital of all this rich country is Washington in the district of Columbia, on the high banks of the beautiful Potomac River, which comes down from the Blue Mountains.   This magnificent city, " founded and planned by George Washington, the first Presi-

dent of the United States, long before it was born," has the stately Capitol as its centre, from which splendid avenues radiate like spokes from the hub of a wheel; fine Government buildings and monuments of marble appear amid their beautiful setting of trees and open spaces.   Its half-million people are mainly employed in Government offices.

New York.

But the largest city in the United States, Americans say in the world, is New York, which first grew up on the narrow rocky Manhattan Island, and then overflowed to New Jersey, Brooklyn on Long Island and the Bronx, which to-day are linked together by many bridges.   The first of these was the famous Brooklyn Bridge, built in 1883; since then more than fifty

H. J. Shepstone.

ON A CAUSEWAY OVER SALT LAKE

The United States of America is a land of vast distances, and some of its trains cross the continent from one side to the other, bridging many types of countryside between the Atlantic and the Pacific Oceans. Such a train is illustrated above, and in the picture we see the " San Francisco Overland Limited Express " pulled up by signal on its way over the Great Salt Lake in the State of Utah. Utah is in the Rocky Mountains area

others of various sizes have been built, including a great new bridge recently constructed across the Hudson.

Land became so dear, and room for building so restricted at the southern end of crowded Manhattan Island, that the only thing to do was to build *upwards*, since building outwards was impossible. That is why New York is the " City of Skyscrapers," with streets like ribbons at the bottoms of great deep canyons of masonry, shut in by giant buildings of fifty storeys high and more, one of which may house ten or fifteen thousand people during the working hours. Fleets of street cars, overhead railways, three underground tunnels one above another, crowded ferries and thronged bridges can hardly take the millions of workers home each day and bring them all back next morning. All the chief railways of the North American continent focus on this city, and to its crowded wharves come the products of the whole vast land behind it away to the Pacific. All nations have a home there. Fifth Avenue is the street of millionaire palaces, but in the lower quarters there are " great dingy box-like tenement houses where dwell the most motley mixture of human beings the world possesses."

The Waterfront.

Those who come to the United States from Europe enter at New York, welcomed by the famous Statue of Liberty, which at night has great flood-lights around its base and a gleaming torch on high. Behind it is Ellis Island, where incoming people are examined to see if they can be admitted to the country, and beyond is the waterfront—the most amazing in all the world, with its skyline broken by the soaring blocks and peaks of the skyscrapers.

From aerodromes near New York, the United States Air Mail starts on its relay journey of 2,665 miles across the continent to San Francisco. Along the

Ewing Galloway, N.Y.

IN THE CITY OF CHICAGO

New York is not alone in the possession of skyscrapers, for they are erected in many of the cities of the U.S.A. and Canada. Here, for example is the Board of Trade Building in Chicago. There are so many monster edifices grouped round that this is the only spot from which a photograph can be taken to give one an adequate idea of the great pile with its countless windows in serried rows.

TWO GLIMPSES OF CHICAGO

Chicago is the chief grain market for the Middle West and has great stockyards in which cattle and pigs are turned into tinned meat. The city possesses many lofty buildings, as is here depicted, and the foreground is filled with a view of the Buckingham Memorial Fountain. This fountain is said, with its seventy-two jets, to be the largest in the world.

Here is another view of Chicago, the massive building being the Art Institute in Michigan Boulevard. The Institute contains a magnificent collection of works of art, and an average of 3,500 people visit it every day. Chicago has a population of three and a half millions, and is situated in the State of Illinois. It counts as the second city in the U.S.A.

CROSSING THE PLAINS

H. J. Shepstone.

A HOLE DUG BY A BOLT FROM THE SKIES

Above is a photograph of Meteor Crater, to be found in Arizona, U.S.A. This enormous hole in the earth was made by a meteorite which descended unknown years ago. The cavity is 1,333 yards in diameter (*i.e.*, across the mouth), so we may say the opening is nearly a mile in width. In depth the hole is still nearly 600 feet, despite the constant filling-up that is going on.

H. J. Shepstone.

You will have heard the term " The Covered Waggon," and such vehicles are illustrated above. Long years ago the Mormons, to avoid persecution, travelled in covered waggons, with all their belongings, upwards of 1,000 miles across desert land to find new homes in the uncharted West.

You will have heard of the Stars and Stripes, the name by which the Flag of the United States of America is known. If you look in the top left-hand corner of this flag you will see there are six rows of stars, with eight stars in every row. Each of these forty-eight stars represents one state in the Union, the largest being Texas, which is double the size of the United Kingdom, and the smallest Rhode Island, just below Massachusetts. In such a vast country as the U.S.A. there are many climates and so each State has its own particular industry, as is shown in the above pictorial diagram.

336

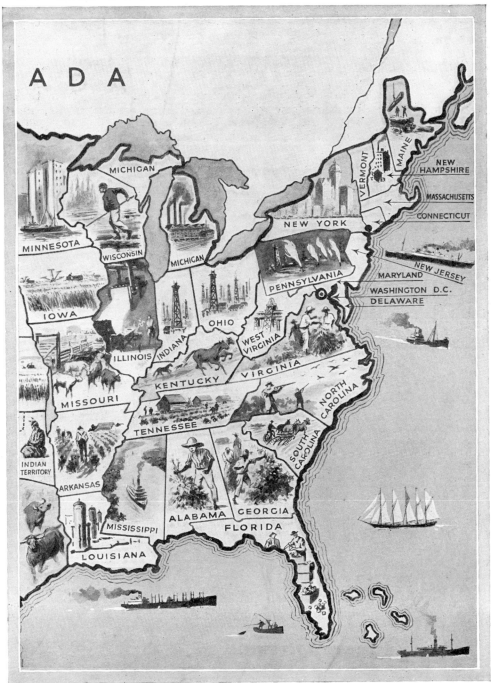

That portion of the U.S.A. formed by Maine, New Hampshire, Vermont, Connecticut and Massachusetts has a climate not unlike our own and the district is known as New England. Below we come to the Atlantic States and then to the Southern States, where cotton and other tropical crops flourish and labour is largely in the hands of the descendants of negro slaves. We have now the great Middle West, with such States as Iowa and Missouri. These are followed by Kansas, Texas, Colorado and others known as the Western States. Next, in the Far West are the Pacific States of California, Washington and Oregon.

route, which is by way of Cleveland, Chicago, Omaha, Cheyenne and Salt Lake City, great landing fields have been prepared, each with its giant flood-light of five million candle-power, and five hundred huge beacon lights flash their welcome guidance by night. For Uncle Sam's mails must go forward at top speed—despite darkness, wind or storm, or heat or cold.

The Black Country of U.S.A.

North and west of New York is the busiest part of industrial America, where rich coal-fields and oil-wells, natural gas and water-power make manufacturing possible on a huge scale. The heart of this busy region is Pittsburgh, where " long lines of coal cars, huge ovens that turn coal into coke for blast furnaces, smelting furnaces that look at night like volcanoes, clouds of smoke, streams of fiery metal shooting out into moulds, great presses and rollers at work shaping white-hot iron and steel, monster cranes, clanging metal, shrieking whistles and toiling men," make this city the most important metal-working centre in the world.

Chicago.

Farther west is another giant city—Chicago—with three and a half millions of people, its stockyards crammed with cattle and pigs from the western ranches or the neighbouring maize country, awaiting their turn to be converted into canned meats, meat extracts, and all the animal products that modern science can devise. Other large towns in the surrounding country share in this tremendous meat-packing business. Chicago is a city of skyscrapers, too, and the chief grain market for the Middle West.

There are two places which visitors make a point of seeing on their journey across the continent—the beautiful Yellowstone Park and the Grand Canyon of the Colorado River in Arizona, both worthy of their places among the wonders of the world.

In Yellowstone Park.

Yellowstone National Park is in the north-west corner of the State of Wyoming on the " Great Divide " of the Western Cordillera. Through it runs the Yellowstone tributary of the Missouri in deep canyons. It is not

Ewing Galloway, N.Y.

WASHINGTON, THE HEART OF THE U.S.A.

The Capitol of Washington, in which Congress meets, and where the Supreme Court holds its sittings, is a magnificent building. The lofty dome shown in our picture is 285 feet in height, and in some respects resembles that of St. Paul's Cathedral, London.

A MONUMENT TO WASHINGTON

H. J. Shepstone.

The city of Washington, capital of the United States of America, was named after George Washington, the first President, and this magnificent obelisk was raised to his undying memory. The monument towers to a height of over 550 feet. Washington was a great statesman and soldier. He was born in 1732 and died in 1799.

A A 2

The above house, so plain and yet picturesque, is known as " Mount Vernon," and was part of an estate which George Washington inherited. It was from this house that the man who was afterwards to be President of the U.S.A. organised a force of colonists to defend the settled parts against marauding and warlike Red Indians.

Photos : H. J. Shepstone.

In our newspapers we often read of the " White House," here shown. It is the mansion provided by the country and the official residence of the President of the United States of America. The building is about 170 feet in length, but consists of only two storeys. Its most arresting feature is the portico, carried out in the Ionic style.

WASHINGTON, CAPITAL OF THE U.S.A.

The above apartment, with its half-circles of chairs and desks, making one think somewhat of a lecture theatre or school, is the Senate Chamber in the Capitol at Washington. Parliament in the U.S.A. consists of the Senate and a House of Representatives. The former corresponds to our House of Lords and the latter to the British House of Commons.

Photos : H. J. Shepstone.

This stately memorial, dedicated so recently as 1921, stands in Washington and was erected by the State of Virginia. The severely classical building stands to keep evergreen the memory of Abraham Lincoln, a President of the U.S.A., who fought for the overthrow of slavery. Lincoln guided the Northern States through the Civil War and led them to victory.

except in the North Island of New Zealand.

The Grand Canyon.

The Grand Canyon of Arizona is easily reached by the " Sunshine Route " of the Southern Pacific ; a branch line runs to the very edge of the Tonto Rim, where are large hotels for visitors.   The canyon itself is " a terrific trough 6,000 to 7,000 feet deep, and from ten to twenty miles wide, and hundreds

HIGHEST IN N. AMERICA
This wonderful vista is that afforded by Mt. Whitney in California, the highest peak in the U.S.A. and on the North American Continent. Note how deeply the snow lies up among the clouds at an altitude of 14,501 feet.

only a region containing some of the most wonderful scenes in the United States, but also a sanctuary where trees and flowers, birds and animals, are strictly preserved from the risk of extinction.   The geysers and hot springs, however, are the most astonishing of all its wonders.   Four thousand hot springs and over a hundred geysers provide spectacles which can be witnessed nowhere else,

Photos : H. J. Shepstone.

The wild, rugged landscape here portrayed is that of the actual summit of Mt. Whitney, with its snowy carpet and rough, shapeless boulders outcropping from the surface of the earth.   The little house, for hardy folks who scale the summit, is the highest building in the U.S.A.

IN CALIFORNIA—AMERICA'S FAR WEST

California is a wonderfully fertile state, bordered by the warm Pacific Ocean, and is a great producer of peaches, grapes, figs and other fruits. Even dates are extensively raised, and the scene above shows us girls gathering in the harvest in a date grove in the Coachella Valley.

Photos: G. P. A.

San Francisco is the principal business city on the Pacific seaboard of the U.S.A., and we see above the pleasure beach with an enormously wide highway behind. The city is built on a beautiful bay, and the route vessels take to reach the open ocean from the Bay is through a straight known poetically as "The Golden Gate." The term "Golden State" has been applied to California as a whole because of its great natural wealth.

of miles long, within which are hundreds of peaks higher than any mountain east of the Rockies, yet whose heads are below the floor level of the Colorado Plateau," in which this enormous gash has been cut by the power of running water. From its rim you can look down through a mile of clear air to the yellow ribbon of the Colorado River which has cut this mighty trench by age-long erosion. Its tributaries, too, have cut similar, but smaller canyons, which enter the main canyon, dissecting the dry plateau into a system of profound gorges.

Beyond the Great Basin, with Salt Lake City and its irrigated fields and gardens near Great Salt Lake, and over the Sierra Nevada, famous for its forest giants, the traveller descends into the rich valley of California—a land of flowers and luscious fruits, rich in grain and cattle—where careful irrigation during the dry summer makes it possible to grow things all the year round. California's great city is the port of San Francisco on the Golden Gate.

Golden California.

Gold made San Francisco. But the land had greater riches than gold, and these—the wealth in timber and grain, cattle and fruit—were first developed by those who came seeking gold but finding much more lasting sources of income. Gold is still got in the Sierras, and in the lowlands, where monster gold-dredges eat their slow way across country, extracting the gold and leaving behind them a desolate trail of waste gravel like strips of

H. J. Shepstone.

AMONG THE STUDIOS OF HOLLYWOOD

You might think at first glance that you were looking at a series of warehouses in some dockland district. Yet, strictly speaking, these buildings are used for a purpose you would hardly guess. They are indeed typical studios such as you would find at Hollywood, the beautiful films in strange contrast to the plain buildings in which they are produced. The stages in these studios are 150 feet deep and 350 feet long.

HOMES OF SOME FILM STARS

Hollywood, the great film centre, is situated in one of the most lovely parts of the State of California. On the seaward side of Hollywood come the famous Beverley Hills, upon which so many well-known film stars have made their homes. Some of the houses are of princely grandeur, the gardens laid out with exotic trees, so that they give one a glimpse of fairyland in real life.

A STRANGE FREAK OF NATURE

G. P. A.

If you could visit the Chimney Rock Mountains in the North Carolina district of the United
States of America you would not be long in joining the thousands of visitors who go to seek
out this strange freak of Nature known as the " Devil's Head." It is certain that this head,
formed in the rock, has existed for upwards of four centuries, and it was once the meeting-
place of Red Indian tribesmen.

CARVED IN THE ROCK

Keystone View Co.

This illustration is a great contrast to the one on the opposite page. The " Devil's Head " was formed by Nature, but the one above was carved under the direction of an eminent sculptor in the Black Hills of South Dakota, U.S.A. The effigy in stone is that of George Washington, and you can form some idea of the size of the face by comparing it with the hut.

desert. In southern California there are rich oil-wells, and the land is covered with oil-derricks.

Los Angeles, south of San Francisco, is the centre of the fruit business. Hollywood, whose clear air and sunshine have made it the " home of the movies," is not far away. But one need not go many miles to the southwest of Los Angeles before he comes to real desert country, with weird flowering cacti, and strange Indian tribes who still live in their pueblos or communal houses of sun-baked adobe or clay, much as their forefathers lived a thousand years ago.

Cotton.

United States lands bordering the Gulf of Mexico are districts of cotton-fields, rice-fields and sugar plantations. Texas, the biggest of the States, however, has very rich oil-wells, in addition to being the largest cotton producer. The great cotton ports are New Orleans, Galveston and Mobile on the Gulf, and Charleston and Savannah on the Atlantic.

New Orleans, once an old city of French and Spanish houses that reminded one of the people who founded it and first made it a place of importance, has now a growing horizon of skyscrapers that recall those of the other great American cities of the north-east. It stands nearly 100 miles up the winding Mississippi from the seaward extremity of the delta, on Lake Pontchartrain, over which a five-mile-long toll-bridge of concrete has been built. Its chief street is Canal Street, which the city claims

Will F. Taylor.

IN THE YOSEMITE VALLEY

For scenery of the most majestic type there is little to equal the Yosemite Valley, adjacent to the Sierra Nevada Mountains. Here the United States Government has established another of its great national parks. In this picture we see the trio of peaks known as the " Three Brothers."

THE SCULPTURE OF THE WILDS

H. J. Shepstone.

Few more beautiful pictures could be imagined than this view of the famous Bryce Canyon in Arizona. It is as though Mother Nature had herself turned sculptress, and the broken strata of the rocks indicates some mighty upheaval in earth's earliest ages. One of the greatest wonders of Arizona is the Grand Canyon of the Colorado River.

to be the widest business thoroughfare in the world.

Lovely Florida.

Rivalling California in the production of fruits is Florida, whose peninsula, like a projecting thumb, points southward into the warm waters of the Gulf Stream. Its Atlantic shores are studded with seaside resorts and winter beaches, popular with Americans of the colder north, Palm Beach, Miami, and Daytona, famous as the scene of record-breaking motor trials. Away out in the Atlantic, 600 miles or so from Cape Hatteras, are the Bermudas, which belong to the British Empire, and are serious rivals to Florida, not only as a winter resort for American visitors, but also as a source of early vegetables, flowers and fruit. The Bermudas are coral islands; their chief town is *Hamilton*.

Owing to the fact that they are founded on coral, there are almost as many islands in the Bermudas as days in the year, and one could count 360 of them at least. Of this number, however, only about a score are inhabited. The biggest of the islands is known as Great Bermuda, and the name of the group comes from the Spanish mariner Bermudez, who sighted them in 1515.

G. P. A.

A DAM MADE UP OF DOMES

For the purpose of providing water for two vast tracts of territory and to reclaim a great desert, the above unusual dam has been constructed in Gila River Valley, Arizona, U.S.A. The dam itself is composed of egg-shaped domes more than 250 feet in height, the distance across the valley being 550 feet. This is the first multiple dome type of dam ever constructed, and there is a road for motor cars along the top.

The Story
of the
World and
its Peoples

Our Neighbours
and Friends
in
Other Lands

H. J. Shepstone.

ENTERING THE TEMPERATE ZONE

The Tropic of Cancer, which you will see marked on your maps, is the dividing line betwixt the Torrid and Temperate Zones of the earth. In this photograph, taken just northward of Mazatland, in Mexico, we see a signpost indicating where the imaginary line crosses the earth's surface. The motor car running on a railway track has just entered the Temperate Zone.

THE LAND OF THE MIGHTY AMAZON

THE first glimpse of South America that most of us get on coming out from Britain is of that high shoulder of tropical Brazil which heaves itself out of the Atlantic at Cape San Roque. It was this same shoulder which de Cabral, the old Portuguese navigator, saw when he discovered Brazil in the first half of the sixteenth century.

Rio de Janeiro.

Eighteen days out of Southampton our steamer calls at the beautiful harbour of Rio de Janeiro, the Brazilian capital, with over a million people. Its lovely islands are dotted with the white villas of wealthy Brazilians, and the tall Sugar Loaf that rears its strange cone over the bay forms a fitting approach to the city's wide curving promenades planted with palms, its straight streets and fine open squares, and its pretty houses on the rising ground behind the business quarters of the city. A wonderful view of Rio can be got from the Corcovado, a mountain behind the city, or from the giddy peak of the Sugar Loaf itself, which has a cableway to its summit, and at night is brilliantly lighted.

Rio is one of the great coffee ports of Brazil, as well as its splendid capital. But even more coffee comes out of Santos, the next port at which we call on our voyage south. A few miles inland from Santos is the coffee capital of Sao Paulo, a city whose fortunes depend as much on coffee as those of Kuala Lumpur on rubber, or Kimberley on diamonds.

Sao Paulo is considered one of the

finest cities in South America. At the back of it and in most of the hill country of the Sierra do Mar right away to Rio there is the rich *terra rossa*, the red soil on the well-drained slopes ideal for coffee-growing.

The workers on the coffee *fazendas* (estates) are Brazilians, or negroes, or Indians, or immigrants into Brazil from Spain, Portugal and Italy. A fazenda may support as many as five or six thousand people, for not only does it grow coffee, but it has its own cattle pastures, its own grain-lands, and its own gardens and fruit plantations, as well as its own mills, bakeries, repair shops, blacksmiths' shops, and its store where the thousands who live on the fazenda can buy anything they require.

A really up-to-date fazenda in Brazil is a world in itself. It is a wonderful sight when the green of the myriads of neat rows of coffee-bushes change to a delicate white in blossom-time, filling the air with their perfume. It is the beginning of a story that ends (so far as South America is concerned) at Santos, where we see long processions of dock labourers— black, brown, yellow or olive-skinned— carrying the heavy sacks of coffee " beans " to the waiting steamers.

Interior Brazil.

This is only the rich " doorstep " of Brazil. If you go inland and north from the coffee-lands, you come first to high tropical grass-lands with many cattle and with great flat table-lands of bare rock here and there. Down in the deep valleys of their southern edges are gold-mines and gravel-beds

Mondiale.

A TREE-ENCLOSED LAKE, AS SEEN FROM THE AIR

In this picture we are looking down, as from an aeroplane, upon a vast tract of dense, primeval forest in the midst of which is the entrancing lake of Petha, near Chiapas in Mexico. Because of the trees, we could only obtain such a comprehensive view of the lake from the air.

Specially painted for this work.

MARKET-DAY IN A VILLAGE OF MEXICO

Long before the white man went to Mexico native Indians held markets in the village streets
and the custom still remains, as is shown in the gay picture above. In this tropic land shops
as we know them do not exist in the villages and so the fruit-seller, the cloth-weaver, the potter,
the hatter and representatives of all the other callings assemble in the market-place, plying
their wares in a scene of vivid colours and burning sunshine. Above we see both Spaniards and
Indians and the cultivation of fruit and vegetables is still mainly in native hands.

AN INDIAN BELLE OF PANAMA

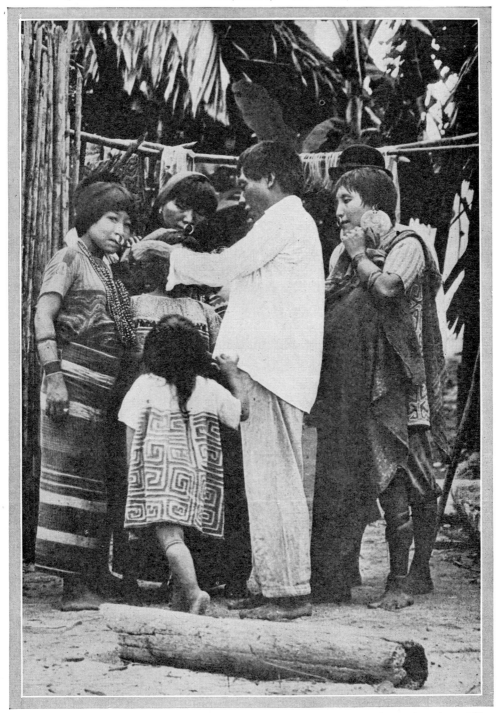

Ewing Galloway, N.Y.

Indian tribes of many different types inhabit the Western Continent, and the people seen above are natives of the Panama district of Central America. Their home is Sasardi, one of the group of 365 islands; and, in the picture, a young girl of the tribe is having a ring put into her nose. Nose-rings among some of these races are regarded as ornaments of great attractiveness.

BY "THE RIVER OF JANUARY"

A wonder city, Rio de Janeiro was called " The River of January " by the early discoverers, who mistook for a river the estuary upon which the city stands. Rio is the capital of Brazil, and is a place of perpetual sunshine. The chief square boasts of 60,000 different species of plants.

Photos : Will F. Taylor.

Here we have another view of Rio de Janeiro with the well-known Sugar Loaf Mountain beyond, rising from the bay on which the city has been built. Rio is the second city in importance in South America and is surpassed only by Buenos Aires. The early voyagers discovered the site of the city on January 1st, 1502.

that yield diamonds and other precious stones. Go on beyond the high grasslands and you come at last to the greatest forest in the world, the Selvas of the Amazon Basin, where trees and creepers grow so luxuriantly that they almost crowd out men and animals, and where the only easy way of getting about is by canoe or river-steamer along the giant waterways.

The best way to see what the forests of the Amazon are like is to take the steamer (from Liverpool) that will bear you across the equatorial Atlantic to the city-gate of the forests at Para, and then up the mighty yellow flood of the Amazon as far as Manaos, the magic city in the very heart of the Selvas on the Rio Negro, tributary of the "mother of waters."

The Mighty Amazon.

Your ship may be steaming up the Amazon without your realising it, for in places nearer its mouth this vast river is so wide that you cannot see its banks if you are in mid-stream. It is only when your ship follows the deep channels as they swing near to the shore that you realise what this forest is, and begin to wonder what awful secrets it holds behind that steep precipice of living vegetation which faces you with its myriad shades of green in a wall 200 feet high.

Will F. Taylor.

ASCENDING THE SUGAR LOAF

The world-famous Sugar Loaf Mountain at Rio de Janeiro, illustrated on the previous page, may be ascended by carriages suspended from wires, forming an aerial cableway. The man seen standing so calmly on one foot in this illustration of the cableway is engaged in lubricating the machinery.

Great flowering creepers fling carpets of scarlet or yellow over the forest wall; flights of brilliant birds wheel out and back again into the depths of the forest, giant butterflies with five or six inches of delicate blue wing-span flit across the deck, and in the yellow swirling flood, swarms of alligators float like almost submerged logs, or great tangled

BB2

SNAPSHOTS FROM RIO DE JANEIRO

Our photograph was taken very early in the morning before many people were about. It shows us the Copocabana Beach at Rio, and we may be sure it will be crowded with men, women and children later in the day. During the hours of bathing an armed guard occupies the crow's nest at the top of the post seen along the esplanade. A guard is necessary because of the sharks.

Photos : Will F. Taylor.

In this illustration we have a view of the Avenida Rio Branco in Rio de Janeiro, a stately promenade. The handsome edifice in the centre is the Municipal Opera House. This fine avenue is one of the chief thoroughfares of the city, and is named after a well-known Brazilian statesman.

UP=COUNTRY IN SUNNY BRAZIL

Here, in imagination, we are " up-country " and about eighty miles from Rio. The ox-cart is standing outside a village tavern at a place called Belem (a word having the same meaning as Bethlehem). Belem is an important junction where two long-distance railways cross.

Photos : Will F. Taylor.

Above is a quiet street in the Brazilian town of Quro Preto. The place was founded early in the seventeenth century during a great gold rush when prospectors came from all parts. Quro was then known as the richest spot in the world and had a population of over 80,000. To-day far less than a quarter that number of people inhabit the township, which was the summer home of the Emperor before Brazil became a Republic.

floating islands drift by. You know that beneath that smooth surface full of blinding sun reflections there lurk shoals of savage *piranhas*—saw-toothed fish that would strip the flesh from your bones in a few minutes—and that along the edges of the river where water and vegetation mingle in a gloomy tangle there are probably anacondas 30 feet long awaiting easy prey.

Yet in the heart of all this there is the wonder-city of Manaos ; its busy wharves accommodate large steamers from European and American seaports, its wide shady streets, its fine Opera House and beautiful buildings, its electric trams, and its cheerful cafés and restaurants make it an island of civilisation in an ocean of primeval and savage forest.

The Rubber Gatherers.

Down the dark Amazon streams comes the rubber collected in the forest depths by sweating *seringueiros* who brave the fevers and the forest dangers to earn a scanty living by tapping the rubber-trees and smoking the white juice on paddle blades to turn it into thick balls of brown and black rubber. Some goes by river steamer or dug-out canoe, some in great rafts of floating balls of solid rubber, to the port of Manaos for shipment. But wild rubber is not so important as it was ; the much finer plantation rubber of Malaya and Ceylon has taken its place to such an extent that only about 15 per cent. of the rubber used in the world to-day is " wild " rubber.

Some of the natives of the Selvas live in thatched villages by the riverside, growing cassava roots from which the *farinha*, used everywhere for making bread and cakes, is made, and also maize, plantains, cacao, sugar-cane and cotton from which the native cloth is woven. Others are primitive savages and head-hunters living in the remote parts of the forest, building great houses called *malokas* in which a whole tribe lives, each family in its own little compart-

Keystone View Co.

DRYING THE COFFEE BEANS

Brazil is a most fertile country and produces all the crops to be raised in a tropical land. It is an important coffee-raising state, and we see here myriads of beans being spread out in the sun on drying floors. The native workmen deal with this harvest of the coffee plant by means of large wooden shovels.

ment, with a great open floor of split logs for general meetings of the tribe in the middle.

The Selvas.

This forest of the Selvas fills the whole of the great heart of South America; it is mainly in Brazil, but stretches into the Guianas, Peru, Colombo, Venezuela, and Bolivia as well. Its heavy rains and hot sunshine give it a steamy, unhealthy climate, and its hordes of stinging and biting insects make life a misery to all, except those who come prepared with mosquito nets to sleep beneath, mosquito veils to their sun helmets, and mosquito boots to protect

Mondiale.

BY THE AMAZON'S HEADWATERS

In this illustration we are surveying dense jungle land set amidst the headwaters of the mighty River Amazon. The Amazon is shorter than the Mississippi or the Nile, but is yet 3,500 miles in length. It rises in the great Andes Mountains and empties into the Atlantic. Near its main mouth the river is 50 miles in width.

their ankles from the winged pests. Yet out of this forest come not only rubber but valuable medicine, like cinchona bark (quinine) and sarsaparilla, and wonderful orchids for whose blossoms fabulous sums are sometimes paid, as well as beautiful cabinet woods.

Ports of the Plate River.

Continuing this voyage southwards from Santos, the South American liners proceed to Montevideo, the capital and

port of Uruguay, and Buenos Aires, the capital of Argentina and the largest city in the southern hemisphere. Both are the great ports of the Plate River, which is Nature's gateway to the grasslands of the Pampas and their cattlelands, sheep-farms and granaries. Buenos Aires, like many other great cities in the New World, is laid out on the chessboard plan into fine streets intersecting at right angles. Here and there are beautiful *plazas* or squares

A TRIO OF SNAPSHOTS OF—

In this view we are looking through a tangled mass of vegetation on to the placid waters of the Amazon. The river and its various tributaries flow through Peru, Bolivia and other South American countries, and the plain across which the goliath stream makes its way contains some of the densest forest in the world.

The Amazon is a giant among the world's rivers and it has actually many mouths. Here is one view in the Delta, showing a small sailing-boat making its way across the harbour of Vigia. This is a part of the Rio (*i.e.*, river) Para, the main mouth of the Amazon.

THE GIGANTIC RIVER AMAZON

G. P. A.

It is summer all the while along the banks of the Amazon, and the rigours of a wintry climate are quite unknown. The above is typical of the river scenery, and you will note that the very trees are quite different from those to which we are accustomed. An ocean-going steamer which has crossed the Atlantic can proceed about 2,500 miles up the Amazon, reaching the wonder-city of Manaos, set like a gem in the mighty jungle. From Manaos cargoes of rubber, obtained from trees in the forest, are shipped.

adorned with statues and fountains, and shady parks. Museums, theatres and galleries and magnificent shops make Buenos Aires the most splendid city in South America. Six great terminal stations receive the many lines that converge upon it, and its docks are crowded with ships from all parts of the world. Its chief business is in meat, grain and wool from the Pampas.

"The great ocean of waving grasses rearing their silvery plumes to a height of eight or nine feet," seen by the Spaniards when they first visited the country, are now partly turned into grain-lands or into pastures for huge herds of cattle and flocks of fine sheep, which have displaced the native herds of deer and guanaco.

Estancias and Frigorificos.

The large *estancias*, some covering half a million acres, centre upon the home of their owners or managers, around which trees have been planted, and ranges of sheds and corrals built. For the families of the peons and the gauchos (cowboys) there are adobe huts farther away from the home paddocks. The gauchos themselves, like the Canadian cowboys and the Australian stockmen, may be absent for many days, or even weeks, tending cattle and horses on these great estates, branding the animals or rounding them up for other purposes, and seeing that the long wire fences are kept in good repair.

In the neighbourhood of the Plate River ports are large freezing establishments called *frigorificos,* where the flesh of the animals reared on the Pampas is prepared for export as chilled or frozen beef or frozen mutton. There are great factories, too, which can the meat, make meat extract, and pack tongues into glass containers.

Will F. Taylor.

THE PARLIAMENT HOUSE OF ARGENTINA

Buenos Aires is the capital of the Argentine Republic and is considered the finest city in South America. In this view we see the Plaza Congreso or Palace of Congress, corresponding to our House of Commons. Buenos Aires stands about 150 miles inland from the Atlantic on the de la Plata or Plate River.

Cattle flourish on the warmer and moister parts of the Pampas, sheep on the cooler and drier lands towards the south. You will find busy *frigorificos* even on the Straits of Magellan and in the lonely isle of Tierra del Fuego.

Northern Argentina is much better than the rest of the country. On the plantations there cotton and sugarcane are grown, as well as maize and fruits, and in the unsettled region of the Chaco native South American Indians live by hunting and fishing or growing several sorts of grains and fruits in their small gardens.

Over the High Andes.

From Buenos Aires we can take train right across the Pampas and over the high Andes to Chile and the port of Valparaiso on the Pacific. Leaving Retiro Station at Buenos Aires at 10.30 either on Sunday or Thursday, we arrive at Valparaiso either on the following Monday or Friday at 23.42 Chilean time, which is forty-four minutes slow of Argentine time. This first part of the journey is over the Pampas, whose level expanse is broken here and there by the trees round the buildings of the great estancias. Enormous herds of cattle and wide areas golden with grain or blue with the flower of the flax tell of the wealth being made there.

Next morning we are in Mendoza, a city in a fertile valley of vines and fruit trees, within twelve miles of the foothills of the Andes. Changing

A BRIDGE SHAPED BY NATURE   *G. P. A.*
The above rock bridge is perfectly natural and was not the work of man, particularly of the romantic Incas, as some people may suppose. It is known as the "Bridge of the Incas" and is one of the sights of the Argentine. Beneath the bridge flows the River Mendoza.

here into the narrow-gauge train, we begin to climb in steep curves up to the great tunnels at the top of the Uspallata Pass, 12,000 feet above sea-level, catching glimpses of Aconcagua (23,000 feet) and of other snowy giants of the Andes up side valleys, and doing our best to accustom ourselves to the thin air at this height. We stop at Puente del Inca on the way to see the famous statue of Christ upon the Cumbre Pass where Argentina meets Chile ; on its pedestal is an inscription which, translated, reads :

"Sooner shall these mountains crumble into dust than the peoples of Argentina and Chile break the peace which at the feet of Christ the Redeemer they have sworn to maintain."

At Los Andes we change into the Chilean train, and after a quick run of four hours from Andean snows to the flowers and orange groves of the lowlands we reach the port of Valparaiso on the sunny Pacific.

Chile.

Chile is a country remarkable for its narrowness and its great length, for it is squeezed in the small space between the Pacific and the high Andes. It has many different climates, for it extends from within the Tropics to cool, temperate latitudes like those of the north of Scotland.

Northern Chile is a thirsty land. Much of it belongs to the Desert of Atacamá, where rain hardly ever falls. Yet if we look at the map we see along its shores a string of ports of which Iquique and Antofagasta are the chief, and cannot help wondering what it is

that makes men live in a land that is by nature rainless and barren. But if we visit some of these towns we learn their secret. There we see large vessels being loaded with nitrates from the desert to fertilise the fields and plantations of Europe and many other parts of the world. We are astonished, too, to see fruits and pleasant gardens here and there, and soon discover that, like the people who live there, they get the life-giving water from the Andes, many miles away, through long pipes.

Nitrate Factories.

The factories or *oficinas* where the nitrates are prepared lie out in the open desert, and have thousands of men and their families living in their many buildings. Some are splendidly equipped with libraries, gymnasiums, and even swimming baths. They are little centres of busy life, like islands in a barren desert. The nitrate is prepared from the hard rocky material which lies several feet below ground and must be

WORK IN A NITRATE REFINERY   *Ewing Galloway, N.Y.*

The print here reproduced affords us a glimpse of the crushing plant in a nitrate refinery in Chili. Nitrate of soda, which is won from a rainless part of the country, is prepared in such refineries for export. The material is largely used as a fertiliser on farms and in gardens.

THE SIGN OF THE CROSS

H. J. Shepstone.

Extending almost from end to end of the continent, the Andes Mountains form the backbone of South America, and it is most interesting to note that high amidst the snows stands an enormous figure of Christ and the Cross. This statue, emblematical of Christianity, is placed just where the frontiers of Chili and Argentina meet, as a token of international peace and friendship.

broken by blasting before it can be removed to the factory. From this stuff, not only the fertilising nitrate, but iodine also is prepared.

Middle Chile is a different land altogether. Here rain comes in the winter, but the summers are long and dry and the grain-growers and fruit-farmers must carefully irrigate their land in order to ensure rich crops. The most fertile lands are in the Central Valley, where vineyards and orange groves, wheat-fields and maize-fields, vegetable gardens and olive yards flourish.

Southern Chile is yet another different land, where heavy rains fall, and dense forests clothe the slopes; where the coast is broken into myriads of inlets and fringed with thousands of islands, and where Indian fishermen have their villages.

Three hundred and seventy miles away in the Pacific off the Chilean coast is the island of Juan Fernandez, where Alexander Selkirk (the original of " Robinson Crusoe ") lived for nearly five years. Visitors can still see the cave in which he made his home.

In the Chilean Andes are several rich copper-mines and iron-mines worked by American companies.

Ewing Galloway, N.Y.

READY TO BEGIN THEIR DANCE

The couple in the foreground are Chilean natives, preparing to dance the cueca, which is very rhythmic though most sedate. The guitar provides the only orchestral music for the dance. Our illustration was obtained at Los Andes, a township high in the mountains on the Trans-Andino Railway, as the line across the Andes is called.

IN BOLIVIA AND ECUADOR

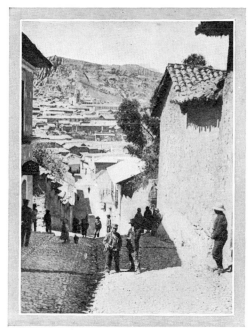

Bolivia is a republic of South America at least five times as large as our Motherland. Here we see the " ups and downs " of one of its townships, La Paz, the capital.

This busy scene emanates from the same town and offers to us an excellent idea of the market throngs on a Sabbath morning. Bolivia is entirely an inland country.

Ecuador, as its name suggests, stands on the equator and has a long seaboard to the Pacific. Above we see a typical native home with the family and friends.

Photos : Will F. Taylor.

This illustration shows us natives of Ecuador doing their marketing on Sunday morning. Some of the people we see are Spaniards and others natives.

The Land of the Incas.

North of Chile is the country of *Peru*, famous in history as the home of the Inca people whom the Spaniards of the sixteenth century found living in cities adorned with splendid temples and palaces. It was a wealthy and prosperous land among the plateaux of the Andes, where great roads linked the towns and a happy people lived upon the produce of their well-tilled farms and their pastures. But Pizarro, the Spanish adventurer, was greedy for gold, and treacherously caused the Inca Atahualpa to be slain, although the Inca had caused his prison to be filled with gold from stripped palaces and temples as the price of freedom. All that remain to tell of the past glories of the land of the Incas are the ruins of mighty temples and giant walls made of worked stones and so wonderfully fixed together without mortar or cement that they have defied the winds and the weather of the centuries. Silver is still mined up on the plateaux, but much less is got now than formerly. Cuzco, the old capital of the Incas, stands at a height of 11,400 feet above sea-level. There you may see the cathedral built by the conquerors, and around the city the mighty ruins of the empire they destroyed.

Pizarro's bones you can see for yourself in their glass-fronted coffin in the great cathedral at Lima, founded by him in 1535. Lima is the capital of Peru; its port is Callao on the Pacific, only eight miles away.

From the Peruvian and Chilean ports wonderful mountain railways make their way up to the high plateaux among the Andes to the shores of Lake Titicaca, 12,000 feet above the sea, and to the rich tin and cattle country of *Bolivia* and its capital of La Paz. These high Andean lands are the home of the llama, which is the chief beast

Ewing Galloway, N.Y.
A CITY OF FOUR NATIONS
Beyond the archway through which we are looking is the main street of Quito, the capital of Ecuador. On the same site Carios, Mayas, Incas and Ecuadorians have all had cities. This place stands on the equator, nearly 10,000 feet above sea level, and has snow-clad peaks beyond.

A NEW RACE IN VENEZUELA

Wide World Photos.

The extraordinary figure here depicted is a member of the Pishauko tribe, only recently discovered by a young explorer in Venezuela.   The tribe lives in almost impassable jungle and the
men are most warlike among themselves and towards all their neighbours.   If these people are
overtaken by illness they resort to self-torture as a cure, and this strange custom is known to
prevail among other savage races in different parts of the world.   The queer fellow seen above
is a dancer in full regalia on the occasion of a festival.

of burden, and the alpaca and the vicuna kept for their soft wool. Railways run along the length of the Peruvian plateau—perhaps the highest railways in the world and far above the clouds.

The Northern Republics.

The giant volcanoes of the Andes are chiefly in *Ecuador*, where Chimborazo and Cotopaxi rear their mighty cones ; but Sorata, who lifts his snowy head over 21,000 feet above the sea, is in Bolivia. Ecuador, whose capital is Quito—a city of eternal spring 9,000 feet up—is the real home of the so-called " panama " hats, made by the Indians from the fan-leaves of a kind of palm tree.

The northern countries of South America—*Colombia, Venezuela* and the *Guianas*—are lands of cacao and sugar, of cotton and tobacco, of bananas and rubber. Dense forests clothe the mountain slopes and deep valleys, although parts of Colombia and Venezuela fall within the Llanos of the Orinoco—great tropical grass-lands.

In these hot countries most people live on the highland plateaux, where the climate is cooler. Bogotá, the capital of Colombia, is over 8,000 feet above the sea, and Caracas, the capital of Venezuela, is in an upland valley at an altitude of over 3,000 feet. From Bogotá a hydroplane service connects with its ports of Barrabquillas and Cartagene on the Caribbean Sea.

Mondiale.

A VOLCANIC AREA IN ECUADOR

The Republic of Ecuador is extremely mountainous, for it embraces the great double range known as the Cordilleras, among whose peaks are many volcanoes. The picture here reproduced affords us an interesting idea of the wild, rugged country in the volcanic region, where any signs of civilisation are few and far between.

The Story
of the
World and
its Peoples

Our Neighbours
and Friends
in
Other Lands

Will F. Taylor.

THE GREAT WALL OF CHINA

The Great Wall of China, which was begun in 246 B.C., extended at least 2,000 miles, and was from 15 to 30 feet in thickness. The wall was erected as a barrier against Tartar horsemen, and it is estimated that more brick and stone was used in its construction than in all the buildings in the United Kingdom put together.

CHINA

CHINA makes a brave show on the political map of Asia. Next to that great triangle of territory in the north belonging to the U.S.S.R., China is by far the largest division of the Asiatic continent, and when we read of the many millions of people who live in China we are not altogether surprised, for on the map the land of the Chinese is a very roomy one indeed.

But when we know a little more of the geography of China we begin to see why people speak of China as a crowded country where, in spite of the fertile soil and the warm summer rains, men must toil long and laboriously to grow the food necessary to support themselves and their families. For a

great deal of China is very unsuitable as the home of many people. Look at the western half of it—more than half, in fact—that spreads itself over a large part of the heart of Asia. This region is chiefly high plateau, very hot in summer, bitterly cold in winter, and almost rainless, save for a few favoured spots. Large parts are so dry that they are sandy or stony desert; there is the Desert of Gobi, which fills the greater part of Mongolia; and farther to the south-west is the Takla-Makan, a desert still more terrible. No wonder those Mongol traders who come down with their long caravans of laden camels to the gates of Peking wear thick coats of sheep-skin—they have travelled from the desert plateau,

371

Will F. Taylor.

CHINESE COOLIE

The word "coolie" is the general term applied to Asiatic labourers. In our picture we show a Chinese coolie bearing cabbages on his back and easing the strain for a moment or two by the use of a resting pole which takes the weight of the load. In Southern China three crops a year are produced from the same piece of ground.

where even in summer the nights are cold.

The Crowded Plains of China.

It is in the eastern part of China that most of her 400 millions of people live, and even there, mountains and hills occupy a great part of the country south of the Yangtse, which is the biggest river in China, with the great port of Shanghai near its mouth. We can see clearly how crowded the real China must be if we find on the map the plain-lands and river valleys of the east, and imagine most of these 400 millions of people packed into those spaces. Nature has, fortunately, given China fertile soil and the most favourable conditions for growing heavy crops, for most rain and sunshine come at the same time of the year. But not even those advantages could feed China's millions of mouths if the farmers and their families did not work hard every working hour. Nowhere else in the world, except in Japan, is the habit of work—hard and constant labour on field and farm—so deeply engrained in the lives of the people.

A Land of Toilers.

Nothing but constant and diligent toil can make even the rich lands of Southern China yield three harvests a year—three distinct crops from the same piece of ground. You can see men, women and children working all day long up to their knees in the slimy mud of the rice-fields, their legs bound with cotton strips to defend them from leeches thirsty for blood, their heads protected from the hot sun by enormous mushroom-like hats of plaited bamboo or rice straw. There they toil all day bent almost double as they plant out by hand the nine-inch-high rice plants grown from seed in some sunny corner earlier in the year.

You can see women carrying to the fields enormous baskets of slime dredged patiently by their menfolk

BREAKFAST TIME IN CHINA

Keystone View Co.

If you could be transported on a magic carpet into a Chinese home at breakfast time this is the sight that would greet your eyes. For the meal coffee is served and food provided in a bowl in the centre of the table. Each member of the party helps himself from the bowl with chopsticks and eats with the aid of the same primitive implements. It would be impossible to say how many centuries chopsticks have been in use.

from one of the million canals that cover the plains of China in a close network to irrigate the land and to provide easy ways of getting heavy loads from place to place. Children in Northern China, where winters are very cold, go up in the autumn to the hillsides and bring down enormous bundles of sticks for winter fuel—bundles so huge that their bearers can hardly be seen beneath them.

On a Chinese Farm.

When you visit a Chinese farm—tiny farms most of them are—you are astonished at the way in which everything is used and nothing wasted.

Every inch of soil that can is growing something ; the banks of earth between the rice-fields carry a fat crop of soya bean, or vegetables, or perhaps long pergolas of fruit-trees so trimmed and tended that all their hanging fruit in autumn is within reach of a man's hand and well open to the sunshine.

As soon as the rice is tall enough, the water in which it has been growing is drained off to let the grain ripen, but not until all the fish have been netted, the luscious water snails collected for food, and the greedy ducks that have lived there fattening on insects and worms have been driven home. When the rice has been harvested by hand and taken bundle by bundle to the farm to dry and yield its store of shining brown grains, the field is flattened out, ridged up, and almost at once a new crop is sown—beans, perhaps, or barley or vegetables. There is no waste of time, or space, or opportunity on a Chinese farm.

The home garden near the farmhouse, that corner where nothing else will grow, is planted with bamboo, whose stout hollow stems are used for scores of things, from building houses to making cooking-pots, and whose tender shoots provide a tasty vegetable as delicious as asparagus. Even the pond, on which lovely pink and white or golden lilies lie amid their pads of floating green, yields lily-roots and water snails that with the fish help to

Will F. Taylor.

A TYPICAL CHINESE JUNK

The sails of Chinese junks vary slightly in shape, though they are mostly made of matting. Some junks are three-masted, and it is by means of these vessels that the Chinese carry on a coast-wise trade. In the rivers smaller boats called sampans are used.

WASH TUB BOATS ON THE YANGTSE

In China, Japan and Korea, food is transferred to the mouth by means of a pair of chopsticks of wood, bone or ivory.

Here is another picture of a Chinese coolie, a woman this time. She is carrying a pair of buckets suspended on a balancing pole.

Photos : Will F. Taylor.

On the Yangtse River, 256 miles from Shanghai, is the treaty port of Wuhu. Steamers arriving here are quickly surrounded by Chinese men, women and children in small boats like wash tubs.

fill the family larder. All the waste from the house and the farm is carefully collected for use as fertiliser, and so changes from waste to wealth, for these Chinese fields and gardens are worked so hard that constant manuring is necessary to preserve their fertility.

The Rice Line.

If you draw a line across China through the northern side of the basin of the Yangtse, you will have south of that line the lands where rice is the chief grain, and north of it lands where wheat and millet are grown rather than rice, which needs warmer weather than you get in many parts of Northern China. Rice is, indeed, the chief food of the Chinese—*if* they can get it— but it is a mistake to suppose that rice grows everywhere in China and that all Chinese live on it. Although China is perhaps the biggest rice-grower in the world, the needs of her people are so great that much rice is imported from other Asiatic lands to the south.

In Northern China—even in Peking —winters are much colder than those we have in Britain. The Chinese there protect themselves against the bitter cold winds by wearing coats thickly wadded with cotton, with long sleeves into which they can tuck their hands, and long boots of leather. The country folk in many parts sleep in winter on a kind of platform with flues beneath it leading warm air from their little fires. This is the origin of tales you may have heard of Chinese who in winter " sleep on top of the stove ! "

Southern China, however, has no winters like those of Northern China,

Will F Taylor

CHILLY OLD LADIES OF CHINA

The two elderly country women evidently feel the cold acutely, for they are warming their hands on brass boxes containing the embers of glowing charcoal. The lady on your left is also instilling some warmth into her feet by similar means. Note that the brass containers have perforated tops through which the heat rises—as did some of the old-fashioned English warming-pans.

tor it is a tropical land where men work in the fields naked, save for a waistcloth, and where only the thinnest of blue cotton clothing is necessary, except in the mountainous areas like Yunnan, where nights are often chilly.

Communications in China.

All this shows what a large country China is. Until comparatively recent years, it has been a land difficult to travel in, and north and south were as far apart as if they were at opposite ends of the world. People of Northern China even now cannot understand those of Southern China ; their languages are in many ways very different, although all speak some form of Chinese. There are

Will F. Taylor.

THE TOWER ON TIGER HILL

We think of China as a country of pagodas, and here is a picture of the famous Tiger Hill Pagoda at Soochow, about 50 miles from Shanghai. Pagodas are merely towers, and most of those built in China are eight-sided, possessing many storeys. There is a pagoda at Kew Gardens, near London.

railways now in China ; even the mighty old walls of Peking have been pierced to let them in, and to-day you can take train from ports on the North Sea or the Channel and go right across Europe to Moscow to join there one of the T.-S.R. expresses, in which you can travel all the way across Siberia to China and Peking, a journey that means a fortnight's living and sleeping in trains.

But although excellent railways have been built almost through the whole length of China, and in and near the chief towns good roads have been made, and motor traffic is a common thing, many of the highways of rural China are unspeakably bad, parts of quite important ones being mere tracks, possible only for camels and other pack animals, for coolies on foot, or for the Chinese wheelbarrow whose single wheel enables it to go where passage for two-wheeled vehicles is out of the question.

The Chinese Wheelbarrow.

Even in large cities like Shanghai, Peking and Hankow, where there are trains, electric trams and motor vehicles of every description, the old Chinese wheelbarrow, piled high with fruit and vegetables or heaped with incredibly large loads, may be seen pushed and pulled by perspiring coolies thinly clad in blue cotton, or managed by stolid country folk come into the busy town to sell their market produce. Away from the towns you may meet such a wheelbarrow carrying a double load of smiling passengers, a row on each side of its high central wheel, or you may encounter another on which the barrow-coolies have hoisted a sail of matting to gain advantage of a following wind.

In Northern China and in Manchuria the " Manchurian cart " is in common use. It is often entirely innocent of springs, and is drawn by the stocky little ponies bred in those parts. In the difficult mountain country the " chair " or palanquin, slung between long bamboos and borne on the shoulders of sturdy coolies, is a common way of getting about.

The Lands of China.

Let us glance at the map and see for ourselves what lands go to make the China of our atlases. There is first of all the Chinese Republic — "China Proper"—with its fertile plains and valleys and its teeming millions of hard-working country folk, and its southern and western mountains where both farming and travel are difficult and fewer people live.

In the far north-east is the great province of Manchuria, with its chief town, Mukden, a land of farmers growing great crops of wheat and soya beans. Large numbers of Chinese, driven from the south by war and famine, are coming to Manchuria as settlers ; the plains are very like the prairies of Canada, and suitable

Will F. Taylor.

A CHINESE " PANTECHNICON "

Wheelbarrows, seeming to carry the most enormous loads, form the chief feature of Chinese transport arrangements. The scene here depicted gives one some idea of what these one-wheeled vehicles can carry, this particular man being the local remover of household furniture.

HOW THINGS ARE DONE IN CHINA

A cheerful little scene in a Chinese school. The Chinese language is extremely difficult to learn, and at least one word has as many as fourteen different meanings.

Rice is threshed and winnowed and is then hulled—the grain separated from the outer covering. Here is a Chinese coolie engaged in hulling.

The two images seen in the picture are made of paper, and head a Chinese funeral procession to frighten away evil spirits.

Photos: Will F. Taylor.

A primitive mill in use near Wei-hai-Wei for the grinding of millet grain. Ground millet yields a fine white flour.

for grain and cattle and sheep, and the climate, too, is very similar to that of the Canadian prairie provinces. At Mukden meet railways from the Trans-Siberian line, from the Japanese protectorate of Korea, and from the city of Peking and Southern China. The chief port is Newchwang, which handles the rafts of timber, and the cargoes of grain and beans from the plains of Manchuria and their surrounding highlands.

In the Heart of Asia.

In the very heart of Asia and in the great central plateaux are three other countries which belong to China only in name and in our atlases. Really they are practically independent of China. They are : (1) the desert and steppe country of *Mongolia*, which fringes Southern Siberia and whose northern part is very much influenced by the Russians of the U.S.S.R. ; (2) the mountain, desert and valley land of *Sinkiang*, which is very much out of the way, and, except for the great wireless station of Urumchi and the camel caravans from China, Turkestan and Siberia, out of touch with the great world outside ; and (3) the mysterious land of *Tibet*, which for long was known as " The Forbidden Land," because the people refused to admit foreigners to their territory.

All three are lands where comparatively few people live, and where a wandering life with flocks and herds is common. All three are parts of the great central plateaux and deserts that form the heart of Asia, and have marked extremes of heat and cold and little rain. In all three the large villages and the towns are either in deep and sheltered valleys or in the oases.

The Great Wall of China.

The Mongols belong to the same great race of desert raiders and nomadic herdsmen as those of ancient days whom the rulers of China tried to keep out of the fertile plains and rich cities by building the Great Wall, whose remains you can still see in a good state of preservation not far from Peking.

The Great Wall of China was begun in 246 B.C. by Chin Shih Huang Ti, and was completed in 209 B.C., seven years after his death. Chin called it " The Long Rampart," and to

Will F. Taylor.

UP AMIDST THE RICE FIELDS

The curious ridges or corrugations here illustrated are the work of Chinese labourers, who till their rice-fields in neat, orderly terraces so that the rain may not wash too much soil into the valleys. The landscape upon which we are looking is typical of the high parts of the province of Yunnan.

build it he employed not only 300,000 of his troops, but all prisoners of war, and even the criminals from the gaols. When it was finished it stretched for 1,250 miles into China from the sea coast at Shanhaikwan to Minchow in far-off Kansu. If we reckon all its windings and turnings, the Great Wall was at least 2,000 miles in length.

The Great Wall strode across country up hill and down dale, without regard to the surface of the land; in certain places it was double or even treble, especially at passes through the mountains, where the hated desert warriors from the heart of Asia and the north were most likely to try to break in.

At the Nankow Pass, through which a modern railway now runs, the wall was strengthened by five additional walls and gates, for this pass formed one of the chief caravan routes from China into Mongolia. The eastern part was strongly built of stone and sun-dried brick, but the western part was only clay ramparts, much of which now lie in ruins—"mere ridges of stones and clay intersected by crumbling towers."

The Great Wall, however, could not keep back the Mongol hordes, who swept into China in spite of its battlements and towers.

IN MANCHURIA'S CAPITAL   *Will F. Taylor.*
Mukden is the capital of Manchuria, and here we see the north-west gate of the city, which is of enormous antiquity. From Manchuria came the Manchus, who ruled China for nearly three centuries. The original walls of Mukden were about 10 miles round, this fact giving us some idea of the size of the place.

The Mongolian Desert.

The Mongolian Desert long ago was probably much more fertile than it is to-day, for explorers tell of the ruins of great cities almost buried in the wind-blown sand and of other traces of a former thriving population. It was on this desert and its borders that American explorers and naturalists discovered not only the fossil bones of great prehistoric dinosaurs, but also the fossil eggs of these strange and long-extinct monsters.

THE TEMPLE OF HEAVEN

Mondiale.

China's capital is Peking, and the city is rich in buildings of great age. Among the most interesting structures is the Temple of Heaven, illustrated above, and known to have been erected more than 500 years ago, though Peking was the chief city some time before that.

Will F. Taylor.

Yun-nan-fu is the capital of that widespread province of China known as Yunnan, and the city is surrounded by a vast and fertile plain, of which we obtain an excellent idea from this picture. Beyond the plain, however, this south-westerly province rises to a mountain range in which is found considerable mineral wealth.

Will F. Taylor.

This full-page picture gives us an even closer view of the Great Wall of China than does the one on p. 371. Here we have an aerial impression and can fully appreciate the width of this mighty rampart. The people who, in days long gone, built this wall were convicts taken from the gaols and prisoners of war, as well as more than a quarter of a million soldiers.

TIBET'S "FORBIDDEN CITY"

Will F. Taylor.

Tibet is almost a mystery country, situated in Central Asia and forming a buffer between China and India. Upon the rugged rock formation here shown stands Gyantse Jong, an old Tibetan fort. All round the base of the hill nestles the town of Gyantse, with its Monastery at the extreme left. The rulers of the populace in Tibet are known as lamas.

P. and A. Photos.

Lhasa is the principal place in Tibet, and is often referred to as "The Forbidden City" because it is death for a white man to enter its walls. Here we see a group of the priests of Lhasa on their way to the Temple of Haiden. Photographs of this strange country are most difficult to procure because of the grave risks a cameraman has to face in order to obtain them.

Will F. Taylor.

The object of veneration carved in stone and framed in mortarless walls is the famous " Red Idol," which gives its name to the gorge or pass of the great main route from Lhasa to India. Though Tibet has so many strange superstitions, the religion of the country is Buddhist.

Camel caravans cross the desert and the steppe of Mongolia regularly to-day, as such caravans have done for ages, but nowadays you can get from Kalgan (which is on the railway from Peking) to Urga and the Trans-Siberian railway by desert motor cars that maintain regular service once or twice a week.

The Forbidden Land.

Tibet is one of the most remarkable countries on the globe. It is mainly plateau whose average height is from 12,000 to 16,000 feet above sea-level, where strong winds rage and winter cold is terribly severe. It is so defended by natural ramparts of mountains that it is difficult to enter, even if the Tibetans welcomed strangers, and even now they do not. When the Mount Everest expeditions wanted to enter

Tibet to approach the great peak from what appeared to be the easiest side, the leaders had to get permission from the Dalai Lama, the priest-statesman, who is the real ruler of Tibet.

The easiest way into Tibet is from China by steep, difficult and winding ways up the valleys of the Yangtse and the Hwang-Ho, and by this route comes the brick-tea from the Yangste valley on the backs of Chinese and Tibetan coolies who return with the borax and the wool of Tibet. From India the only ways are over snow passes as high as the topmost Alps, where the sturdy Tibetan yak, whose strong legs and sharp hoofs give it foothold on steep and slippery surfaces, and whose long hair protects it from the severe cold, is the only possible beast of burden, except the Tibetan

Mondiale.

AT THE BRIDGE OF NINGPO

There is something delightfully artistic in the scene here depicted, with the high, graceful arch of Ningpo Bridge, through which we can see the wharves beyond. The light in the centre of the arch is to guide boatmen during the hours of darkness. The bridge is very solidly constructed of masonry, and has withstood the wear and tear of many centuries.

WATER GIPSIES OF SOOCHOW CREEK

Mondiale.

Che-kiang is a large province of China, one of its towns being Ningpo, whose bridge we can see on the previous page. If we could enter the town, here is a typical street scene which would greet our eyes, and no doubt we should be intrigued by the, to us, curious signs in the native alphabet. These signs refer to the goods offered for sale inside the shops.

Will F. Taylor.

Throughout China, wherever there happen to be rivers or canals, we find water gipsies, who live with their families on boats, carrying on business through the same agency. The busy scene depicted above shows us the Soochow Creek at Shanghai, with the tall tower of the Chinese General Post Office beyond. Some of the boats are mere barges, but many of them are floating homes, plying to and fro along inland waterways.

sheep which are sometimes used to carry bags of borax over the Himalayas to the plains of the Ganges.

The Tibetans.

Many Tibetans are herdsmen living in black tents of yak-hair, and facing the bitter winds of the high plateaux that make even the faces of the young men the colour of old leather and seamed with a thousand wrinkles. Other Tibetans live in the towns and villages in the valleys where the climate is much less severe and a little grain and some fruits can be grown in fields and gardens. The chief city is Lhasa, where the most splendid building is the Potala, the palace-monastery of the Dalai Lama.

Old and New China.

We have said little so far about the Chinese who live in the towns of China Proper, where skilled artists and craftsmen still carry on the marvellous work for which the Chinese have been famous throughout history ; nor have we space to describe as they deserve the wonderful temples, pagodas and palaces, the great canals and their beautiful old humpbacked bridges, and the splendid old houses of noblemen and merchants.

Side by side with these reminders of a glorious past are the creations of modern civilisation in China, the fine buildings of Shanghai's European quarter, and the great iron and steel works of Hankow, for example.

A Land of Many Races.

When considering China and trying in imagination and without the privilege of travelling to understand what the country is like, we must bear in mind first of all its colossal area, which amounts to about two millions of square miles. Within this area are gathered together almost a quarter of all the men, women and children of the world ; some of the districts being more densely populated than any on the face of the globe.

If we speak of the people who inhabit this great country as being Chinese we shall be sadly incorrect. We could indeed pick out more than fifty separate and distinct races in the score or so of provinces that go to make up China, and they are all more or less different in manners and customs, dress and appearance, and even in the languages they use.

Mondiale.

A PLACID HARBOUR OF HONG-KONG

Hong-Kong is an island belonging to Great Britain at the mouth of the Canton River, washed by the South China Sea. It is a most important centre for the trade between our Motherland and China and has even a British university. The entrancing view shown above is that of the fishing village of Aberdeen, with its harbour, on one of the coastal inlets of the large island.

The Story
of the
World and
its Peoples

Our Neighbours
and Friends
in
Other Lands

WHERE IT IS ALWAYS SUMMER

E. N. A.

This picture gives us a charming idea of the scenery of Japan, with its leafy trees, trails of wistaria and quaint style of architecture. The buildings at which we are looking form part of the Futawarasan Temple at Nikko, Japan. Nikko is a great centre of religious fervour, for it has many temples, as well as the tombs of Emperors.

JAPAN: THE LAND OF THE RISING SUN

A FORTNIGHT'S journey from London by way of Berlin, Moscow and the Trans-Siberian railway will take you to Mukden in Manchuria and on to Fusan, the port for Japan. This means that nowadays you can reach Japan in about sixteen days from London by the continental route. If, however, you elect to go by sea, you have a voyage of about five weeks before you.

The Japanese Empire stretches from the cold and misty Kurile Islands in the north to the forest-clad tropical island of Formosa in the south. Such a great range of latitude means that in the Japanese Empire there are all sorts of climates and all sorts of products, and many different ways of living. The fisherfolk of the Kuriles live in a very different way from the highly-civilised people of the main islands, and these again live very differently from the savage head-hunters who still dwell in their high forest retreats in the middle of Formosa.

The Real Japan.

The real Japan is the main group of large islands between the Japan Sea and the deep Pacific. Honshiu is the largest, and contains Tokyo, the capital, with its port of Yokohama, Osaka, the biggest manufacturing city in Japan, Kobe, another great port, and several other of Japan's most important towns. North of Honshiu is Hokkaido, with Hakodate as its chief town and port. South of the great main island, and shutting in the lovely inland sea with their northern coast-lines, are Kiushiu and Shikoku, with the important Japanese port of Nagasaki.

Japan has important interests on the Asiatic mainland, for Korea (or Cho-sen as the Japanese call it) is a Japanese protectorate. Its capital is Seoul (Keijo); travellers approaching Japan by the continental route pass through Keijo and the whole length of Cho-sen before they arrive at Fusan, where they can take steamer across the Korea Strait to Japan itself.

A Volcanic Chain.

The Japanese islands are mostly very mountainous and all volcanic. They are, indeed, a long range of volcanic uplands partly sunken in the sea. You can trace this great line of volcanoes from the cold peninsula of Kamchatka in north-eastern Siberia, and through the Japanese islands to Formosa and on to the East Indies, where the Dutch island of Java has more volcanoes to the square mile than any other country in the world.

Japan is on what is called " a line of weakness " in the earth's crust, where the stupendous forces of volcanic eruptions and earthquakes are frequently active, proving that this part of the world is still " in the making."

Some of the most appalling volcanic outbursts the world has ever known have occurred in Japan, and some of the worst earthquake disasters. In 1923, for example, the great city of Tokyo was practically destroyed by an earthquake shock and by the fire that followed as a result.

Japan's most famous volcano is Fujiyama or Fujisan — " O Fuji," the Japanese call it —" the Honourable Mountain." You can see it on a clear day as your steamer enters Tokyo Bay, a perfect snowy cone of peerless

Will F. Taylor.

A HOMELY, WAYSIDE SCENE IN JAPAN
No picture could better illustrate the workaday world in a village of Japan. Here we see children and wayfarers partaking of a rest, whilst the highway is shaded by pleasant pine trees. The view was obtained at Suzukava, on the road from Tokyo to Kyoto.

FUJIYAMA, THE SACRED MOUNTAIN

E. N. A.

The peak of Fujiyama, with its snow-clad cap, is the highest point in Japan, and forms the summit of a sleeping volcano. At the very top are shrines at which faithful Buddhists pray; and, during the climbing season, from 15,000 to 20,000 pilgrims ascend the slopes. The mountain is 12,365 feet in height, and is one of the most beautiful sights in the Japanese Empire.

CHERRY BLOSSOM AND MAPLE LEAVES

Will F. Taylor.

Lake Hakone is a beautiful small lake near the watering place Hakone. Here there are health-giving thermal springs of pure, sulphurous and saline water at temperatures ranging from 98° to 168° F. In spring one sees the cherry blossom, and maple leaves bedeck the autumn.

Will F. Taylor.

One of the most charming, and at the same time one of the most progressive, races are the Japanese. They are fond of their tea-houses, dance-houses and theatres. In the evening such places are illuminated with paper lanterns and the tea-house streets are filled with noise, laughter and singing. Our illustration shows the exterior of a Japanese theatre.

Will F. Taylor.

Kyoto is the centre of art-ware in Japan, and is one of the most beautiful cities imaginable. The former capital, Kyoto possesses wonderful gardens and temples.

Will F. Taylor.

Korea is separated from Japan by a strait some two hundred miles wide, but the country was annexed by Japan. The girl in this picture is dressed for her wedding.

Will F. Taylor.

These Japanese craftsmen are stencilling on silk. Silkworms are reared in large quantities, and the raw material obtained is woven into fabric.

E. N. A.

Not far from the seaport of Kobe is Hyogo, with its giant Diabutsu or statue. The figure below is that of a priest with his boy attendant.

beauty, and at the sight you understand once and for all why Fuji appears in so many Japanese pictures and decorations, and why every year thousands of pilgrims clad in white ascend the mountain as an act of piety.

The greatest of all, however, is the enormous old crater of Aso-san, which is several miles across and now has many villages and fertile fields within its broken rim of red and black volcanic rock.

Skilful Farmers.

So much of Japan is mountainous that her crowded population must make every possible use of the limited amount of land fit for cultivation. You will see not only the plains bearing rice and other crops to the utmost limit, but also the very hillsides terraced far up to provide extra land for growing things. Like the Chinese, the Japanese farmers are hard and patient workers, who have learned to make use of everything and to waste nothing.

Because the land is so filled with mountains, the Japanese rivers are as a rule short and very swift—useful only for rafting down the timber from the highlands, or for providing cheap power for electricity. One of the thrills experienced by visitors to Japan is to shoot the rapids on one of the swift rivers in a boat that is by no means as clumsy as it looks.

The New Japan.

The Japan about which we used to read in school books has changed a

Keystone View Co.

MEAL-TIME IN JAPAN

The above is quite a characteristic scene and shows a Japanese family at breakfast, sitting upon the floor. Each member of the party is using chop-sticks, and the food consists mostly of spaghetti. The neat tea-tray is typical of homes in Japan.

A PERCH FOR SINGING BIRDS

E. N. A.

Our photograph was taken on the Island of Miyajuma, and the curious structure in the water is known as a " torri." It was constructed originally as a perch upon which the wild birds might rest to sing their morning greeting to the gods. The water is that of Japan's famous inland sea, in which a fifth of her national supply of fish is caught and which is used by ocean-going, coasting and ferry steamers, though well-skilled pilots must be employed at the helm.

great deal, even in the last twenty years, for the Japanese of the large towns—especially the ports—have learned all that Americans and Europeans can teach them. Electric trains and trams, motor cars, picture-houses, hotels, theatres and restaurants much like those you find in Europe and America are common sights.

Great up-to-date mills, factories, foundries and shipyards tell very plainly how well the Japanese have learned the business of modern manufacture. In Yokohama some of the business offices remind you distinctly of the skyscraper monsters of New York, Chicago and San Francisco; the buildings are not so high, it is true, but the idea is unmistakably there. You will see Japanese business men dressed much as business men are in Europe and America

hurrying off to their offices in the mornings; and Japanese business girls, too, with short skirts and bobbed hair just like their sisters of the West.

The Old Japan.

But in the country, away from the ports and the large cities, there is still the Old Japan with its fine old-world courtesy and love of beauty, its wonderful old temples and fascinating houses, and its craftsmen and artists, who sometimes spend their whole lives in the creation of a single work of art.

There, too, you can feel the real charm of Japan, enjoy the loveliness of the cherry blossom in spring, and see the gorgeous colours of the maples in autumn.

Life still flows peacefully on in the old-fashioned way in the country villages of little brown houses, and in the

Will F. Taylor.

IN THE STREETS OF YOKOHAMA

Yokohama is the principal seaport of Japan, with a vast harbour enclosed by breakwaters and a population of nearly half a million people. In the above picture we see a typical scene in one of the streets. The old woman's boxes are filled with toy whistles ornamented with feathers.

E. N. A.

A JAPANESE SUBURBAN GARDEN

Like all large cities, Tokyo has its suburbs where better-class folks reside, and a feature of the pretty suburban villas is a beautiful garden such as the one illustrated. Bridges, fish-pools, and massive stone ornaments invariably figure in such gardens, as well as clipped shrubs and most artistic rockery work.

thousands of tiny farms scattered in plain and valley. Unceasing work in the rice-fields or in the tea-gardens and mulberry groves on the hill-terraces, or wood cutting and fuel-gathering on the upper slopes, fills the whole day for these patient toiling peasants. In the attics of the farm-houses live the silk-worms on their flat trays—greedy creatures that keep the girls and boys ever busy in gathering fresh mulberry leaves to satisfy the growing appetites of their crawling charges until the time comes when they spin their cocoons of wonderful lustrous silk and set their keepers the new task of gathering, unwinding and drying the silk and making it into pale yellow hanks to be sent to the silk factory in the town.

Yokohama.

Those who come to Japan by sea usually enter the country at Yokohama, the chief port, where they are perhaps a little disappointed at first to find so many of the menfolk dressed in European garb and wearing hard bowler hats, but the bright clothes of the women and children make up for this. Many of the buildings are distinctly American in appearance, and the New and the Old Japan flow through the streets in a mingling stream of motor cars and blue-clad coolies with mushroom hats and the name-badge of their employers marked on their backs; of rickshaws and bicycles bearing peaked-hatted, skirted schoolboys; of queer little lorries drawn by small shaggy ponies, and electric cars.

One of the places to visit from Yokohama is Kamakura, which you can reach in less than an hour. There people go to see the famous Bronze Buddha, which is nearly 50 feet high, and whose eyes are said to be of pure gold and its forehead of silver. Or if you wish to enjoy the beauty and peace of the countryside, you can go out to the Hakone Mountains, forty miles away, and stay for a few days at one of the many good hotels. On this line is Gotemba, where you can leave the train to climb Fuji if you wish, leaving your hotel at three in the morning and reaching the summit in late afternoon. You spend the night at one of the rest-houses and descend next morning.

Tokyo.

Tokyo is only half an hour from Yokohama by electric train. It is practically a new city, which has arisen out of the ruin caused by the terrible earthquake and fire of 1923, which left behind thousands of acres of smoking waste that only a week before was a prosperous city. In six years the city was well rebuilt; "six new bridges spanning a river as wide as the Thames in London, 400 smaller bridges over the city's moats and inlets, 600 miles of new roads, three new parks, fifty-one open spaces, and houses, shops and factories." Three days of rejoicing were proclaimed in March, 1930. The Emperor himself drove through the city in his motor car at the head of a procession, and "paid reverence at the Hall of the Nameless Dead to the enshrined ashes of 33,000 people who perished in the flames."

Tokyo's principal street is "the Ginza," which runs through the heart of the city, where you can buy anything that can be purchased in the great towns of Europe and America.

The Temples of Nikko.

Nikko is a pleasant place at which to stay. It lies ninety miles north of Tokyo amid wonderful scenery, and is renowned for its beautiful temples, some of which may be visited if you take off your

LARGEST IN THE WORLD   *E. N. A.*

No suspended bell in the world is larger than this one, which hangs at the Chion-in Temple at Kyoto in Japan. Kyoto was once capital of the Empire, and is a city with broad streets, electric traction, fine buildings and many other Western innovations that betoken progress.

A TREE SHAPED LIKE A BOAT

Trained trees and magically dwarfed specimens are a feature of Japanese gardening, but the example shown is of outstanding interest. It is a spruce fir known to be centuries old ; and, in the course of time, monks have cut and trained the branches till the whole tree has assumed the shape of a boat. The tree may be seen in the Kinkukuji Gardens at Kyoto.

Photos : E. N. A.

The many-storeyed structure here depicted is the castle at Najoya in Japan. The strangely curved eaves are a feature of Japanese architecture, and we notice the same peculiarity in many of the pagodas. Japanese pagodas, or towers, are different in form from those of China.

boots or shoes before entering and wear the special slippers provided by the temple guardian. One of these temples —"Yeyas Temple"—bears the famous carving which is copied in millions of Japanese trinkets, a carving in wood of three monkeys, one with his hand to his mouth, one with his hands before his eyes, and the other with his hands over his ears. "*Speak* no evil; *see* no evil; *hear* no evil." The Japanese think much of Nikko; they have a proverb that runs: "He who has not seen Nikko cannot say, 'beautiful!'"

Famous Cities.

Kyoto is another beautiful old city where you can see the emperor's palace surrounded by its great wall with six gates, and in whose shops you find some of the most exquisite pottery and other works of art in the world. From Kyoto you can go up to lovely Lake Biwa, the biggest lake in Japan, which gets its name from the fact that it is shaped like a *biwa* or Japanese lute.

The wonderful old city of *Nara* was the centre of government a thousand years ago, and the ruins of palaces and temples there bear witness to its former greatness. *Osaka*, whose many waterways make Europeans call it the "Venice of Japan," is a great manufacturing city with mills and factories on the most up-to-date lines. *Kobe* is its great port, which, like Yokohama, is now thoroughly modern as well as thoroughly Japanese.

Then there is the great seaport and dockyard of *Nagasaki*, standing on a bay on the Island of Hyushiu. In olden days this was the only Japanese port open to European traders, and it is now a vast commercial centre, spreading to the hills which rise behind the harbour.

Of all the countries in the world, Japan has one of the most dense populations, and on this account she is ever seeking further territory.

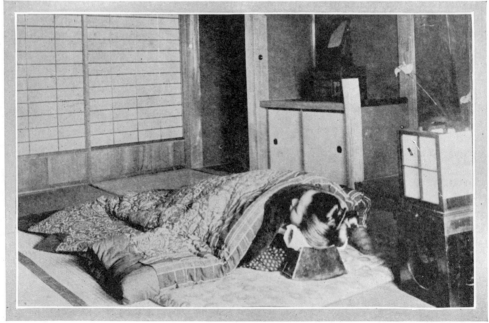

Keystone View Co.

HOW A JAPANESE GIRL SLEEPS

It seems all topsy-turvy to us, but Japanese girls sleep with the mattress and bed-covering on top of their bodies, as is here shown. For her head, instead of a downy pillow, the girl has a block of hard wood, into which the base of the skull just fits. It would never do for the Japs to turn and wriggle from side to side during their hours of slumber!

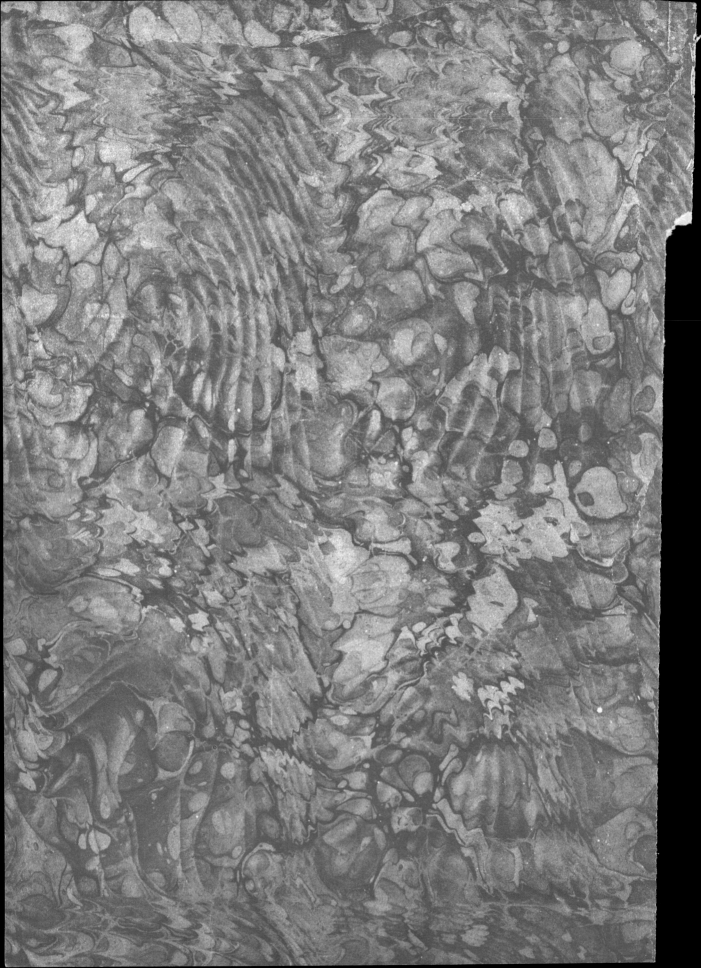